The four dimensions of power

MANCHESTER
1824

Manchester University Press

SOCIAL AND POLITICAL POWER

Series editor: Mark Haugaard

Power is one of the most fundamental concepts in social science. Yet, despite the undisputed centrality of power to social and political life, few have agreed on exactly what it is or how it manifests itself. Social and Political Power is a book series which provides a forum for this absolutely central, and much debated, social phenomenon. The series is theoretical, in both a social scientific and normative sense, yet also empirical in its orientation. Theoretically it is oriented towards the Anglo-American tradition, including Dahl and Lukes, as well as to the Continental perspectives, influenced either by Foucault and Bourdieu, or by Arendt and the Frankfurt School. Empirically, the series provides an intellectual forum for power research from the disciplines of sociology, political science and the other social sciences, and also for policy-oriented analysis.

Already published

The four dimensions of power

Understanding domination,
empowerment and democracy

Mark Haugaard

Manchester University Press

The right of Mark Haugaard to be identified as the author of this work has been asserted by him in accordance with the Copyright, Designs and Patents Act 1988.

Published by Manchester University Press
Altrincham Street, Manchester M1 7JA
www.manchesteruniversitypress.co.uk

British Library Cataloguing-in-Publication Data
A catalogue record for this book is available from the British Library

ISBN 978 1 5261 1037 4 hardback

First published 2020

Typeset by Newgen Publishing UK

The book is dedicated to my daughter Vanessa Haugaard, who has a wonderfully ironic sense of humour, which I profoundly appreciate.

Contents

Acknowledgements

I would like to acknowledge Jeffery Alexander's and Steven Lukes' support and suggestions on an earlier, and less streamlined, version of this book. I would also like to thank my many colleagues in RC 36 (the IPSA research group on political power), as well as colleagues and postgraduates at the School of Political Science and Sociology, National University of Ireland, Galway, with whom over the years I have discussed these ideas. Last but not least, I would like to thank my wife Patricia for proof-reading and making many useful comments upon the manuscript.

Introduction: Conceptions of power and an overview

What is power?

Bertrand Russell argued that *power* is to *politics* what *electricity* is to *physics*. Power essentially concerns energy: the energy that humans use to get things done (Russell 1938). Just like physical energy, such as electricity, it can be used virtuously or malignly, for the purposes of creating light or to electrocute someone as part of a death penalty.

Russell's energy conception accords with Robert Dahl's (1957) definition of power, which is expressed in terms of cause and effect: 'A has power over B to the extent that he can get B to do something that B would not otherwise do' (Dahl 1957: 202–3). Rephrased in the language of cause and effect: A causes B to do something that B would not otherwise do.

The capacity of A to cause B to do something, which B would not otherwise, is linked to the potency of A. There are two sources of this potency. One is the physicality of A: electricity, tooth and claw; the other power source is a complex system of meaning and structure, which both A and B inhabit and which, usually, predates their interaction.

Since Aristotle's (1941) *Politics*, political systems have been defined in terms of power structures. The virtuous rule by one Aristotle termed monarchy, while the malign rule by one was tyranny. The virtuous rule by a few was aristocracy, while the malign rule was oligarchy. The virtuous rule by the majority was constitutional government, while its malign – or, more correctly, selfish – form was democracy. Social political power can take many forms and has both the capacity for good or evil. In everyday speech, when we use the concept 'power', there is a tendency to equate it with its malign form. However, this is not inherent to social and political power.

One of the most influential definitions of power was Max Weber's, expressed as follows: ' "Power" (*Macht*) is the probability that one actor within a social relationship will be in a position to carry out his own will despite resistance, regardless of the basis on which this probability rests' (Weber 1978: 53). There are issues with translation here because *Macht* has a narrower, more coercive focus than the English word *power*. However, this definition has influenced the power debates towards a normatively negative appraisal of power, as something malign, coercive and dominating (see Lukes 2005: 83–85; Lukes in Hayward and Lukes 2008; Morriss 2002: xiv). Hence, the assumed focus is on the power that the powerful exercise over the less powerful, to the detriment of the latter.

When power is viewed as normatively negative the implicit agenda concerns how to get rid of power, as some malign tumor that should be excised. However, as we shall see from a more sociological orientation, there is no getting rid of power; it is ubiquitous.

In my experience, the negative view of power, as domination, resonates with the everyday speech usage of the concept of power. In everyday conversation, when people ask me what my academic specialism is and I answer *social and political power*, the follow-on question frequently concerns the evils of Stalin or Hitler or the wisdom of Lord Acton's adage that 'power corrupts and absolute power corrupts absolutely' (Dalberg-Acton 1887).

In contrast to the above, in the academic literature there is also a view of power in terms of empowerment. Working in the republican normative tradition, Hannah Arendt is the most notable political philosopher to concern herself with power in normatively positive forms, analyzing what virtuous forms of power might look like (Arendt 1970 and 1998). Working on an empirical level, in sociology Talcott Parsons (1963) was the first exponent of the power-as-empowerment position. He compares power to money as a facility for action. This was followed by the work of Barry Barnes (1988), who integrates the work of Thomas Kuhn with sociological theory to argue that power represents some kind of epistemic consensus. In social philosophy, John Searle (1996 and 2007) has developed a view of power as capacity for action, which is similar to Barnes' perspective.

With the exception of Arendt and Morriss (2002), in mainstream political philosophy, especially in liberal political theory, there has been a remarkable absence of attention to power in its normatively positive, or virtuous, forms. This is partly because power is assumed to be malign. Power is characterized as the opposite of freedom. Freedom from power, or negative freedom (Berlin 2010), is considered a condition of possibility of emancipation. This negative view of power is paradigmatically exemplified by the title of an article by Philip Pettit: 'Freedom as Antipower' (Pettit 1996).

To return to our observation that power is energy, if freedom is to be more than the freedom of Robinson Crusoe (before Friday arrived), if humans are to be more than simple tool-making animals, then freedom also entails the joint capacity for action, or social energy, that is derived from being part of political society. Indeed if freedom entails not just the right to do something but also the capacity to do it, then power is a condition of possibility for freedom (Morriss 2009). In Arendt's felicitous turn of phrase, power is the capacity to act in 'concert' (Arendt 1970: 44; see also Haugaard 2015). If this is correct, then political theorists should think about what normatively desirable power might look like, rather than wishing it away.

Several authors have argued that power should be considered as a *capacity* concept. The first to do so was probably Spinoza, who saw it as *potentia* (Saar 2010), which he conceptualizes as the potency of a person. Similarly, the contemporary analytic philosopher Peter Morriss has argued that power constitutes a capacity concept that refers to a person's ability or 'ableness' to do something (Morriss 2002: 80). Stewart Clegg (1989) argues that power is both an episodic (momentary) and dispositional concept, the latter indicating capacity for action. The flipside of power as domination is power as empowerment. As we shall see, most exercises of power (excluding slavery) entail some level of empowerment. In fact, dominating power is usually parasitic upon the empowering aspects of power relations. To take a simple example: when an exploited person works for another without overt signs of resistance, one explanation for acquiescence (there are many others, including 2-D structural constraint, 3-D cognitive bias and 4-D ontological predispositions) is that they have an immediate desire (or need) for the empowerment (including a wage and collective membership) that this relationship offers. So, in such a case domination is fused with empowerment.

To cover some of these usages, Amy Allen (1999) developed a distinction between *power-to*, *power-with* and *power-over*. As a dispositional concept, potential, or ableness, implies an emphasis upon *power-to*, while the more dominating view entails *power-over*. If we speak about 'black power' or 'women's power' the emphasis is upon the empowerment of these groups. As a collective group they create power-with. However, while this is all emancipating, this power-with and power-to may manifest itself in the capacity to exercise *power-over* others (Morriss 2002: 33). The power-over that social movements have is a consequence of their power-to. This has led Pamela Pansardi (2012) to argue that, contrary to everyday usage, *power-to* is the primary concept, and *power-over* the derivate one. With respect to the supposed opposition between freedom and power, if we take freedom to entail the power-to realize our desire, then power, as ability, becomes a condition of possibility of freedom, rather that its opposite (Morriss 2009).

As the above illustrates, once we move beyond the overarching perception that power is energy, the concept differentiates into many forms. The joint capacity for action, which Arendt, Parsons, Morriss and Pansardi have in mind, and the insidious power of Joseph Stalin are both forms of power.

Both virtuous republics and the Gulags are essentially power machines, which generate social power for different ends but, as we shall see, often using similar methods. It would be neat if we could separate these forms of power into different entities. However, social life is not that tidy because both enabling and dominating aspects of power often have similar bases and much of the time are operative simultaneously. As we shall see, there are deep theoretical reasons for this, as most forms of domination entail, and are parasitic upon, modes of empowerment.

At this point I do not wish to provide a further overview of the power debates. Rather, I wish to discuss what this diversity tells us about the concept of power. For the reader who wishes to have a short overview of the power debates, I have written such a survey in *The Encyclopedia of Political Thought* (Haugaard 2014) and in collaboration with Kevin Ryan (Haugaard and Ryan 2012: chapter 2). However, this background is not required. Some readers who find conceptual analysis tedious may wish to skip what follows down to the subheading 'The four dimensions in brief' or they may wish start with Chapter 1.

Power as an essentially contested concept

The multiplicity of meaning of power has led some theorists, most notably Steven Lukes (1974 and 2005) and William Connelly (1983 [1974]), to argue that power is an *essentially contested concept*. The idea of essentially contested concepts comes from a well-known article by Walter B. Gallie (1956) in which he argued that many concepts, such as *democracy*, *art* and *Christian*, are somehow inherently resistant to agreed definition. The reason that they are essentially contested is that they appear analytic but are inherently evaluative. For instance, if we term something a *democracy*, or *art* as opposed to *craft*, or an action is characterized as *Christian* (in character), these are not simply statements of fact. They constitute a positive normative endorsement of something. Conversely, according to Lukes (2005; Hayward and Lukes 2008), if we say that someone is subject to power, this implies a negative normative evaluation to the effect that they are dominated or that their interests are thwarted.

In arguing that power is an essentially contested concept, Lukes was moving in the right direction, in the sense that he was moving us away from any overarching essentialist claims to a singular correct definition of power. While Lukes' position has certain strengths, it does not go far enough in my opinion. First, supposedly *essentially* contested concepts are not actually inherently evaluative, as claimed – only so within specific language games. Second, this view does not emphatically ditch the idea that there should be a singular definition of power; rather, it claims that there is one but we will never be able to agree on what it is.

Dealing with the first point (and the second later), while it is true that for normative political theorists power is perceived of as normatively evaluative, I do not think that appraisal of normativity inherent to the concept. In fact, many of the concepts that Gallie considers essentially contested are only contested in certain contexts or within what I will later term language games. For instance, the supposedly essentially contested signifier *Christian* is only positively evaluative among Christians who (rather narcissistically) tend to assume it is *a good thing* to be a Christian. To an atheist or agnostic sociologist/political scientist/anthropologist, *Christian* is simply a descriptor, without any normative connotation, positive or negative.

In social science, part of our work involves taking concepts that are used with normative connotations in everyday speech and stripping them of those connotations, viewing them, as dispassionately as we can, as empirical facts. The paradigm instance of this can be found in the first explicitly sociological study: Durkheim's 1897 *Suicide: A Study in Sociology* (Durkheim 1989). At the time, everyone assumed that suicide was a terrible thing, which any social scientist would wish to condemn. Durkheim shocked his contemporary readers by talking about societies as being more or less *developed* at suicide (Durkheim 1989: 160) or groups having greater/lesser *aptitude* or *talent* for suicide than others (for instance, Durkheim 1989: 155). By using normally positive terms (developed, aptitude and talent) in combination with suicide he was making the point that as a sociologist he was not viewing suicide normatively, as a blight to be cured. Rather, Durkheim viewed suicide dispassionately as a social fact (Durkheim 1982).

Another instance of non-evaluative usage is early sociologists' fascination with understanding what was unique about *modern* society. At that time, in everyday speech *modern* was a term of commendation. In that language game *modern* was opposed to *backward* or *primitive*. However, *modern* is not *essentially* normative. Part of learning the practice of the discipline of sociology was (and is) learning to use *modern* in a purely analytic sense, methodologically bracketing (or putting aside) normative connotations. Of course, in certain instances, even great sociologists such as Weber and Parsons slip into using the term *modern* normatively. However, within the discipline such usage is regarded as a lapse, as a failure to live up to the standards of the discipline (no doubt I lapse, too).

In this work, power is analyzed both empirically (without normative connotations) and also normatively, and the switch of language game will be clearly signaled. Generally speaking, I begin with non-normative usage, understanding how power works, before making any normative evaluation. The latter will be interdependent on the former – it will be possible to accept my empirical theory and reject my normative conclusions, but not the other way around.

As a qualification, of course, it must be acknowledged that normative usage frequently slips into what purport to be empirical statements. As we shall see, one of the techniques of domination is precisely to present something as empirical that is really normative. However, that point conceded, this is not an either/or phenomenon. Statements are more or less normative; therefore, it possible to be more or less evaluative – a point I will later return to.

Power as a family resemblance concept

As I have argued elsewhere at greater length (Haugaard 2010), Ludwig Wittgenstein's characterization of *family resemblance concepts* is better suited to the purpose of making sense of the usage of the concept of power than essentially contested concepts. Family resemblance concepts are analogous to the members of a family, with overlapping characteristics – John has the nose of his mother and the sense of humour of his father etc. Wittgenstein used the word *game* to explain family resemblance concepts (Wittgenstein 1967: § 66). We might say that all games entail winning and losing, yet a solitary child bouncing a ball is also playing a game, which has no winning or losing. To take a different example, at this moment I am sitting at a *table*. However, in a short while I intend to go sailing, so I am about to check the time of high tide using a tide *table*. I doubt that any definition can cover both usages of *table*.

I would categorize the social and political power family as gesturing at social and political energy, as in Russell (1938). In turn, this subdivides into a cluster of family resemblance concepts that have overlapping synergies and characteristics. The family-wide concept explains little in itself, as it is too wide and vague. Rather, the kind of construct required by sociological and normative theory is one focused on power concepts, including: coercion, the exercise of power, power resources, authority, power-over, power-to and power-with, and the various dimensions of power.

Language games and conceptual tools

Closely associated with Wittgenstein's (1967) view of *family resemblance* concepts are the ideas of *language games* and words considered as *conceptual tools*. Essentially, one should not think of a language as a singular phenomenon. Rather, languages are made up of micro systems of meaning that have their own systemic form within the larger linguistic system.

The meaning of words is relationally constituted. If you take chess as a local language within other systems of meaning, the meaning of the word *queen* is relationally constituted relative to the words *king, bishop, knight, castle* and *pawn*. A game of chess constitutes a local language game. The meanings of the words in chess have some resemblance to everyday usages, for instance: as with reference to a feudal kingdom, so in chess, the *king* and *queen* are the most important pieces. Yet, knowledge of feudal politics will not inform you precisely how the *king* and *queen* move in chess.

In everyday life, we are continually part of local language games in which words gain a qualified, or specific, meaning relative to a local way doing things. This is not simply between dialects of the same language but also within small groups. Even small social units, such as families, frequently have jokes among themselves, which presuppose shared local meanings, or local language games. Similarly, specialist groups develop their own local language that serves specific purposes for them. Within the latter language games, words should be thought of as conceptual tools, specifically developed for the pragmatic purpose of getting a job done. Local language games within families and other collectives serve the purpose of signaling collective belonging, which is a different phenomenon.

The paradigm instance of the development of a local language game and conceptual tools is to be found in the square-rigged sailing ships of yesteryear. These ships were immensely complex and, especially towards the end of the days of sail, hugely under-crewed in order to compete with the new technology of steam propulsion – it is ironic that the end of the age of sail produced some of the greatest and most disciplined sailors of all time. Learning to be a crewmember of such a ship was not simply a task of learning the correct set of the sails; it also entailed being able to respond accurately to an order given. In order to accomplish that task a precise language was developed. This language was every bit as much part of the tools of the trade as the knife and marlinspike, which every sailor carried in their pocket. They were conceptual tools, analogous to physical tools.

Just like the physical tools, of which the ship itself was the largest (a ship is a sailing tool or sailing machine), over the centuries, these conceptual tools changed to become more fit for purpose. It was not that there was one correct meaning that they found, or some hidden essence. Rather, relations between signifier (word) and signified (referent) were constantly adapted to produce more precise conceptual tools. For instance, the signifier *starboard* came from the Viking ships that had a steering oar (literally, a steering board) on the right-hand side of the ship, which was always kept away from a quay wall to protect it from damage. The other side of the ship, the left, went alongside and was used for loading. In Danish the verb to load is *lade* (literally, to laden), so the left was the loading side, or *ladebord*, which became *larboard* in English. Logical as this was, *larboard* and *starboard* shouted upwind in a howling gale were relatively indistinguishable to the ear. Therefore, by order of the British Admiralty, in 1867, *larboard* officially became *port*, which still suggested the loading side but had a different sound. The change to the word *port* constitutes, in essence, the creation of a new conceptual tool, replacing the now obsolete conceptual tool *larboard*, in much the same way that the introduction of physical tools (such as halyard winches) was an improvement. In a language game, words are conceptual tools, and their worth is judged by their usefulness. The same applies here. As we shall see later, in the analysis of 3-D power, thinking of words as conceptual tools has significant theoretical implications for the everyday assumption that convention equates to arbitrariness. If some conventions can be said to be better (for getting a job done) than others, they are far from arbitrary.

Thinking of words as conceptual tools renders essentialist debates on *the correct definition* of power, or power-related concepts, totally beside the point. *There is no general definition of power that is better than all others.* Claiming that *I have the best general definition of power* is as absurd as claiming that I have just invented *the best* carpenter's tool. For this reason any suggestion of a best definition of power must be abandoned. There are *saws*, *drill-bits* and *chisels* all of different sizes and shapes, each developed for a specific task. However superbly made a *chisel* or *drill-bit* may be, it does not qualify as *the best, or essence, of all tools*. The same goes for conceptual tools associated with power. The point is that what makes a tool useful is whether it is fit for purpose. Do these conceptual tools aid understanding or do they confound it? If the latter, then change them, just as the sailors of old replaced *larboard* with *port*.

A local language game is a way of throwing certain features of social life into relief by developing use-particular conceptual tools. This language game is a linguistic system, within the larger language. Chess is a largely self-contained language game in which each piece refers to the other and to the rules of the game. Most everyday language games are not as perfectly self-referential as chess, but even so, they have a self-referential systemic quality. The vocabulary of the sailing ship was a language game aimed at providing conceptual tools for managing the ship efficiently, which was a local language game largely known to sailors. Of course, some of the words of that language game are part of wider usage. However, the full nuances and implications of the language game of sailing were only appreciated by these disciplined and expert sailors.

In any academic discipline there is a conceptual vocabulary that goes with a paradigm or specific theory. Within these language games definitions are not right or wrong relative to a final-vocabulary-out-there. There is no holy grail of the essence of things-in-themselves. Rather, there are local definitions that are evaluated relative to their effectiveness within that language game. What matters is internal consistency, usefulness, clarity and, in the final instance, the usefulness of the language game as a whole. What is the language game for? Why do we need this set of conceptual tools? These are the types of questions that we should focus upon, not what is the essence of power.

To take an instance: in the next chapter, while discussing one-dimensional power, I will distinguish between political power and violence. Echoing some of the ideas of Arendt (1970), I argue that physical violence usually is a sign of the loss of political power and so, in a sense, they are opposites, which is an observation Arendt was often criticized for (for instance, Breen 2007). Similarly, in a special issue of the *Journal of Political Power* (11(1)) on Forst's theory of noumenal power (Forst 2014 and 2017), Pablo Gilabert (2018) takes Forst to task for opposing power and violence. To simplify Forst's theory, political power requires justification to ensure compliance, while violence does not. However, these criticisms make the mistake of thinking that there is some kind of essence to either power or violence. The better way of thinking about this is in terms of the language game being developed and the usefulness of the conceptions as conceptual tools. With regard to my or Forst's claimed distinction between power and violence, the question should not be: have Forst or Haugaard missed the essence of power or violence? Rather, it should be: is this a useful distinction that enables the reader to understand the particular sociological or normative explanation of the nature of social and political power that Forst or Haugaard are constructing? Or, put more simply: does this distinction enable Forst or Haugaard to accomplish the tasks they wish to?

I can well imagine a different language game in which the power/violence distinction does not make sense. For instance, a theorist may wish to construct a language game where power equates to *having an effect* on someone. Within this language game, to say that violence is not power appears absurd. Violence is one of the biggest effects one person can have on another; they can use violence to kill someone – Pablo Gilabert makes this point with regard to Forst (Gilabert 2018). So it follows that violence is the ultimate form of political power. I would not disagree with the logic of this, or say that this use of concepts is categorically *wrong*. Rather, I simply assert that this is not the language game I or Forst are engaged with.

As we shall see, the reason that I wish to distinguish social and political power from simple violence has to do with understanding the relationship between power that is based upon some level of *consent* and power that does not presuppose any consent. I wish to understand the difference between coercive domination and domination based upon phenomena such as authority and reification. In order to do so, I require political power and violence as different referents. To be clear, this is not a transcendental claim about the true essence of things; it simply reflects the need that I have for particular conceptual tools designed for a particular task of understanding.

The main danger of these local usages is the hazard of switching language game while not being aware that the same signifier, or word, has changed referent. Thus we are not speaking about the same thing. For instance, when a social theorist such as Parsons uses the term *power*, the referent is *power-to*, while for Weber the referent for power is *power-over* or *power as domination*. For this reason it is important to be specific in usage, to write about *power-to* and *power-over* (or *domination*), and avoid the temptation to make one of these referents just *power* in general. Equally, it is important to be aware, and to signal, when language games are being switched.

In what follows, my language game also includes local usage with regard to gendered pronouns. Rather than using both at once (*he* and *she*) or combinations (*s/he*), I use both singly. In other words, I sometimes use a female-gendered pronoun and at other times a male. I have adopted this convention for two reasons. First, I find the use of both or the made-up combination linguistically clumsy. Second, it is useful to be gender-specific in describing an interaction because there are two or more actors involved. If the powerful actor, A, is one gender and the less-powerful, B, is another, it is clearer who is the referent once we slip into gendered pronouns. I have not counted the numbers of gendered pronouns but my guesstimate (and intention) is that the number is roughly equal.

Another aspect of the local language game of this book is that from now on the four dimensions of power will generally be referred to using an abbreviated form, as follows: 1-D, 2-D, 3-D and 4-D.

The normative and empirical language games

In the power literature the two most significant language games are the *empirical* and the *normative* language games. Examining power as an *empirical* phenomenon is different from claims concerning when is it *right* or *wrong* to exercise power. Speaking generally, the former is a sociological concern, while the latter is a normative one, or a concern of political theory.[1]

In the power literature the two claims are frequently not separated, which leads to confusion. For instance, in a review of the second edition of *Power: A Radical View*, which is a book I admire, I argue (Haugaard 2008a) that Lukes conflates the two language games. Lukes stated that power is not reducible to individual decisions and nondecisions and entails the 'social structured and culturally patterned behaviour of groups, and practices of institutions, which may indeed be manifested by individual's inaction' (Lukes 2005: 27). In that context Lukes approvingly quotes Marx's adage about people making history but not in circumstances of their choosing (Lukes 2005: 26). Yet, later in the same book and, with greater emphasis, in his well-known exchange with Clarissa Rile Hayward, Lukes insists that power entails agency because 'there is a link between power and responsibility: ... part of *the point* of locating power is fixing responsibility ...' (Lukes in Hayward and Lukes 2008: 7).

Lukes is a highly acute sociological and normative theorist, so how does this apparent contradiction arise? The former is a sociological empirical claim while the latter is a normative one. It is a *sociological* claim that the most significant power effects are not reducible to intentional agency. Rather, they entail structured contexts of social action, including the unintended effects of the action of past generations. However, in the language game of normative and moral theory, responsibility is key. For instance, at the Nuremberg Trials could-have-done-otherwise agency implied *guilt*, while a convincing-structural-constraint response suggested *innocence*. If the local language game includes fixing moral responsibility to power, then the structured context of action does not constitute power. Thus, there are two language games, which are incommensurable.

While it is essential to separate empirical and normative claims, to know which is which, it is also important to realize that the problems of these language games are mutually dependent. Normative theory without sociology (*ought* without *is*) is like attempting to do biology without physics and chemistry. A normative account of how power should be without understanding how power is created in the social system will only have limited usefulness, as the normative recommendations will bear little relationship to the conditions of possibility of actual societies. I suspect that this is the reason that there is a radical disjuncture between the practice of politics and some of the nuanced debates of political philosophers.

I start with sociological theory and conclude with normative theory. The sociological theory section is much longer, eight chapters, than that of the normative theory, which is confined to the last and concluding chapter. The reason for this is practical, as I had already reached book length with the former. I intend to write another normative book after this and I hope that the single normative chapter will indicate to readers the significant implications of the sociological analysis.

Another qualifier with regard to local usage is that I oppose *normative theory* to *sociological theory*, rather than use the word *social theory*. My reason for using *sociological theory* in place of *social theory* (or social philosophy) is that in everyday usage *social theory* can be normative, while *sociological theory* is not. Otherwise, the two are used interchangeably.

A qualification on *is* and *ought*

In drawing the sharp distinction between a sociological language game and a normative language game, I am assuming that it is possible to distinguish *is* from *ought*. In making this distinction I am going against certain fashionable contemporary trends. Critical realists and most postmodernists would claim that is not possible to separate the empirical and the normative, which is a claim that I concede has some truth to it. However, this observation is not an analytic claim; rather, it is one concerning the difficulties of *practice*. When thinking about how power is practised, it can sometimes be difficult to methodologically bracket normative perceptions. However, distinguishing between the normative and the empirical should not be considered an all-or-nothing phenomenon.

Even if it may not be possible to expunge every vestige of normative bias from sociological theory, it is possible to try your best to keep both kinds of claims separate, which is not an all-or-nothing phenomenon. Rather, normative and empirical claims should be considered as on a scale. The claim that 'the cat sat on the mat' is usually an empirical claim, and 'act according to moral precepts that can be universalized' is usually a normative one. That said, 'the cat sat on the mat' can have normative connotations within a specific context – maybe cats should (or should not) be sitting on mats? Furthermore, the statement 'the cat sat on the mat' uttered by a devoutly religious believer in some Ancient Egyptian ritual of cat worship could have strong normative connotations – it could be a divine sign of great moral provenance. However, in normal circumstances, 'the cat sat on the mat' would contrast with the normative injunction 'act according to moral precepts that can be universalized'. Again, while the latter is largely a normative claim, when giving substance to specific acts, this normative injunction has empirical content. The latter conceded, I would still argue that 'the cat sat on the mat' and the injunction 'act according to moral precepts that can be universalized' usually fall at different ends of a scale. In most contexts the former is close to the ideal, or pure, type of an empirical claim, while the latter is a predominantly normative one.

As we shall see, as the book develops, I am generally hostile to binary thinking, replacing binary either/or thinking with scalar both/and-type thinking. I fully accept that it is impossible to bracket normative considerations *entirely*, in binary fashion, so that a statement is a pure *is* or pure *ought* statement. However, if we think on a scale, where statements are more or less normative, there is a significant difference between normative and empirical claims. With a certain conscious level of analytic rigour and methodological bracketing, it is possible to make empirical theoretical claims about the *is* workings of power, which are qualitatively different from any normative accounts of how we think power should, or should not, be constituted. As we shall see later, in the analysis of 4-D power, it is precisely the capacity to make such distinctions that is central to modern proliferation of *disciplines*, both as subject areas and as a social subject predisposition.

Overall conceptualization of power

This book is structured around a conceptualization of power in four dimensions. These dimensions are inspired by Lukes' (1974) account of the power debates in three dimensions, with re-theorized aspects of Michel Foucault's work added as the fourth dimension, which follows Peter Digeser's (1992) suggested combination of Lukes and Foucault. In addition, my approach incorporates much of the work of more consensual power theorists (including Hannah Arendt, Barry Barnes, Peter Morriss and John Searle), wider sociological theory (especially Jeffrey Alexander, Pierre Bourdieu, Émile Durkheim, Ernest Gellner, Anthony Giddens, Norbert Elias and Max Weber), philosophy (including J. L. Austin, William James, Thomas Kuhn, John Searle and Ludwig Wittgenstein), psychology (especially Erik Erikson and Stanley Milgram) and normative political theory (among others Rainer Forst, Jurgen Habermas, Phillip Pettit, Richard Rorty and John Rawls). To this I have added many years of my own musings upon the subject. As a result, the four dimensions of power as theorized here are significantly different from the manner theorized by Lukes or in the work of Foucault.

For the reader who is unfamiliar with the power debates, and wishes to familiarize themselves with them, I refer them to Haugaard (2014) and Haugaard and Ryan (2012). However, what follows can be read without this background. I would ask readers who are familiar with the debates not to skip over the chapters on any of the dimensions, including the first and second, because I handle them differently from any previous theories – including my own previous work. Obviously, they may wish to skip the synopsis immediately below.

The four dimensions in brief

All four dimensions of power are ideal types. They constitute lenses that render certain perspectives of reality visible. The designation of dimensions of power constitutes a way of understanding particular aspects of power, while momentarily methodologically bracketing the other dimensions.

While I have just suggested that the four dimensions of power are complex in their detail, it is possible to conceptualize them in general terms relatively simply. I propose to do this, so the reader has a sense of where she is going. Viewed sociologically, the four dimensions of power each respectively focus upon *agency* (1-D), *structure* (2-D), *system of thought* (3-D) and *social ontology* (4-D).

In his seminal 1957 article on political power, Dahl describes 1-D agency power in the following terms:

> suppose a policeman is standing in the middle of an intersection at which most traffic ordinarily moves ahead; he orders all traffic to turn right or left; the traffic moves as he orders it to do. Then it accords with what I conceive to be the bedrock idea of power ...
>
> (Dahl 1957: 202)

In 1-D the focus is upon the momentary exercise of power, in which one actor makes another do something that they would not otherwise (Dahl 1957: 203), which was the perspective that interested Dahl most. 1-D is agent-centred and posits a direct causal relationship between two or more social agents, while the external structural conditions of possibility are taken as given.

While the intended emphasis is upon 1-D in the above example, in fact, all four dimensions of power are present. The 1-D aspect refers to the exercise of power by the police officer, which makes the driver do something that she would not otherwise do – turn right instead of left, or vice versa. The 2-D aspect refers to the social structures that make a police officer a *police officer*, with certain dispositional powers, which are reproduced every time there is compliance. If the driver does not comply, then there is 2-D structural conflict. 3-D refers to the tacit social knowledge that the driver and police officer share. The driver imposes the concept of *traffic police* upon someone wearing a particular hat or uniform, and in so doing it appears reasonable for her to comply. If the driver thinks of the police officer as having an absolute right to command, there is reification involved. The 4-D aspect refers to the internalized self-discipline necessary for drivers routinely to obey the highway code, which includes compliance with the demands of traffic police, even when the driver may not wish to do so. As we shall see, a driver with the temperament of a feudal knight would probably cut the police officer's head off.

In most social interaction all four dimensions of power are present, even if we choose to focus upon them one at a time. In this language game, the word *dimensions* is used analogously to the way we use the word to describe the four perspectives of the plans of a house. It is meaningful and informative to break the house into a *plan*, *front* and *back elevations* and two *end elevations* – four dimensions. Just because we focus momentarily upon the *plan* does not mean that the other dimensions have vanished into thin air. The plan gives us specific information about the house, which the other dimensions do not. Yet, we do not really understand the house just from focusing upon the plan. While we look at each aspect singly, full understanding comes from first separating and then combining all four aspects or dimensions.

Overview of the structure of the book

With regard to the first dimension of power, in Chapter 1, I include both power-over, as in Dahl, with power-to, as in Arendt (1970), Allen (1999) and Morriss (2002). By combining them I develop an account of conflict that lies on a scale from coercion to consensual legitimacy. This includes an account of performative authority, as foundational to agency, derived from Austin (1975), Alexander (2010), Searle (1996) and Weber (1978). In understanding everyday authority I explore it by its absence through the analysis of Primo Levi's experiences in Auschwitz (Levi 1991). 1-D authority emerges as empowerment and domination within the system. On the second dimension of power, in Chapter 2, I follow Bachrach and Baratz (1962 and 1963) in emphasizing bias. However, I add the category of structural conflict, which changes the essence of this dimension significantly. The latter is based upon a development of Giddens' (1984) theory of structuration and my own work (Haugaard 1992 and 1997) on structural reproduction. I argue that structural reproduction is interactive, thus with two possible reactions by others, confirm-structuration or destructuration. Structural conflict makes 2-D a significantly more radical conflict than 1-D. In Chapter 3, I bring the first and second dimension of power into dialogue. I argue that 1-D conflict and 2-D conflict are significantly different, and that the creation of systems entails moving from deep 2-D conflicts to shallower 1-D conflicts. This includes an account of various forms of resistance, including passive resistance, and revolutions.

With regard to the third dimension of power, in Chapter 4, I drop the idea of false-consciousness, which is replaced by consciousness-raising. To this are added theories of paradigms and epistemes, from Kuhn (1970 and 1977) and Foucault (1970 and 1989), respectively. By refracting this against Austin (1975), what counts as *knowledge* emerges as performatively felicitous reasoned justification. In Chapter 5, I develop the third dimension of power to include reification, the distinction between the sacred and profane (as influenced by Alexander 2010). This includes a critique of the popularly held belief, which has been hugely influential in many fields, including postmodernism and modern art, that the conventional nature of structures renders them arbitrary, which is not the case. In Chapter 6, I engage with Truth (with a capital T) as reification, which includes a playful critique of Descartes characterized as a theologian, rather than as a philosopher. The latter is done while maintaining a theory of truth. This is intended as a clarification and re-theorization of Foucault's theory of power/knowledge/truth (Foucault 1980 and 1994), combined with Kuhn (1970 and 1977) and the earlier theory of knowledge in terms of performative success.

In Chapter 7, I discuss the fourth dimension as the social construction of social subjects, which is influenced by Elias (1995), Erikson (1995), Garfinkel (1984), Giddens (1984), Foucault (1979) and Milgram (2010a and 2010b). From Erikson, Garfinkel, Giddens and Milgram, I develop the concept of ontological security as core to 4-D. Using Elias and Foucault as correctives to each other, I look at modes of internalization of self-restraint, as both enabling and constraining, in both fields of knowledge and politics. As observed by Elias, in a complex system of interdependence internalized restraint replaces external coercion, which I argue is key to democratic politics. However, as observed by Foucault, this self-restraint has dominating aspects. Overall, new forms of 4-D have significant implications for the extent and nature of violence in contemporary society. In Chapter 8, I explore the social construction of social subjects in extreme situations, including social death. 4-D is theorized with respect to slavery and solitary confinement, which is influenced by the work of Patterson (1982) and Guenther (2013).

The last chapter is normative and is significantly different from any current normative perspectives in political theory. It is based upon an understanding of how power works and the orientation is pragmatist. What defines *ought* is evaluated relative to the question: what are power structures for? In particular: what are liberal-democratic power structures for? I argue that most normative theorists think in a binary way, dividing the world into oppressors and oppressed. They assume that power is zero-sum, which constitutes a profound theoretical mistake. I argue for a scalar theory of power, where the dual empowering and dominating aspects of power play a crucial role. Key to the theory is the idea of normative desirability as positive-sum power, which respects all social actors as ends in themselves. Most systems are more or less desirable, while normative theories seeking perfection, inspired by imagined utopias (see Cooke 2006), violate what we know about the nature of social and political power. Consequently, utopian thinking invariably leads to totalitarian nightmares. Similarly, reifying discourses including, for instance, appeals to the *will of the people* – current in populist politics (Muller 2016) – also have normatively undesirable qualities. In contrast, pragmatic sociologically informed accounts of power entail an acceptance of imperfection and quest for balance that, ironically, in their lesser ambition, lead to better societies than more ambitious idealistic utopian and reifying visions.

Note

1 Hindess (1995) observes this distinction but concludes that only normative analysis is interesting. As he does not explain why, this is left as a subjective preference, which is difficult to engage with theoretically.

1

The first dimension of power: Violence, coercion and authority

The first dimension of power is attributed to Dahl. We will expand upon it to include accounts of positive-sum power, authority, coercion and (in Chapter 3) contrast 1-D with deeper forms of 2-D conflict. This chapter builds upon the work of Allen (1999), Austin (1975), Barnes (1988), Clegg (1989), Parsons (1963) and Searle (1996).

Routine power as agency

In Dahl's model an exercise of power takes place when an agent makes a difference in the world by making something happen that would not otherwise have happened if it were not for that agent's actions. Dahl uses the example of a police officer directing a motorist in a direction they would not otherwise have gone (Dahl 1957: 202). As Dahl was a democratic theorist, who developed his vocabulary of power as a conceptual toolkit to test the quality of democratic participation (Dahl 1961), the democratic process also constitutes a paradigmatic instance of the routine exercise of 1-D power. Through the use of elections and parliaments one political party prevails over another and individual citizens have an effect.

The police officer and the democratic process of 1-D power presuppose some level of legitimacy relative to the less powerful compliant social actor. However, 1-D power also includes more coercive and illegitimate exercises of power. The command from a highway robber (*Your money or I shoot!*) constitutes an exercise of 1-D power. Unlike the police officer, this is based upon coercion and is regarded as illegitimate. In everyday speech, it is the coercive form of power that springs to mind. As we shall see, in actual social life both aspects of 1-D power co-exist. In short, the distinction between legitimate and illegitimate 1-D is what Weber would call an *ideal type* (Weber 1970: 294 and 2011: 47–66), which is an abstraction that constitutes the essence of a social phenomenon but rarely exists in its pure form.

Power-over, power-to and power-with

Since Dahl's work, Allen has introduced the distinction between *power-over*, *power-to* and *power-with* (Allen 1999). In 1-D, the *power-over* aspect of agency is obvious. A police officer exercises power-over drivers and in a democracy the winning party exercises power-over those who lose an election. However, as has been emphasized by Morriss (2002) and Pansardi (2012), this power-over constitutes a manifestation of a wider capacity for action, which presupposes power-to. Both police and winning parties have a generic capacity for action, or power-to, which is a condition of possibility of their capacity for interactive power-over.

In a successful exercise of power-over, the capacity for action, or power-to, is not only possessed by the more powerful but also the less powerful. For an exercise of power to be successful, the respondent B has to have the power-to do as A commands. It is for this reason that power-over is usually exercised over persons with some power-to. The ultimate exclusion is to be so powerless that you are unworthy of having power exercised over you – the poorest of the poor fall into this category. The abjectly powerless fall outside, or are excluded from, the social system. Or, they find themselves included only through their vulnerability, in demeaning ways, including slavery.

In the case of legitimate power, the exercise of power-over feeds back to *empower* B. Compliance with the authority of the traffic police delivers B *power-to* drive in an ordered system of traffic. This is in contrast to purely coercive power, as in *Your money or I shoot!* By handing over her money the responding actor loses capacity for action (she no longer has that money), while in the case of legitimate power-over, the response feeds back into the reproduction of the responding actor's power-to. In an ordered traffic system, responding appropriately to the rules of the road empowers drivers.

Typically, power-with refers to collective organization between A and B in order to enhance their collective power-to (Allen 1999). Minorities joining forces are an instance of power-with. Also, organizations created for a collective goal are instances of power-with. Furthermore, there is a sense in which all collectives, even informal ones, entail power-with. Much of everyday interaction concerns ritualized greetings that are expressions of solidarity. The phatic communion greeting *Hello, how are you?* constitutes an expression of solidarity *with* the other, or collective power-with. This results in collective dispositional power-to resources that may or may not be activated by individual members.

Reinforcing feedbacks between power-over and power-to

The power-over and power-to aspects of interaction are not necessarily separate events but often constitute a duality. The fact that drivers accept the power-over of the traffic police and follow the highway code enables them to drive in an ordered manner, which gives them a capacity for action.

In the democratic process, there are winners and losers. However, in a properly functioning democratic system, the loser is not an absolute loser. When the election is over, the structures of the election are reproduced and this gives the loser the capacity for action (or power-to) to fight another election. Consequently, in a well-balanced democracy there is a virtuous cycle between power-over and power-to.

While 1-D power can be mutually empowering, it is frequently not so. In instances of power-over as pure domination, the feedbacks from power-over to power-to are absent. If the more powerful, dominant, A exercises power-over the less powerful, or subordinate, B in a manner whereby the power-to gain is all in A's favour, B is dominated and has little pragmatic reason to comply. Consequently, such a relationship requires coercion as a base for power-over. If someone holds a gun to someone else's head, and says *Your money or I shoot!* the compliant B gains nothing from the interaction. Consequently, the sole reason for B's compliance is her response to coercion.

Domination

Typically, domination is not either/or but on a scale. Many relationships of power-over entail a mix of domination and mutual empowerment. For instance, in economic exploitation, the exploited party gains some power-to, while the more powerful person typically gains comparatively greater power-to.

In the power debates there was a tendency to assume that 1-D was inherently and therefore solely dominating power. Domination refers to a power relationship where A gains at the expense of B. This dominating view of power is exemplified by Lukes' 1974 definition of power, which is as follows: 'A exercises power over B when A affects B in a manner *contrary to B's interests*' (Lukes 1974: 27; italics added).

Following the discussion in the introduction concerning language games, there is no singular correct definition of power. I am not saying that Lukes was categorically wrong to define power in this way. Rather, from a sociological point of view I wish to emphasize the complexity of power relations and to explore how empowerment and domination are nearly always mixed. This enables us to understand the relative stability and dynamics of complex power systems.

From a normative perspective the assumption that power is inherently obnoxious leads to the belief that what is the most normatively desirable objective is the total abolition of political power-over. In reality, the aim of removing all conflict, and all power-over, entails the suppression of conflict. Often this is presented as a utopian vision of power-with replacing power-over. In everyday discourse, this is characterized in terms of a vision of cooperation replacing domination, or love replacing war. However, as we shall see later, in greater depth, an entire society based purely upon power-with and power-to is impossible. Systems that appear this way create the illusion of the absence of power-over by suppression of conflict of interests, which entails massive 3-D and 4-D social control to block all potential dissent.

Power as variable-sum: zero-sum and positive-sum power

As argued by Baldwin (2015), the negatively evaluative perception of power (power as domination) was not inherent in Dahl's conceptualization of power. Rather, it was a later attribution. If we emphasize only the negative aspects of power, only domination, understanding why actors often consent to power-over becomes difficult.

The perception that power-over is necessarily dominating comes from the assumption that power-over is zero-sum. *Your money or I shoot!* is a classic example of zero-sum power. In zero-sum power relationships the gain of the powerful is entirely at the expense of the less powerful. However, sophisticated structured relations of power are usually not zero-sum but are positive-sum. In positive-sum relationships both parties gain something, even if the more powerful usually gains the most.

Zero-sum power relationships are unstable relationships. When a subordinate gains nothing, the only reason for the subordinate's compliance is fear of coercion. Consequently, the subordinate remains a potential revolutionary, biding her time until she has the chance to overthrow the elite. Usually, pure coercion begets a coercive response, which is akin to constantly living on the side of a volcano. Zero-sum systems are inherently unstable, and consequently often characterized by violence.

From the perspective of the more powerful there is a short-term advantage to coercive relationships because coercion enables the more powerful to disregard the desires of the less powerful. However, in the longer term the instability of the relationship is to the disadvantage of the more powerful. For this reason there is a tendency for complex systems to become positive-sum. The only exception to this is terrorization of the less powerful subjects. In that case there is a 4-D power effect that renders the compliant social actor particularly docile, fatalistically accepting her domination. It is also possible to build complex systems this way, but this is exceptional. We will discuss this qualification further, with regard to slavery and solitary confinement, in Chapter 8.

Positive-sum relationships tend to be more stable, as resistance is low. This is most obviously the case with respect to power-with organizations that are directed at goals desired by the less powerful. An educator exercises power-over a student. When this is a genuine pedagogic relationship, the student gains a capacity for action, or power-to, from the power-over of the teacher. That power-to constitutes an incentive for the student to accept the legitimacy of the power-over of the teacher. In the ideal type, perfect instance, the power-over of the teacher constitutes a power-with relationship between pedagogue and learner. Of course, as observed by Willis (2016), many working-class children resist teacher authority, which could potentially empower them, because they find the status difference objectionable in principle.

As a qualification on the above, moving from ideal types to reality, we must not forget that even though educational institutions and other power-with organizations are in principle empowering, they do presuppose everyday power-over relations that are open to uses other than those intended. It is quite likely, without checks and balances, that those with power-over may use that power for their own interests, rather than the goals of the less powerful. Such use of power-over is domination because the power-over only serves to enhance the power-to of the more powerful. In supposedly power-with relations, domination is often less visible than in more overt domination where no pretext is made of serving the interests of the less powerful. A variation on this is when those working for an organization reify the organization above its intended purpose. So, they protect the organization from the normatively legitimate contestation or resistance of the less powerful. In the eyes of the more powerful, protecting the organization can appear altruistic.

Less positive-sum than sharing goals, but still positive-sum, are attempts to manage conflict in such a manner that they cease to be zero-sum. The democratic process is the classic procedure for stabilizing power relationships by turning conflicts into positive-sum power-over relationships. When political party A prevails over political party B, there is a recognition of real conflict and the gain for A may be significant. Yet, the loss for B is not absolute. The democratic process consists of a set of political structures, which entails that those with the most votes win and take power. The moment the loser concedes defeat the democratic structures are reproduced and, once reproduced, those structures exist as a resource for B to prevail over A in the next election. Consequently, when party B loses, he does not lose absolutely or in a zero-sum manner. Once B acknowledges his defeat, he contributes to the reproduction of democratic power structures, which in the longer term are enabling to B. Next time around it may be party A who concedes defeat.

Resolving conflicts by turning zero-sum power-over into positive-sum power-over is distinguishable from the resolution of conflict based upon creating a relationship of pure power-with. The latter suggests turning adversaries into allies and collaborators. This solution to power conflict is more idealistic but also more utopian. Communist and other utopian models are premised upon turning conflict, and power-over, into power-with. In contrast, democratic models do not seek to eliminate conflict; they re-channel it from zero-sum power into positive-sum power.

As we will see in greater depth in Chapter 9, in most instances democracy emerges out of an attempt to stabilize social relations. Over time elites buy off resistance by offering some stake in the system to the less powerful, with democratic norms emerging as a result. This more pragmatist and realist view of the emergence of democracy is in contrast to a more idealist image of populations becoming converted to justice and fairness.

The continued existence of the democratic process presupposes that the less powerful have a stake in the system, whereby they also gain some power-to. However, this empowerment of B has to be real, not just theoretical, in order to result in stability. If B represents a permanent minority who always find themselves in opposition, then the gain is not real, and so the relationship is zero-sum, even if the trappings of democracy, including regular elections, exist. Normatively this is an insidious form of domination, as the name of democracy is invoked and election rituals take place, but this is not real democracy. In such cases, the system tends to be unstable. Over time, permanent minorities tend to resort to violence and coercion because the democratic process does not offer the possibility of positive-sum empowerment. Models of consociational democracy (Lipjardt 2008) are an attempt to stabilize this kind of situation by making it mandatory that government includes the minority. Thus a minority gains a stake in the system.

Episodic and dispositional power

In theorizing democratic power-over it is useful to distinguish between episodic and dispositional power (Clegg 1989; Wrong 2009). Episodic power is momentary power, while dispositional power refers to the capacities that an actor has. In the election example, the winner gains power-over episodically. However, dispositionally both parties gain, as the democratic system constitutes a resource that gives them both the dispositional power to prepare for another election, where the episodic result may be different.

In making sense of both the dominating and emancipatory aspects of power it is essential to move away from binary either/or thinking. Power relations are usually not binary but on a scale, or *scalar*. In a democratic contest, and in many other political power systems, there will always be winners and losers but as long as the losers are not absolute losers they still have reason to buy into the system. If episodic loss does not feed into dispositional loss of power for those who lose, then the democratic process remains stable.

A perfect circulation of elites, where winners and losers take turns, is the most positive-sum outcome possible. As will be argued in greater depth in Chapter 9, maximally positive-sum power relations are the most politically stable and normatively desirable. However, most actual democracies fall short of this ideal. Modern political systems are not *either* democratic or undemocratic; they are *more or less democratic*, relative to certain criteria (see Hyland 1995).

Political stability is increased the more episodic loss is balanced by dispositional gain. Conversely, the more episodic loss is also dispositional, the deeper the conflict and the more unstable the system.

Resources

1-D power includes power-to and power-with, which entails the joint capacity for action. If actors set up an organization to achieve a particular shared goal (power-with), they are essentially creating a socio-political power machine to give themselves agency, or power-to. Any power-with organization will have some minimal hierarchy, so also entail power-over. Political and organizational institutions exist either to manage conflict (the democratic process would be typical, as would a labour court) or to build capacity.

Dahl was at great pains to distinguish between the *exercise of power* and *power resources* – a distinction he developed with great clarity in his encyclopaedia article on power (Dahl 1968). Resources are what social actors draw upon in the exercise of power. Resources exist outside the momentary exercise of episodic power. Resources are the *potentia* of power (see Saar 2010), which constitutes the dispositional power of the social actors in question.

There are three broad categories of power resources: coercive resources, authoritative resources and economic resources. Let us examine each in turn.

Coercion

Coercive power is the most direct and, I would argue, the crudest form of 1-D power resource. As we are about to see, it is not tied into the other dimensions of power in the substantive way authoritative and economic resources tend to be. For that reason it tends to be less stable.

Coercion works upon the subordinate B through the threat of deprivation and is one stage removed from violence. Arendt famously, and controversially, argued that power and violence are opposites (Arendt 1970). What she had in mind was direct physical violence where the compliance of the subordinate (B) comes purely in response to the actions of the more powerful (A). This is ideal type thinking, where violence has no structured and symbolic content, which is actually relatively rare. Typical actual instances of pure violence would be a random shooting or stabbing attack.

In contemporary socio-political systems pure violence is the exception, not the rule. Most actual violence has symbolic content. For instance, violent rape and slavery are deeply symbolic and tied into wider aspects of gendered and structural domination (3-D and 4-D).

At the opposite end of the scale from pure violence lies authority. In an authority relationship the power of the powerful (A) is directly linked to the cognitions and perceptions of the subordinate (B). The subordinate recognizes that A has authority, which entails meaning and structure.

If considered in a scalar manner, with violence at one end of the scale and authority at the other, coercion falls between pure violence and authority. In coercion the reason for compliance by the subordinate comes from a fear of deprivation, either through violence or material/economic deprivation. However, if coercion is structured, in the sense that the subordinate is informed that if she complies then potential violence/deprivation against her will not be actualized, this has symbolic content and, in that sense, the interaction is communicative.

Weber argued that *social action* is distinct from action that is non-social. Two cyclists structuring their cycling to avoid each other is social action, while the same cyclists colliding randomly is action of a physical kind. The former presupposes shared communication, while the latter does not (Weber 1978: 4–24). Using this distinction, pure violence (as an ideal type) does not presuppose communication, while coercion is communicative.

Coercion can be one-off, such as *Give me your money or I shoot!* However, in complex political systems coercion is usually structured. In complex social systems there are rules around how to avoid coercive sanctions, which the subaltern learns and consequently structures their behaviour appropriately. There are exceptions to this, when coercion is used to terrorize the subordinate, by disordering their lives, which is a point we come to in the discussion of 4-D power (Chapter 8).

Legitimate coercive power-over

We have already observed that power-over is often linked to power-to. While in everyday speech we tend to think of coercive power-over as inherently dominating, this assumption is not correct. The modern state has a monopoly of violence, which is usually justified following Hobbesian-type normative justification. The Hobbesian normative legitimizing justification for state coercion comes from the problem of collective actions. In game theory this is referred to as counter-finality, which is exemplified by the tragedy of the commons (Elster 2015; Laver 1997).

As a thought experiment, imagine ten farmers who share a commons that can support 100 sheep without environmental degradation. With this number there is an optimal yield of grass-to-sheep ratio. Hence, the most mutually beneficial use of the commons is for each farmer to keep ten sheep. However, if this arrangement is purely voluntary, there is a tendency for each individual farmer to reason as follows: *if I were to keep just one or two extra sheep above my quota that will not make any real difference, overall. However, the gain to me will be significant.* Or, they may be less selfish and reason as follows: *my neighbours are not trustworthy, so I had better get my extra sheep up there ahead of the rest before they spoil the commons.* Either way, the aggregate effect of each farmer thinking individually is that the commons becomes over-grazed, to the collective detriment. To avoid this suboptimal outcome, the farmers agree to set up an enforcer of the 'ten-sheep rule', who has coercive power resources to ensure compliance. Hence, in this instance coercive power-over works to counter the individual temptation to make an exception of self.

When coercive power is used to overcome suboptimal tragedy-of-the-commons-type situations, it is in the interests of those who are coerced, thus coercion is not dominating from a dispositional perspective. This form of coercion works to ensure resources are used in a positive-sum manner. However, in these situations the *coercive* aspect tends to become *auxiliary* to the phenomenon of *authority*, as social actors understand why coercion is necessary, and in so doing confer authority upon the enforcer. Similarly, in the instance of the traffic police or democratic elections coercive enforcement tends to be auxiliary to a perception of legitimacy in the system.

In everyday life, the tendency for social actors to make an exception of self requires mutual coercion to rectify that defect. The combination of coercion and authority delivers the desired effect. Coercion and authority are ideal types that in the real world usually exist in combination. As a qualification to the above, there is always the problem that the powerful enforcer will make an exception of self, in which case what was set up as normatively legitimate coercion deviates from the ideal type and becomes domination.

Authority

Authority is a symbolic and communicative phenomenon (for a fuller account of authority see Haugaard 2018). It follows a pattern set out by Searle (1996 and 2007), which is as follows: *X counts as Y in circumstances C*. Any object or person (an X) counts as Y (a figure or institution with authority) in circumstances C (the structured institutional context). For instance, the individual Barack Obama was an ordinary person (an X), who won an election in the USA (circumstances C), and so became president (Y). The President of the USA is a powerful figure. Yet, this authority power is largely premised upon subordinate actors (citizens of the USA), who perceive X as Y in circumstances C.

As argued by Barry Barnes (1988), a president's authority is premised upon the response of those over whom he exercises authority. In everyday speech we may say, *President A has power*. However, sociologically, this means, *President A has authority power conferred upon her by members of the polity*. Authority is created by those who perceive persons in a certain way (as a Y) and react appropriately. The responding others constitute *a ring of reference* for that authority (Barnes 1988: 51).

Theoretically, what is the difference between the real-life Napoleon and the 'psychiatric napoleons' with delusions of grandeur? It is that Napoleon had a ring of reference composed of the French public who were willing to confirm his authority, while the latter napoleons do not have such a ring of reference (Haugaard 1997: 30). If no-one believes you are a Y, you are not a Y, however deep that self-belief in Y-ness. It is the belief of others that is key.

As argued by Alexander, authority is fundamentally tied to meaning (Alexander 2011: 82). Coercion presupposes some meaning; the powerful A must communicate to the subordinate B what to do, and how failure to do so entails sanctions. However, when X counts as Y in circumstances C, it is the meaning of Y-ness that defines the nature of the resources involved. In this case it is the nature of shared concepts and their implications that are constitutive of power resources. Authority is a cognitive phenomenon, which gives it a profound epistemic 3-D aspect (Chapter 4).

Authority and scope of resources

Dahl was at great pains to point out that resources are usually confined in scope (Dahl 1968). For instance, *university professors* (Y1) have authoritative power-over what students read and write, while the *traffic police* (Y2) have power-over where they park their cars.

The scope of authority power resources is tied to meaning. In class, when lecturing on the subject of authority and power resources, I routinely perform an informal breaching experiment of the norms of society. I (an X) in the capacity of Y (*university professor*) give all my students a two-day extension on the due date of their essays. They treat this as something serious, which is a reasonable exercise of power-over. However, I then follow this with an instruction that they should all take a cold shower when they get home. They stare at me as if I have gone slightly mad and then laugh. The meaning of the concept *university professor* is structurally incompatible with giving the order to take a shower. While perhaps a less onerous task than writing an essay, ordering students to take a shower is beyond my Y-status authority.

Authority is specific in scope relative to meaning. Authority power has a more confined scope than coercion. For instance, a *concentration camp guard* has power that is largely based upon coercion (not authority). As a consequence he has the power to determine what the inmates read, when they take showers and so on.

Relative to students, both university professors and traffic police have authority power resources. However, they do not constitute a singular elite because the scope of their authority resources is different and not combinable. In contrast, in order to govern society a single power elite must either have power resources that are of wide scope, or their resources must be easily combinable. As argued by Dahl (1961 and 1989), a plurality of elites is compatible with democratic politics, while the existence of a single elite is not.

In contrast to authority, coercion does not work through the formula *X counts as Y in circumstances C*. Consequently, coercion is a power resource that is wide in scope. It is for this reason that singular elites (dictators and so on) constantly revert to coercion. While authority has the virtue of being self-reinforcing in its exercise (the more authority is exercised, the stronger it becomes as it sediments in the ring of reference), it has the disadvantage of being highly specific in scope. In contrast, when coercion is exercised it is not usually self-reinforcing (except at a subtle 3-D level whereby agents come to take coercion for granted, and at a 4-D level, where it reinforces a resigned fatalistic timorous personality type) but has the advantage over authority that it is less confined in scope or is more fungible.

Everyday authority

We generally tend to think of authority in terms of elites in powerful positions, which ignores the fact that authority is actually an everyday phenomenon, tied to social roles and identity. This everyday authority is particularly strong in Western liberal democracies, where being a *citizen* entails having significant authority. This authority was something that was fought for over centuries but is currently so taken-for-granted as to be virtually invisible. Because we tend to take everyday authority for granted, we underestimate the extent to which the fabric of social order is built around authority.

The best way of making everyday authority visible is by examining its absence in social situations where one would normally take it for granted. Primo Levi was a professional chemist who was, by his own definition of his identity, 'an Italian *citizen* of Jewish race' (Levi 1991: 4; italics added). However, in early 1944 he was captured by the Fascists and then deported to Auschwitz, where he worked as Jewish slave labour. At first he worked in the open air doing physical slave labour but in November 1944 Levi became an assistant inside the camp chemical laboratories of IG Farben's Buna-Werke, which saved his life, as it spared him the worst cold of winter and enabled him to secure extra food. In other words, this was a gain in material or economic resources.

While Levi gained in material resources, he did not gain authority relative to the norms he had left behind as an Italian citizen or as a professional. Usually, a professional chemist has a relatively high Y-status authority inside the laboratory. This gave Levi a momentary misapprehension that he had gained that authority once he entered the laboratory. Not only did he not regain the authority of a professional chemist; he did not regain the Y authority of *a citizen*. Inside the laboratory the cleaners were German and resided outside the camp. According to the racial hierarchy, they were Aryan, which entailed a high Y-status function. The manager of the laboratory was a political prisoner. The Y-status function of the latter was not nearly as low-status as the Jews; they were more like regular prisoners in contemporary jails. In the following extract Levi describes his interaction, or lack of it, with one of the German cleaners.

> When they [German cleaners] sweep, they sweep our feet. They never speak to us and turn up their noses when they see us shuffling across and the laboratory, filthy, squalid, insecure in our shoes. I once asked Fraulein Liczba [German cleaner] for some information, and she did not reply but turned with an annoyed face to Stawinoga [laboratory manager – a political prisoner] and spoke to him quickly. I did not understand the sentence, but I clearly grasped '*stinkjude*' and my blood froze. Stawinoga told me that for anything to do with work we should turn directly to him.
>
> (Levi 1991: 168)

As has been argued by Taylor (1989), part of the modern process of democratization, which gathered pace from the seventeenth century onwards, was a slow affirmation of the value of the *ordinary life*. This entails the recognition, or social construction, of the equal moral worth of all citizens. Obviously, this idea spread slowly through the hierarchies of society. First, all *property-owning men* were of equal moral worth, then *men*, then *women*, then people of different colour and so on. This equal worth was not simply about the vote but also a much deeper phenomenon. To be of equal moral worth, every member of society has a shared minimal Y-status function, which confers authority. I term this *citizen's authority*.

In European states that are not republics, where the members technically remain *subjects* (not citizens) relative to a monarch, that status also translates into the everyday authority of equal moral worth. In practice, in European democratic monarchies being a *subject* is equivalent to being a citizen in a republic. Hence, although not technically accurate, I will use the term *citizen* for both.

Minimally, to have a citizen's authority means to be the author of your own acts. It is, to echo the work of Pettit (1997, 2012 and 2014; Haugaard and Pettit 2017), the opposite of slavery. The slave does not have the full authority to interact with others because he exists for the sake of his master.

The most basic form of citizen's authority is to have the status function of a person with whom others interact. That the cleaners swept Levi's feet was a symbolic representation of the fact that he did not have the status of a person. Much of everyday trivial interaction, or phatic communion, such as saying *thank you* at the checkout, constitutes an acknowledgment of the fact that the other has the status authority of a person of equal moral worth. There is a *person* at the till, as distinct from a machine.

In contrast, in deeply hierarchical societies, the less powerful become invisible to the powerful. In practice this does happen in so-called democratic societies, with regard to certain groups, in subtle ways. Speaking *about another person*, who is present, without acknowledging their presence, has the effect of delegitimizing their claim to the status function of full authority. They remain an X without the Y-status function of a person. For instance, speaking to a third party *about* a person in a wheelchair or who is elderly, yet who is physically present, without acknowledging their interactive presence would be an instance of not endowing them with the Y-status function authority of equal moral worth. Typical in this regard would be the following: *Does he take sugar? Can she use the shower by herself? Does he understand? Can she go out on her own?* etc. In a recent study Mik-Meyer and Haugaard (2019) explored to what extent persons in Danish homeless shelters have citizen's authority with respect to social workers. This is an interesting case, as homeless persons do not have a lot of authority, yet their citizen's authority was still present.

Authority as performative action

Authority is a phenomenon that Austin refers to as *perfomative* action. As with the Levi example, Austin uses the absence of authority to show the essence of authority. Let us for a moment examine Austin's thought experiment characterization of performatives.

> Suppose for example, I see a vessel on the stock, walk up and smash the bottle hung on the stem, proclaim 'I name this ship the Mr. Stalin' and for good measure kick away the chocks: but the trouble is, I was not the person chosen to name it (whether or not – an additional complication – Mr. Stalin was the destined name: perhaps in a way it is even more of a shame if it was). We shall agree
>
> 1) that the ship was not thereby named;
> 2) that it is an infernal shame
>
> One could say that 'I went through a form of' naming the vessel but that my action was void or without effect, because I was not a proper person, had not the 'capacity', to perform it: but one might also alternatively say ... it is a mockery, like marriage to a monkey.
>
> (Austin 1975: 23–4)

Austin did not have the authority to name ships, just as Primo Levi did not have the authority to speak to Aryan Germans.

Failure in the reproduction of authority has an element of unreasonableness versus reasonableness. It is unreasonable for Austin to think he can name ships, while it is reasonable for the Queen of England to think she can. The conceptual tools that Austin devised to express this dichotomy were *felicity* and *infelicity*. Austin's actions were infelicitous, while the Queen going through the same actions would be felicitous.

Notice that it is the interacting others who decide what is felicitous or what is not; it is not for the person claiming the authority. It is the ring of reference that determines whether an action is felicitous or infelicitous. It was Fraulein Liczba, as a member of the Nazi ring of reference, who decided that Levi's interaction was infelicitous. An infelicitous action is not simply wrong but suggests some kind of deep unreasonableness. This (supposed) unreasonableness means that the person engaging is infelicitous and can be *ignored as irrelevant* or as part of the furniture, in the case of Levi. The infelicitous-cum-unreasonable do not have the Y-status authority for agency.

The difference between Austin and Levi is that, while Austin does not have the authority to name ships, he does have the authority of an average citizen or person. Levi's authority is significantly less again because of the epistemic logic (3-D power aspects – Chapters 4–6) of the Nazis. However, from a sociological point of view, the process of non-recognition or infelicity-cum-unreasonableness is the same while, of course, normatively it is entirely different.

Referring back to the breaching experiment with my students, when I gave my students a two-day extension upon their essay, that was *felicitous* with regard to the meaning of *professor*. In contrast, my order for the students to take a cold shower was entirely *infelicitous* and unreasonable, which is why it provoked laughter. As observed by Arendt (1970: 45), laughter and authority power are opposites.

Authority as variable-sum

Authority is decreased when used inappropriately – what in everyday speech is termed *corruption*. When a person in authority uses their authority inappropriately relative to their Y-status function they are running the risk of a reaction of infelicity. When that happens there is the further risk that members of the ring of reference will withdraw the Y-status that X enjoys. Because authority is conferred externally, the person in authority cannot by themselves will new forms of authority resources into existence, as they would be inconsistent with their ring-of-reference-defined Y-status function. The authority of a person or office is directly proportional to the strength of their surrounding ring of reference. Authority used well will reinforce the ring of reference, while authority misused undermines the ring of reference.

In order not to deflate the ring of reference the misuse of authority must be kept covert and singular (although there can be lots of singular events). So, for instance, if a politician or professional asks for personal sexual favours or bribes in exchange for access to their Y authority, that may be effective in a particular episodic instance. As long as that member of the ring of reference does not communicate this to the rest of the ring of reference, the overall ring of reference is left intact and so the dispositional power of the powerful remains. However, when knowledge of this misuse becomes generally known to the public the Y-status authority of the powerful is damaged.

The *#MeToo* campaign is essentially a campaign to delegitimize the authority of persons in public life who have abused their authority. When many women state that they have been inappropriately propositioned as part of an abuse of authority, they are essentially undermining the ring of reference that constitutes that authority. In the case of film stars this authority is informal social power authority. In the case of more formal political authority there are usually procedures for the removal of such individuals. Even where this is not so, as in the informal case, once knowledge of the inappropriate use of authority becomes widespread, irreparable damage is done to the political authority.

The variable-sum nature of authority also points towards the positive-sum increase of authority. When authority is used appropriately the responding social actors gain trust in the authority. So, the authoritative power of those in authority increases.

In most complex societies a bureaucratic office entails training, which is aimed at internalizing the self-restraint necessary to ensure that the X does not abuse their Y-status function. This entails social subject formation, thus 4-D power. Authority is linked to the overall internalization of restraint of a society. As we shall see in the discussion of the work of Elias, in Chapter 7, modernity entailed an increase in the self-restraint that was functional to the evolution of modern bureaucracy.

In instances of charismatic authority, the special qualities of the X person have a positive feedback into the Y-status function. If an X is particularly trustworthy, or considered unlikely to abuse authority, then the ring of reference will be likely to confer greater Y-status function. Often, as we shall see in the discussion of the sacred, charismatic authority has a kind of magical quality about it. People attribute the individual X with special powers that make the members of the ring of reference willing to confer extra Y-status function.

It is one of the ironies of authority that the unrestrained desire to increase authority undermines it, while the appropriate use of authority, evidenced by the lack of any illicit or infelicitous attempts to increase it, actually augments authority. Generally, those who want authority to empower only themselves tend to lose it, while those who use authority cautiously, in order to empower others, increase it.

Simulacrum authority

When authority decreases through its inappropriate use, coercion can serve as a substitute. Eventually the amount of legitimate authority is significantly less than coercion. Those occupying such positions will still *claim* to have authority but it is in *name only*. Where authority is only a simulation of real authority, I will call this *simulacrum authority*. A person who takes power by force will proclaim their authority, or their Y-ness, which imitates real authority. This is why the leaders of military coups usually attempt to reinforce their power with a rigged (so-called) democratic election to the office of president. If the respondents do not accept the Y-ness as genuinely deserved and in reality compliance comes from coercion, this constitutes simulacrum authority. A military leader who becomes 'president' through a rigged election has the simulacrum Y-status authority of a president.

In everyday speech we do not distinguish between real authority and simulacrum authority. So, this constitutes a discipline-specific conceptual distinction, or specially made conceptual tool, which I am constructing to signal the different source of compliance. To be clear, I am not claiming that in everyday life despots do not claim authority power or that they are not referred to as having authority. This is an instance where everyday speech and sociological conceptual tools diverge.

It is also important to emphasize that real authority and simulacrum authority are not an either/or phenomenon. At the time of writing (2020), President Assad is engaged in a civil war in order to hold on to power. His presidential power largely rests upon coercion but it is also the case that he has loyal followers, mainly from the Alawite and Christian communities, from whom he enjoys genuine authority. So, he has both simulacrum and genuine authority.

Typically simulacrum authority imitates real authority, in order to stimu-late a change of view in the audience. Simulacrum authority figures will be particularly keen to exhibit the trappings of authority so as to emphasize their Y-status, in order to make it real. So, they may have elaborate uniforms or highly formalized and pompous modes of speech or interaction. This can be coupled with great ceremonial displays. Again, it has to be emphasized that to the extent to which these displays convince the people (according to the everyday logic *if it walks like a duck and quacks like a duck it must be a duck*) the president gains real authority. Over time it is possible for simulacrum authority to become the real deal.

A presidential inauguration or royal coronation is all part of the pro-cess of creating the belief in Y-status (see Bellah 1967). If that belief is in doubt, the ceremony may be made more elaborate to mask the simulacrum element of the authority. Normatively speaking, as I theorize democracy, Donald Trump is not a *democratically elected* president of the USA, as he had nearly 3 million votes fewer than Hilary Clinton. However, Trump gained the Y-status of president through a technicality of procedure (the Electoral College), as set out by the US Constitution. Immediately after his inaug-uration, Trump claimed that he had as big a crowd as the democratically elected predecessor, although photographic evidence suggested otherwise (Rein 2017). Recently, after a visit to France, Trump suggested that Fourth of July celebrations should be upped in pomp and ceremony to include a full military parade (Vazquez 2018). I conjecture that Trump understands that a ceremony presided over by the president, with large crowds as a visible ring of reference, could increase his democratically questionable Y-status presidential authority.

Economic resources

Economic resources have two 1-D aspects to them. On the one hand they can be used analogously to violence, as a form of coercive 1-D. A more powerful actor can exercise significant coercive power-over a subordinate by threatening the deprivation of material resources. Similar to the distinction between authority and coercion, the symbolic content of such an interaction is relatively simple. To be successful the powerful have to convey to the less powerful the nature of the deprivation promised. In these cases, beyond the communication of desired reactions the symbolic content ends.

Just as complex political systems require authority, advanced economies require a symbolic circulating media. As noted by Parsons (1963), there is a direct parallel between authority and money. An X (such as piece of paper with '50 euro' printed on it) counts as a Y (currency) in circumstances C (within the structures set out by the European Central Bank). Again, as with authority, currency Y-status function constitutes a unit of meaning that confers resources upon its possessor by virtue of that shared meaning.

The performative conventional nature of money is not apparent to the average user in a stable economic system. As argued by Parsons (1963), this becomes apparent if we consider the history of paper currency. Early money currency started as metal coins, made of gold, silver and copper, where the unit value was equivalent to the value of the metal content – a pound sterling was originally equivalent to one pound weight of silver with a purity of 92.5% (hence sterling silver as 0.925 silver). This type of coinage was a commodity in its own right. As economies expanded, paper money was issued, which could be redeemed against scarce metals. In the twentieth century the value of currency slowly became entirely socially constructed by convention only, or fiat currency. However, in the early stages paper money was viewed with suspicion. The equivalent today would be Bitcoin, which some claim as currency and others refuse to give the Y-status function of currency.

In times of economic crisis the conventional nature of currencies becomes manifest. From a theoretical point of view, commanding goods and services using paper money is a performative act, analogous to authority. In times of economic collapse and consequent hyper-inflation, the X (paper) ceases to have Y status (as currency with value) in circumstances C (hyper-inflation).

The symbolic and coercive aspects of economic resources are ideal types, and often are found together. In relations of exploitation, the person selling their labour may sell that labour at a price that is below its value because they are coerced by their need for scarce resources. Yet, by selling their labour power for so much an hour, they also reproduce the deeper Y-status function performative aspect of economic resources.

Beyond the Y-status of currency, they also reproduce the concept of abstract labour power as measured in clock-time. The symbolic equivalence required by the equation of labour-time and Y-status currency is particular to a given economic and interpretative system. As we shall see in the discussion of 3-D power, the symbolic nature of money and measured labour-time constitute epistemic phenomena characteristic of a historically specific system of thought.

2

The second dimension of power: Conflict over structures or deep conflict, and dominant ideology

In the analysis of 2-D power the focus is upon the structural aspects of power relations. Bachrach and Baratz (1962) described the second face of power (2-D) in terms of organizational bias, whereby certain issues were organized into politics, while others were organized out. While the perspective is agent-centred, the analysis lacks any engagement with the phenomenon of structural conflict. They had in mind covert agenda-setting, which takes place behind the scenes, rather than more overt dynamic agent-centred interactive structural conflict.

In this chapter we will explore structural bias and structural conflict. In routine structured 1-D power, such as the traffic police example or the democratic process, social subjects exercise agency within the parameters of social structures. Democratic conflicts take place within the structures of the democratic system. However, those structures came into being as the consequence of conflict *over* feudal/monarchical/colonial/patriarchal social structures. In 2-D conflict the social subject exercises agency by engaging in conflict over social structures. As we are about to explore, structural conflict has a very special quality that renders these events a deep form of social conflict.

Following on from this dynamic view of structural conflict, the less powerful are often fully aware of 2-D structural bias against them, yet they apparently acquiesce in their own domination. This phenomenon, known as the *dominant ideology thesis*, contradicts *some* of the assumptions of traditional Marxist false-consciousness-type arguments. The qualifier *some* is significant, as epistemic acquiescence (3-D) is a real and important aspect of social life (Chapters 4, 5 and 6).

In terms of structure, we will focus upon structural conflict and structural bias and conclude with dominant ideology. In the following chapter, we will look at some examples of 1-D and 2-D conflicts before going on to 3-D.

Social structure as interactive

In the literature there is a tendency to see structure as external to social action; agency entails action while structure constitutes external binding constraint or determinacy of action (see Hayward and Lukes 2008). This comes from imagining structure as some kind of solid skeletal form, analogous to scaffolding, that gives a system shape. However, a number of sociological theorists, most notably Elias (1995), Giddens (1984) and Bourdieu (1990), have been responsible for a rethinking of this conceptualization of structure. Rather than thinking of structure as a thing-in-itself, we should think of it as a *process*: as *structuring* or *structuration*.

It is a truism that society would not exist without individuals who are constantly reproducing those structures. This assertion is often taken as some kind of liberal individualist stance, often termed *methodological individualism*, where it is claimed that social actors are characterized as some kind of free choosers of social structures. This is entirely mistaken. In 2-D conflicts a given actor may wish to structure in a certain manner but that act of structuration may not be validated by others, and so remains an unsuccessful attempt at structural reproduction. The conditions of possibility for successful structural reproduction are hugely constrained. However, this constraint does not turn individuals into dupes of the system. They constantly monitor and evaluate the conditions of possibility and structure accordingly. In place of methodological individualism the perspective used here can be characterized as *methodological interactionism*.[1]

Routine reproduction of social structure

Following Wittgenstein's private language argument (1967) and Austin's account of performatives (1975), I argue that much of social action is characterized by *interactive structural conflicts* (Haugaard 1997: 119–162 and 1992).[2] In this perspective, all meaningful social interaction has a structured and goal-oriented aspect. The structured aspect of social action is the systemic element, which entails meaning. For instance, when a social actor uses a 50-euro note to make a purchase (their goal), the structural elements include, among others: the Y-status meaning of a 50-euro note, structures of language, structures of capitalist modes of production and so on. When I structure the economic Y-status function of a 50-euro note the interaction is successful only because there are others who are willing to confirm that Y-status. The same applies to authority. The Y-status of a president exists only because there is a ring of reference that is willing to confirm any Y-status-based exercises of the authority (structuration) by the president. In validating Y-status, for both the euro and the president, the ring of reference essentially *confirms* the Y-status structure of the initial acts of structuration. In short, an individual *structures* and the ring of reference *confirm-structures* and in that instance the social structure is reproduced.

Much of structure is reproduced as the unintentional effect of intentional action – when buying a pound of sugar the average customer and cashier do not reflect upon the fact that they are interactively co-reproducing the value of money and, following that, the structures of the capitalist system of exchange. However, while in routine interaction these elements are taken for granted, they can equally be the subject of conflict and contestation.

If the structures are not contested, this is 2-D *structural bias*. However, if these structures are contested then we have 2-D *structural conflict*. The latter conflicts hinge around the need for interactive collaboration of others, which gives the less powerful potential for resistance.

1-D and 2-D conflicts compared

2-D structural conflicts have a very different quality to 1-D structured conflicts, as they are conflicts *over* structure, while 1-D structured conflicts are *within* structured context. In the latter, the social structures are reproduced unproblematically. Felicitous exercises of authority are instances of 1-D, while infelicitous interactions are often structural conflict, thus 2-D. In 1-D structured conflict, such as the democratic process, conflict is ordered, which feeds back into the wider systemic social order. In contrast, in 2-D conflict there is fundamental disagreement over the rules of the game, which is a deeper form of conflict.

In 1-D authority or economic relationships both actors take the performative X counts as Y-status in circumstances C as given and in so doing gain power-to and power-over. In contrast, in 2-D structural conflict they forgo these powers because they have some principled objection to the structures in question. In many instances this objection may be over the bias in question. In those cases, a remediation of the biases, rather than their removal, may be sufficient. Workers may go on strike for higher wages. A strike is partly a 2-D refusal to reproduce structure. However, if by using given procedures, such as labour courts, higher wages are negotiated and the workers return to work, this is resolved as a 1-D structured conflict. This is qualitatively different from workers going on strike as part of a communist revolution, in which case the offer of higher wages, without system change, would be refused and would signal ongoing 2-D conflict.

Examples of 1-D structured conflict versus 2-D structural conflict

On 25 September 2017, the people of the Kurdish province of Iraq held a referendum on Kurdish independence, with overwhelming support. Similarly, on 1 October 2017, an independence referendum was held in Catalonia, which was won by those desiring independence. In response to hostile reactions from central government in Iraq, the Kurds froze their result on 25 October, while, in contrast, based upon that mandate, on 27 October, a Catalan Republic was officially declared, with all the pomp and ceremony that typically goes with these types of events.

The declaration of a Catalan Republic was a performative act, in which a group of people (an X), tried to give themselves Y-status as a republic and sovereign state. However, this action was deemed infelicitous by their rings of reference. Although both the Kurds and the Catalans engaged in structuration of independence, neither were (in the short term) successful in reproducing the structures of an independent sovereign republic because other states were not willing to recognize the felicity of their actions. So, while they structured referenda leading to a *republic*, they did not achieve the authority Y-status of a *republic*.

What makes the Kurdish and Catalan referenda examples of 2-D conflict (rather than 1-D structured conflict) is not the defeat but their relationship to social structures. In contrast, in October 1995, Quebec held an independence referendum that was lost by the independence movement. Similarly, on 14 September 2014, Scotland held a referendum that was also lost by the independence movement. In both cases the margin of defeat was relatively narrow. However, unlike the Kurdish and Catalan cases, had the referenda gone the other way both Scotland and Quebec would have been recognized as independent states by the central governments of Britain and Canada. Furthermore, the actions of Scotland and Quebec would also have been recognized as felicitous by other sovereign states, and international organizations, including the UN. The nature of the independence defeats in Quebec and Scotland took place within a set of rules of the game, a set of social structures, which were recognized by a ring of reference comprised of other states. In both instances the central governments were willing, in principle, to accept the outcome of the referenda. So, these were 1-D power structured conflicts, as there was an overlapping consensus about the structures. In the Kurdish and Catalan cases, it was a 2-D conflict because there was no willing ring of reference that recognized the validity of these acts of structuration.

Structuration, confirm-structuration and destructuration

In 1-D structured (as opposed to mere coercive) conflicts, structures are reproduced because structuration receives recognition, which I term *confirm-structuration*, while in a 2-D conflict the more powerful other refuses to confirm-structure. Contrary to Giddens (1984), I would argue that structuration in itself is insufficient for structural reproduction. A structure only becomes a systemic structure when it is confirm-structured by others (Haugaard 1997).

Giddens' (1984) emphasis upon structuration alone made his theory too voluntaristic because it appears as if agents can reproduce structure singly. In contrast, in this model interactive collaboration is a prerequisite for successful structural reproduction, which constitutes a highly effective external source of constraint, as the interacting other may contest the act of structuration. Both the Catalans and Kurds structured the structures potentially leading to an independent republic but they failed to achieve confirm-structuration from others. This failure of collaboration constitutes structural constraint. As structural constraint comes from others, the external ring of reference constitutes a manifest external force that cannot be wished away, as in voluntarism. However, as the other is an agent, this externality is not like some mechanical determinate constraint, as in structuralism.

In both the Catalan and Kurdish cases the central governments opposing them were active social agents in their acts of not confirm-structuring the validity of the referenda. In the Catalan case ballot boxes were destroyed and election centres disrupted by the Guardia Civil, acting on behalf of the Madrid government. In the Kurdish case the Iraq government sent tanks into Kurdistan. As this is active non-recognition of an act of structuration, as opposed to simple ignoring, we can term such responses *destructuration*.

Structural conflicts represent deeper systemic disorder, and consequently destructuration is often coupled with violence. This reversion to violence is symptomatic of a deeper breakdown of social order. In 1-D structured power relationships mutual recognition of social structures facilitates social interaction, as *power-to*, *power-with* and *power-over*. Interaction directed at some goal reproduces social structure, thus social order. In contrast, structural conflict implies the breakdown of authority – X fails to count as Y-status. Consequently, in order to exercise power-over successfully, dominant actors must revert to coercion. So, for the powerful to have an effect they must coerce the other. 2-D structural conflict leads to 1-D coercion or violence.

In contrast to 2-D conflict, in 1-D structured conflicts all agree to abide by the outcome of the structured process (structuration and confirm-structuration) take place even when the outcome is adverse to the confirm-structurer, as in the democratic process. So, even if the less powerful is not the overall beneficiary from the outcome, if they recognize the validity of the act of structuration and therefore confirm-structure, social structures are reproduced.

Confirm-structuration and destructuration as ideal types

Like all sociological categories, 1-D and 2-D conflict are ideal types. The Kurdish independence referendum did receive some recognition. It received confirm-structuration from the state of Israel and the Catalan declaration received significant support from Slovenian politicians, although the Slovenian government never officially recognized Catalonia. Both received recognition from various sub-national nationalist groups, such as Sinn Féin in Ireland, and the minister-president of the Flanders region of Belgium, Geert Bourgeois. However, in order to really count, to be felicitous in a sense that gives power-to or -with, these acts of confirm-structuration should come from powerful sovereign states or important international organizations (the EU or the UN).

When 1-D and 2-D occur simultaneously

In many instances a conflict may have both 1-D structured and 2-D structural conflict aspects. On 29 November 1947 a vote was taken at the UN to partition British Mandatory Palestine into two states: a Jewish and an Arab state (Israel and Palestine). The vote resulted in 33 countries in favour of recognition, with 13 against. Significantly, the Palestinians rejected the plan and all the Arab countries neighbouring Israel were in the rejectionist camp. On 14 May 1948, Israel declared independence and the result was simultaneously a 1-D and 2-D outcome. The Soviet Union, the United States, Iran (under the Shah) and a whole plethora of other, largely Western, countries recognized Israel (confirm-structuration). Simultaneously, within Israel a civil war broke out between Palestinians and Jews, while the surrounding Arab states made war on Israel. The latter constituted a destructuration rejection of the Y-status authority of Israel as a sovereign state. Since then Israel has had an existence characterized by structural recognition from Western powers, plus Egypt and Jordan, and 2-D rejection of its existence by the majority of Middle-Eastern states. After the Islamic revolution of 1979, Iran switched from being a confirm-structurer to one of the most implacable destructurers of the Y-status function of Israel.[3]

It is also interesting to note that back in 1948, following the recommendations of the UNSCOP plan and the UN General Assembly Partition Resolution of 29 November 1947, which split Palestine into two states, the Palestinians could have structured their own state. That act would have been confirm-structured by Western powers, including the USA and Israel, but would probably have been destructured, as infelicitous, by Arab states, who had walked out of the UN in protest at the resolution (Morris: 2001: 180–7). As Israel's Y-status action was part of a partition plan, a similar act of structuration by the Palestinians would also have implicitly suggested confirm-structuration to the recognition of the state of Israel. At that time the Palestinians and their allies were not willing to do this. Later, one of their concessions, as part of the Oslo process, was Palestinian confirm-structuration recognition of Israel, symbolically represented by a handshake between Arafat and Rabin, in front of US President Bill Clinton, on 13 September 1993.

The Boycott, Disinvest and Sanctions (BDS) movement is a Palestinian movement that calls for boycotts, disinvestment and sanctions against Israel (see BDS website (BDS Movement 2018) and Thrall 2018). This is 2-D structural conflict, in which the other – the Israelis – are refused the Y-status function of a normal state. Boycotts and similar activities are symptomatic of 2-D structural conflict, whereby one party refuses to recognize the Y-status function of the other.

Moving from 2-D structural conflict to 1-D structured conflict

2-D often takes the form of *anti-normalization* with the opposite party – a phrase frequently used by the BDS movement. In contrast, in a 1-D conflict the authority Y-status function of the other is recognized and power is exercised within an agreed sense of the normal. The preliminary moves towards resolving a deep 2-D conflict are aimed at finding a way to turn the conflict into 1-D structured conflict. The cut-off between 1-D and 2-D can be unclear. At first a limited set of shared social structures is created in which power conflict is constrained. These are then used to widen the area of shared structural reproduction.

The first stage is usually simple recognition of equal moral worth. In the Northern Ireland peace process this mutual recognition of Y-status was embodied in the principle of *parity of esteem*, whereby each side essentially agreed to recognize the other as having an equal moral claim (Ruohomäki 2010). This is the conceptual equivalent of recognizing the personhood of the other as the basic foundation for authority. Normatively, it entails a willingness to engage and take seriously the justifications of others and to offer them justification in turn (Forst 2007) – this will be developed further in Chapter 9.

The mutual structuration-cum-confirm-structuration to authority Y-status function equality acts as a platform for drawing in other structures of reciprocity. It is noticeable that once power-sharing was set up in Northern Ireland the mutual affinity between the two leaders Martin McGuinness and Ian Paisley was crucial to allowing power sharing to continue. Even though before the talks they were sworn enemies, they became known as the 'chuckle brothers' because of their shared sense of humour (*Irish Independent* 2017). While the ability to share jokes may appear trivial, it is in fact much deeper, as it is symptomatic of mutual recognition of equal moral worth.

At the time of writing (2019), the Northern Irish executive had collapsed, and what is crucial to this collapse is the lack of willingness of the DUP to recognize the equal status of the Irish language in Northern Ireland. Language is, of course, symbolic of identity, thus Y-function. The campaign by the DUP was accompanied by a period of mockery of the language (Moriarty 2014), which is symptomatic of the collapse of parity of esteem. Mocking the identity of the other is supposedly humorous, yet it degrades the other as infelicitous (see Billig 2005) and creates in-group inclusion and out-group exclusion (see Mik-Meyer 2007). It is a way of withholding consent to Y-status as persons of equal moral worth. While both mockery and joke-sharing are based upon humour of a kind, the former is a weapon while the latter is a mode of recognizing shared Y-status equality. As we shall explore (in Chapter 7), 1-D structured conflict is often characterized by control of emotion, while 2-D structural conflict entails the display of emotion (see Heaney 2011; Heaney and Flam 2015).

Structures as war by other means

Social structures are a way of containing conflict. In a polemical mode Foucault argued that politics is war by other means. Foucault writes as follows.

> Humanity does not progress from combat to combat until it arrives at universal reciprocity, where the rules of law finally replace warfare; humanity installs each of its violences in a system of rules and thus proceeds from domination to domination.
>
> (Foucault 1977: 151)

In one sense I entirely agree, although I would be less pessimistic. The rules of the game are usually not as dominating as naked violence, as suggested by Foucault. Part of moving from violence to a structured political system entails convincing the other that power is positive-sum. This perception of a gain may be illusory, or it may be real. However, I would agree with Foucault that political structures do not represent the dissolution of social conflicts. Rather, they represent the re-inscription of conflict within a set of social structures. In other words, the mutual acceptance of structural constraints means a change of the mode of conflict from 2-D structural conflict to 1-D structured conflict.

Power-over can either be coercive or it may be structured. When it is structured, conflict is tamed as social actors confirm-structure each other's structuration practices. Norbert Elias (1995) and Ernest Gellner (1983 and 1989) both observe that the European transition from feudalism to modernity entailed a taming of everyday violence. In Western European countries, from Italy to Scandinavia, the homicide rate fell from just below 100 per 100,000 to below 1 per 100,000 (Pinker 2012: 75). In the feudal world, class conflict was typically resolved through coercion. There were few structures for resolving conflict in a 1-D structured manner. Rather, 1-D coercion and 2-D conflict were to the fore. In contrast, with the advance of modernity the democratic process entails a massive structuring of everyday conflict. The democratic process is essentially a process whereby everyday social conflict is channelled into structured 1-D conflict. Just as with examples of the recognition of states, this entails massive status function recognition. At first the equal worth of citizens referred to male property owners, then to all males. Further, in the suffragette movement in the nineteenth and early twentieth century women demanded the Y-status function that would allow them to participate in the political process. These women were engaged in a 2-D conflict for Y-status recognition in order to be allowed into a 1-D process of conflict resolution. Once part of the political process, these campaigners would have internalized the 2-D constraints and biases of the political system, which would have a de-radicalizing effect, moving 2-D conflict into 1-D.

Once the suffragettes obtained recognition from the more powerful male politicians, and so obtained the franchise, they gained a capacity for action. In much of the literature there is an assumption that power and freedom are opposites (e.g., Pettit 1996), which is premised upon the equation of power with domination. However, if power also includes power-to, it constitutes a condition of possibility for freedom (Morriss 2009; Haugaard 2016) because power-to is a condition of possibility for agency. In some sense 2-D conflict appears like an act of freedom, in that it constitutes an attack upon the order of things – it is what is meant by freedom by those in favour of, so-called, radical revolutionary politics. On the other hand, once actors buy into a set of political structures, this gives them a capacity for action, thus agency, which is a precondition of freedom. Both contesting the order of things and using the order of things to get what you want constitute acts of freedom, although in different ways.

2-D as structural bias and structural conflict

In their original account of 2-D power, Bachrach and Baratz emphasized that 2-D entailed structural bias. While adding structural conflict, we still include structural bias as part of 2-D. This bias entails exclusion of certain ideas or policies from the agenda. These become outside the conditions of possibility for a given social order. With regard to authority or economic resources, certain possibilities are considered infelicitous and beyond the normal. For those actors attempting to champion such issues, they understand that their cause will be met with destructuration. To be clear, there are two terms: *structural conflict*, which refers to conflict over structural reproduction, and *structural bias*, which refers to the conditions of possibility of a given set of social structures. Typically, structural conflict takes place as a consequence of unacceptable structural bias.

Structural bias can take many forms; it is equally possible that 2-D bias entails the exclusion of certain issues or persons. The significance of the rise of the authority status function of citizens' authority is symptomatic of a long process of democratization, which entails wider Y-status inclusion within the democratic process. However, even today, in most democracies there are still significant 2-D exclusions of persons. For instance, most electorates are defined by nationality, not by residence. Consequently, many sovereign democratic states have long-term residents, who live, work and contribute in their taxes or social security the same as everybody else but are disenfranchised because of their birth nationality. If democracy entails having a say concerning decisions that affect you, this constitutes a person-related 2-D exclusion that is not justifiable relative to the normative principles of democratic theory (as theorized here, in Chapter 9).

It is important to remember that, from a *sociological* point of view, 2-D *structural exclusion* refers to any exclusion, whether it is normatively justified or not. Above I made the case that the exclusion of long-term residents of a polity is a *normatively* unjustified exclusion. From a *sociological* viewpoint I include exclusions under the rubric of 2-D biases, whether normatively justified or not.

Democracy excludes those who are only transitory residents. A tourist passing through a democratic state on the day elections are held is not given the vote. As theorized here, in this language game, that constitutes a bias, as a sociological fact, describing the local conditions of possibility – it is not possible to vote if you are a tourist. However, normatively, I would consider that exclusion justified because, unlike the long-term resident, the tourist is not directly affected by the politics of the state she visits once she leaves. The word *bias* is a negatively evaluative term in the normative language game but not so in the sociological one.

2-D *structural conflict* takes place when social actors decide to contest 2-D structural bias. 2-D structural conflict entails changing the conditions of possibility. It is a fight for a new order of things, for new horizons, and new inclusions. Because 2-D is disruptive, to echo Foucault (1977: 151), this entails a reversion to a kind of war, but the objective is *usually* to replace one set of 2-D exclusions with another, or to replace one system of domination with another one. However, it should be acknowledged that at times social actors prefer continued 2-D conflict, as the creation of 1-D constraints entails the acceptance of compromise.

To use Hobbes' metaphor, 2-D conflict is a momentary reversion to a state of nature (Hobbes 1914: 63–6), in the sense that the rules of the game are no longer taken as given. It constitutes a challenge to the sovereign order of things.

2-D bias and the dominant ideology thesis

Structural bias is often reproduced without overt structural conflict. In the chapter on 3-D power we will see how conflict is suppressed for epistemic reasons, including reification. In this chapter I wish to conclude by analyzing the dominant ideology thesis, whereby biases are often reproduced with the full awareness and acquiescence of the less powerful. This is a phenomenon that superficially appears as 3-D power but is not 3-D, as acquiescence does not come from epistemic or ideological incorporation into the system.

Lukes (1974) characterized the acquiescence of the less powerful in terms of 3-D power, whereby social actors internalize a form of false-consciousness and thus fail to see their real interests. This account builds upon a long Marxist tradition that includes Gramsci's theory of hegemony (Gramsci 1973) and Lukacs' account of class-consciousness (Lukacs 2000). However, shortly after Lukes (1974), Abercrombie et al. (1980) put forward what became known as *the dominant ideology thesis*.

Contrary to traditional Marxist theory, Abercrombie et al. (1980) showed that the working classes are often *less* ideologically incorporated than the upper classes. Contrary to any theory of false-consciousness, the dominant elites are often the only ones who buy into the dominant legitimizing ideology. The mystery of why the working classes reproduce a system that is biased against them does not arise from a failure of conscious understanding; rather, the working classes reproduce the dominant structures due to an acute *awareness* of the constraints confronting them and, consequently, resigned acceptance of the status quo. In contrast, for the powerful the dominant ideology functions as a legitimizing rationalization serving to justify their dominance. The objective of a dominant ideology is not about *ideological incorporation* of the less powerful but *self-justification* by the dominant.

Following the dominant ideology thesis, Scott (an anthropologist who specialized in peasant revolts – Scott 1987) showed that subaltern social actors who appear to willingly acquiesce in their subordination often have a hidden discourse that is at variance with their public ideology (Scott 1990). This hidden script is symptomatic of potential resistance. However, as long as these ideas remain within the private sphere of the dominated, the result is not overt 2-D conflict. Through their interaction the elites are most familiar with the public quiescent script and so may be under the illusion that the less powerful subscribe to the dominant ideology. Or, perhaps less forcefully, the dominant may be aware of the subaltern script of resistance but, in order to maintain self-justification, choose to ignore that discourse. In the latter case, there emerges a kind of mutual complicity, which remains unspoken, between the elite and less powerful, of public pretense that the subaltern discourse does not exist. An interesting variant on this is the creation of safe places for the expression of this opposition. In the feudal system, carnival was used in this way.

In his analysis of subaltern hidden scripts, Scott gives the example of a slave woman who apparently acquiesced, even endorsed, the punishment of her daughter by her white master. Yet, once the master left earshot, acquiescence gave way to an expression of extreme anger, taking pleasure in the thought of seeing her master's blood flow (Scott 1990: 5). During revolutions it is not uncommon for supposedly 'loyal servants' to turn upon their masters. From the perspective of the dominant, this is interpreted as an apparent change in the servant brought about by opportunistic disloyalty or malign influences, while in fact there was a hidden transcript all along.

Dominant ideology often appears more stable than it is. The less powerful B has a public reason, which accords with the dominant ideology of A, while they may well maintain a private reasoning that is extremely critical, often revolutionary. In these cases, what appears as a stable 2-D structural bias is, potentially, unstable, leading to overt 2-D conflict when conditions are expedient.

Scott argues that the existence of subaltern discourses can often be ascertained by subtle acts of resistance, which are often symbolic in nature, the essence of which is captured by an Ethiopian proverb, quoted by Scott: 'when the great lord passes, the wise peasant bows deeply and silently farts' (Scott 1990: v).

In the Israeli occupation of the West Bank there is much overt resistance and violence against the Israeli presence, which is classifiable as overt 2-D conflict. However, for everyday life to go on, Palestinians also routinely reproduce the 2-D structural biases of occupation. In these instances, 2-D acquiescence becomes visible through acts of symbolic resistance. In the territories of the West Bank there are (currently – 2020) numerous security checkpoints. When moving even relatively short distances, Palestinians have to present documents at these checkpoints, which is resented, as this bureaucracy makes everyday life complex and constitutes an everyday reminder of lower Y-status. In order to register resistance, yet comply, Palestinians often produce their ID cards, as requested, but in an overtly unnaturally slow and deliberate way (Johansson and Vinthagen 2015). This is a way of complying, while making it clear that this compliance does not mean ideological incorporation into the discourse that legitimizes the soldiers' structural authority. It is a way of saying: *yes, we will do as you say (because you have 1-D coercive power) but, no, we do not regard any of these social structures as legitimate.*

In her critique of the power debates, Hayward (2000) follows in the tradition of Scott. She argues that what often appears as ideological incorporation is acquiescence brought about by an understanding of structural bias coupled with the desire to make the best of a situation. In *De-facing Power* (Hayward 2000), Hayward analyses two Connecticut schools with student intakes from opposite ends of the class spectrum. Fair View School is an almost all white upper-middle-class school, while North End Community School is an inner-city school with an intake from the unemployed or poorly paid of largely black or Hispanic ethnic background. In North End the students are taught adherence to rules and regulations. In contrast, the students at Fair View continually interrogate structures. At first glance, it might appear that North End is more ideologically incorporated than Fair View. However, upon interview it became apparent that the teachers and students in North End did not buy into the system uncritically. Rather, the obedience to rules reflected the fact that the teachers understood that these students are unlikely to be in situations where they can make the rules. In this context of 2-D bias, the best life skill to give them is how to respond to rules, without challenging them. In contrast, the students and teachers at Fair View expected the students to enter a social class in which they could influence the rules of the game. Consequently, both North End and Fair View schools were teaching the students to structure and confirm-structure relative to what they understood as a realistic appraisal of the 2-D structural biases of the system. In the case of North End, that did not mean 3-D ideological incorporation, as the teachers were in fact critical of the system.

When to resist and when to comply

In terms of 2-D structural bias, understanding how to attain and handle authority entails predicting correctly how others will react to certain performances of Y-status function. When a social actor learns what kinds of performances will receive a felicitous response from others, she is effectively both empowering herself in the short term and simultaneously acquiescing to the current 2-D structural biases.

Gender would be typical in this regard. To put this in a way that echoes Goffman (1971), when a person learns the expected felicitous script of front-stage gender performances, they enhance their capacity to work within the system. Simultaneously, they reproduce existing 2-D gender biases, which define the conditions of possibility within that society.

In our analysis of the democratic process we argued that democracy entails defeat episodically but empowerment dispositionally. This is the reverse of that. Social actors find themselves in a system that is structurally biased against their interests or Y-status function. Through socialization, they become knowledgeable about that system and they learn which strategies work to empower them episodically. In focusing upon their immediate interests they become experts at acquiescence to structural practices that disempower their Y-status group dispositionally.

When to resist or reproduce dominant ideology constitutes a complex challenge for social actors. Hillary Clinton describes an instance of this tension between female politeness and assertiveness. It occurred during her second TV debate with Donald Trump, which she describes as follows.

> We were on a small stage and no matter where I walked, he followed me closely, staring at me, making faces. It was incredibly uncomfortable. He was literally breathing down my neck. My skin crawled.
>
> It was one of those moments where you wish you could hit pause and ask everybody watching: 'Well, what would you do?'
>
> Do you stay calm, keep smiling and carry on as if he weren't repeatedly invading your space?
>
> Or do you turn, look him in the eye and say loudly and clearly 'Back up, you creep. Get away from me. I know you love to intimidate women but you can't intimidate me, so back up.'
>
> I chose option A, I kept cool, aided by a lifetime of dealing with difficult men trying to throw me off, I did however grip the microphone extra hard.
>
> I wonder, though, whether I should have chosen option B. It would certainly have been better TV. Maybe I have over-learned the lesson of staying calm, biting my tongue, digging my fingernails into a clenched fist, smiling all the while, determined to present a composed face to the world.
>
> (Clinton 2017: 136–7)

Clinton's composure was part of her social competence as a female who could control her emotions, as polite and pleasant, even to overbearing alpha males. Yet, in this instance, in a head-to-head contest with such an alpha male this socialization handicapped her. Within the patriarchal language game, a (supposed) *female weakness* is that assertive women tend to lose control of their emotions and become *hysterical* (Clinton 2017: 137). So, to succeed in politics she learned to control her emotions, which is an episodically power-to-maximizing course of action. Based upon past experience, she predicted that had she said *back up you creep*, the likely response in the press would have been negative. In an interview discussion she conjectured that the media spin would have been as follows.

> See, she can't take it. If she can't take Donald standing there like the alpha male that he is, then how's she going to stand up to Putin. A ridiculous argument, but nevertheless one that might get traction.
>
> (Clinton in Beard and Clinton 2017)

The problem for Clinton is that authority is performative and you can't control the reaction of your audience. If you can perform the Y-role status-function of acting in a *presidential manner*, then you might win, but if you act infelicitously you will be deemed unsuitable to become a Y-status president. In Clinton's assessment, acting presidentially means *being in control of a situation*. However, this is a performatively problematic balancing act for women. Being in control means being firm, while being deemed too assertive can equate to *hysteria*, thus lack of self-control. Women's socially constructed reputation for lack of self-control of emotions makes it difficult to handle someone exercising subtle domination, such as invading physical space. The safer performance is to pretend that the invasion-cum-domination is not taking place – Clinton's strategy. In opting for this strategy, Clinton was not suffering from ideological incorporation into Trump's misogynistic values. In fact the way she describes her choices demonstrates that she was acutely aware of the 2-D structural biases and chose to avoid 2-D conflict. Typical of less powerful actors reproducing dominant ideology, she adopted an episodically power-maximizing strategy relative to the 2-D structural bias she found herself in. As a feminist, she was fully aware that these types of social structures disempower women dispositionally.

Consistent with the types of subaltern discourse described by Scott, in private Clinton would demonstrate critical resistance to structural bias. In private Clinton unleashed a 'fuck-laced fusillade' against Trump to her aides. 'Aides understood that in order to keep it all together onstage, Hillary sometimes needed to unleash on them in private' (Chozick quoted in McCarthy 2018). In one instance, she said 'you want authentic, here it is!' as she expressed her views of what a 'disgusting human being Trump was' (Chozick quoted in McCarthy 2018). In other words, the discourse that she personally endorsed was different from the self-restrained public performance of the debates.

In reading Scott's account of subaltern discourse (Scott 1987 and 1990), the use of examples suggests that subaltern discourse is a phenomenon of the abjectly powerless. Following Goffman (1971) on front-stage and back-stage performances, back-stage performances exist right across the spectrum of power. Authority is performative and so even the powerful have to keep certain views back-stage in order to remain felicitous in the eyes of their ring of reference.

In conclusion, in 2-D overt *structural conflict* social actors engage in overt conflict over the social structures. The less powerful are fully aware that the existing social structures are biased against them and so contest them, refusing to co-reproduce them through confirm-structuration. Similarly, in 2-D *structural bias* the less powerful are often (though not always) well aware of the bias but (in contrast to structural conflict) are acquiescent in reproducing that bias because they feel it is the better course of action episodically.

Exploitation often takes the form of the dominant ideology thesis. The labourer who (apparently) 'freely' sells her labour power for less than its value is not really acting freely in an absolute sense. Rather, she needs to provide for herself and her dependents, and this employment may be the best, or only, choice available to her within the existing 2-D structural bias.

Similarly, with regard to authority power, the competent social agent learns which performances of authority positions will be perceived as felicitous. Empowering herself within those parameters entails reproducing role-specific social norms that entail structural bias. However, in the privacy of the home the less powerful may well rail against the injustice of the system. Fairy tales, where the poorest wins out over the wealthy and privileged, are another way of expressing this subaltern discourse. Told at bedtime, when darkness closes out the reality of a long day, characterized by confirm-structuring 2-D bias, these stories provide a welcome release.

Notes

1 I do not like these kinds of labels but, as they will be attributed to me by others, it is better to be pre-emptive and use the label I find least objectionable.
2 I developed the rudiments of these ideas in my PhD, which was published as Haugaard (1992). However, at that stage the presentation was overly complex and the terminology tedious.
3 The historical events behind this account are based upon an amalgam of reading on the Israel–Palestine conflict that has taken place over years, so not precisely referenced. However, possibly the most influential has been the work of revisionist historian Benny Morris, especially Morris (2001 and 2004).

3

The first and second dimensions of power contrasted: Deep versus shallow conflict and resistance

In the previous chapters we looked at the basic principles of 1-D and 2-D power. Before continuing to 3-D and 4-D, let us explore the complex ways in which these dimensions interact. Part of the reason for emphasizing these dimensions of power is the tendency of most contemporary power analysis to focus primarily upon 3-D and 4-D. There is an implicit suggestion that such analysis is *more radical*, as is evident by the proliferation of Foucauldian analysis. However, this perception ignores the fact that 3-D and 4-D phenomena are theoretically tied into 1-D and 2-D conflict. As we shall see in the discussion of the work of Gene Sharp, 2-D conflict is the foundation of radical politics and subaltern resistance.

Distinguishing 1-D and 2-D conflicts

In identifying whether or not a conflict is 1-D or 2-D the researcher should identify whether there is conflict over goals, in which case it is probably 1-D, or whether it is a conflict over structures, in which case it is 2-D conflict. Goal-centred conflicts concern social actors empowering themselves as much as possible without challenging status quo structural constraints.

In a democratic contest each party wishes to win the number of votes necessary to obtain a mandate to form a government but they are not challenging the democratic system. So, they are pursuing goals, which is 1-D structured conflict. Similarly, workers and employers who negotiate over wages within existing labour law structures or companies that try to outcompete each other by increasing profits or sales (i.e., within the rules of competition) constitute instances of conflicts where the defeated party, in the last instance, lets structures override goals. However, to challenge those structures by refusing to recognize their Y-status authority, or the legitimacy of a political or economic system, is 2-D structural conflict.

A complicating instance is where the goal is the reform of the structure, which takes place in the transition from 2-D conflict to 1-D structured conflict, which we discuss later in this chapter.

To reiterate our terminology, at the level of 1-D power, in addition to *structured 1-D conflict*, there are also *coercive power* relationships, which may or may not be structured. And, at the level of 2-D, there is *structural conflict*, and there is *structural bias*. Routine *structured 1-D conflict* takes place within existing *2-D structural bias*, whereby social actors respect existing structural constraints. Coercive 1-D achieves its effect from coercion, so need not be structured but may be.

Conflicts over goals have a different quality to conflicts over structures. Conflicts over goals can be heated and confrontational but, at the end of the day, the contestants are mutually structurally constrained. In that sense, 1-D conflicts are not as deep as 2-D conflicts. In a routine election, however hard it has been fought, the only felicitous response for those with fewer votes is to confirm-structure the victory of the other with the most votes (except in the US presidential system). In 1-D structured conflict there is mutual recognition of Y-status function, what is inside and outside the conditions of possibility. This results in a shared sense of the felicitous, which constitutes a different typology of underlying justification to 2-D conflict.

In 2-D conflict the containment of conflict through structure is absent. When the Catalans held a referendum on independence they were violating the conditions of possibility (2-D structural constraints) of the Spanish constitution, and the central government in Madrid destructured in order to maintain the rules of the game. For those who destructure social change in order to maintain the status quo there is a sense of upholding the order of things. As structures are laden with meaning, those destructuring novel structuration often see themselves as upholding *common sense*, or *the natural-order-of-things*. In contrast, those engaged in 2-D structural conflict see themselves as radical because *they do not accept the status quo*. In this respect 2-D conflict is more likely to entail 3-D epistemic conflict than 1-D.

In terms of justification, 1-D conflict often has a sense of pragmatism about it: *let's do business as usual and do it as well as we can*. Or, less enthusiastically, *Okay, the system isn't perfect but let's make the best of it*. In contrast, 2-D conflicts are over structures that entail meanings, and so often involve appeals to abstract principles or sense-making (see Haugaard 2008b). Typically, 2-D conflicts are characterized by the following types of statements: *I don't care about the consequences; I am willing to fight for my principles*. Or, *You may see the world like that but that is the degenerate past; we are fighting for new beginnings, for justice*.

In structural conflict there is a sense of the fragility of social order, because in challenging the conditions of possibility (by structuring differently or destructuring the status quo) the conventionality of social structure becomes apparent. Often social actors will question structures, arguing that they are *mere convention and therefore arbitrary.* As we shall see in greater depth, challenging the order of things often leads to ontological insecurity. That which is taken for granted suddenly becomes described as arbitrary, thus creating uncertainty, and therefore resistance, which has significant 3-D and 4-D implications. There tends to be a knock-on effect between 2-D structural conflict and 3-D and 4-D conflict. In contrast, 1-D structured conflict entails the status quo with respect to 3-D and 4-D power.

2-D conflict and self-sacrifice

Because every interaction has both a goal-directed and a structured aspect, what type of conflict ensues is often down to which aspect of the interaction predominates (Haugaard 1997: 119–36). Which are most important, goals or structures?

In a case of dominant ideology, the less powerful do not normatively endorse the social structures they confirm-structure, but at the end of the day they let their interest in attaining certain goals override potential structural conflict. The worker who sells her labour power to a capitalist, while she tries to drive up her wages as high as possible, is engaged in a 1-D structured conflict to obtain the goal of higher wages within the existing order of things. In contrast, the Marxist worker who goes on strike and refuses back down unless the system changes is engaged in a 2-D structural conflict.

Dominant ideology shows that a tension often arises between the two types of conflict, where one overrides the other. In the case of dominant ideology, goals override structures.

In contrast to dominant ideology, when structures override goals, 2-D conflict has a very different quality to it. When a structure is unpalatable, yet reproducing that structure would give the actor in question immediate reward in terms of goals (episodic power-to), the conflict is deep and the sense of frustration palpable. For the less powerful, destructuring social structures that could deliver desirable outcomes elicits justifications of self-sacrifice and even martyrdom. 2-D conflict entails avoiding structural reproduction and, at times, this may include avoiding much-desired goals.

To win or not to win?
Iran has a policy of not recognizing the Y-status of the state of Israel. This includes a total ban any on interaction at the level of sport. Participating

in sporting events that entail playing against Israel is interpreted by Iran as confirm-structuring the Y-status authority function of Israel as a legitimate sovereign state. Consequently, it is official policy for Iranians to withdraw from any sporting contests that entail competing against Israeli athletes. In practice, this involves Iranian athletes forgoing the episodic power-to realize their goal of participating and/or winning in many international contests.

Alir Reza Karimi is an Iranian freestyle wrestler, whose goal is to achieve a gold medal. In November 2017 Karimi was wrestling in the under-23 Wrestling World Championships in Poland. Karimi was in the middle of a match, where he was beating Russian wrestler Alikhan Zhabrailov, when from the sidelines his coach instructed him to stop winning, a call that Karimi ignored. During a break in the match, the coach ordered Karimi to lose. As demanded by his coach, Karimi went on to lose in the second half. As it turned out, Karimi was instructed to lose deliberately because winning would have meant competing against the Israeli wrestler Uri Kalashnikov, who had just won a parallel match that the Iranians had hoped the latter would lose. The Russian, Zabrailov (whom Karimi could have defeated), went on to win Gold (Karimi's ultimate goal), while Kalashnikov won Bronze. Not only did Karimi forgo a likely Gold medal (he was beating the eventual winner of Gold); Karimi's sacrifice entailed that he was also suspended from wrestling for six months for match-fixing, and his coach was banned for two years for instructing his wrestler to lose (Haaretz 2018).

Clearly Karimi wanted to win the wrestling championship. In an interview Karimi stated that when his coach told him to lose in order to avoid wrestling the Israeli Kalashnikov, he was bitterly disappointed. He said: 'In a moment, my whole world seemed to come to an end' (Haaretz 2017).

Here is an instance where a goal is highly desired but some principle entailed by structural reproduction (having to wrestle Kalashnikov and thus, implicitly, confirm-structure the Y-status function of Israel as a sovereign state) overrode much-desired goals.

When a social actor gives up some desired goal because of a refusal to confirm-structure some Y-status (Israel-as-a-state, in this case) there is always an appeal to self-sacrifice and principle. In this spirit, the Iranian Youth and Sports Ministry commented upon Karimi as follows: 'Your noble and heroic action in the world competition in Poland, abandoning the medal and podium in support of the highest human values, is a source of pride and praise' (Haaretz 2018).

To take a different example, with regard to economic resources, the #*MeToo* movement has highlighted the issue of the way in which women are routinely paid less than men. In this case pay also implies lesser authority status. Women are aware of the differential, but the pursuit of immediate goals creates its own pressure to go along with 2-D structural bias. However, recently the #*MeToo* campaign has inspired women to refuse, at tremendous cost. An excellent instance of this is given by Sienna Miller at a #*MeToo* summit (March 2018). She spoke as follows.

> A few years ago I was offered a gutsy, powerful role to play that was close to my heart. It was a two-hander on Broadway, but I was offered less than half what my male co-star was being paid.
>
> The decision to turn down this particular role was difficult and lonely. *I was forced to choose between making a concession on my self-worth and dignity and a role I was in love with.*
>
> (Miller quoted in Ford 2018; italics added)

Miller wanted, indeed loved, the role; that was her goal. However, she sacrificed that goal because of a structural imbalance between her pay and that of her male co-star. In her eyes the lesser pay was symptomatic of lesser worth, which suggests lesser Y-status function. She could have gone along with the bias, in order to secure the part, in which case goals would have overridden structures. However, in this case she turned down the part as a matter of principles of dignity and self-worth.

2-D as principle and self-sacrifice

In general, when structures override goals, or 2-D overrides 1-D possible empowerment, there is an appeal to abstract principles because structures have normative systemic implications. In contrast, when goals override structures pragmatism is to the fore. Iranian critics of Iran's sports policy say that 'the ban on competing against Israel has hurt the development of Iranian athletes, forcing them to forfeit or pull out of competitions in which they might face Israeli athletes' (Erdbrink 2017), which is a pragmatic point. In contrast, the official line of Iran's Parliament is as follows: 'Agreeing to play in a game against athletes of a regime that has given humanity nothing but occupation, murder, aggression and betrayal is disrespectful of the rights of thousands of martyrs' (Erdbrink 2017). This constitutes an appeal to abstract principle, coupled with self-sacrifice. There is a clear difference in tone in the two statements.

In 1-D authority or economic conflict, structures are reproduced so there is system stability. In contrast, in 2-D conflict the failure of structural reproduction entails the possibility of disorder. Because structuration does not meet with confirm-structuration, the structuring agent cannot exercise power-over, power-to or power-with relative to the other, except though 1-D coercion. However, if the social actor who refuses to confirm-structure feels strongly about the principles involved she may not even respond to coercion. This may lead to direct violence on the part of the more powerful structurer, where the other is physically manipulated into prison, or killed. On the part of the resistant destructurer coercion will give them authority Y-status associated with being a *martyr* for the cause. If they are killed, through their Y-status as a *martyr*, their agency lives on in a curious way, as an inspiration for further sacrifice.

The other as unreasonable

Due to the performative nature of authority, in a 2-D conflict the common strategy is to de-legitimize the status function of the other. The powerful will claim that the other are *terrorists* or common *criminals*, therefore not worthy of interaction. Conversely, the subaltern will claim that the powerful are *imperialists*, *colonialists*, *Nazis*, *racists* or whatever is considered the most contemptible oppressor in the discourse of the time. These are all negative Y-status functions that legitimize, and often make it imperative, not to interact with the other. Interacting with *terrorists* is appeasing *terrorism*. Such interaction often has the implication of creating a perceived equivalence between the *terrorist militants* and the *state army*.

Similarly, from the perspective of the subaltern, who has carefully portrayed the dominant with a negative status function as (say) a *colonialist*, engaging in structured conflict means normalizing and legitimizing colonialism. This leaves the subaltern open to being outflanked by ideologically purer subalterns. A subaltern group is not singular; among them there are rivalries for the Y-status function of *speaking for the people*. In such circumstances, any action that can be construed as *selling out* is an opportunity for someone else, who is ideologically purer, to claim that Y-status function.

In Afghanistan there have been continual attempts to fight and defeat the Taliban, which have ended in failure. However, if the Taliban cannot be made to disappear through 1-D coercion, there comes a moment they have to be drawn into 1-D structured politics. The Afghan president 'Ashraf Ghani has offered to recognise the Taliban as a legitimate group as part of a process that he said could lead to talks to end more than 16 years of war' (*The Guardian* 2018). Ghani stated that 'We are making this offer without preconditions in order to lead to a peace agreement.' He continues: 'The Taliban are expected to give input to the peacemaking process, the goal of which is to draw the Taliban, as an organisation, to peace talks' (*The Guardian* 2018). The words *to draw the Taliban to peace talks* mean moving the Taliban from a strategy of violent confrontation into a 1-D structured context, which is what a peace process is. That is to say, Ghani is offering to confirm-structure the authority Y-status function of the Taliban, as reasonable political actors, in order to entice them into 1-D conflict resolution mechanisms.

The willingness to recognize the dialogic Y-status function of the Taliban constitutes a major shift and concession for Ghani, 'who has previously referred to the Talibans [sic] as "terrorists" and "rebels"' (*The Guardian* 2018). The designation of a group as *terrorist* may have a descriptive content of their tactics, in the sense that it describes groups who make war without regard for the rules of war, such as the various 1949 Geneva Conventions. However, as a political strategy it signals Y-status disapproval, as is suggested by the everyday saying: *one person's terrorist is another's freedom fighter*. From the sociological perspective, the label refers to someone who should not receive the confirm-structured positive authority Y-status function of *reasonable interlocutor*. The designation *terrorist* constitutes a negative authority designation, a minus-Y status function. As Y-status is performative, it is also a claim that the other is infelicitous and unreasonable.

Once the negative Y-status function is used, it constitutes an impediment to drawing these social actors into negotiations. In that sense, the label *terrorist* not only creates constraints for the group so designated, but also those who constitute the ring of reference that confers it. Entering talks with *terrorists* is often perceived as dangerous because once they are addressed they implicitly gain a positive Y-status function as reasonable interlocutors, which cannot easily be withdrawn. Furthermore, overt recognition of the other has the potential for the designation of *appeasing terrorists*, which is a negative Y-status function that the more powerful will wish to avoid.

Margaret Thatcher was in the Grand Hotel during the 1984 Brighton bomb attack. Partly as a consequence, she prided herself on not giving in to *terrorists* (on the cognitive bias created by this kind of experience, see McCullough et al. 2013). However, in 'one of her final acts before she was deposed as prime minister, Lady Thatcher allowed her Northern Ireland Secretary, Peter Brooke, to talk to republicans [the IRA] through a secret "back channel" after MI5 advised the government that the IRA was looking for ways of ending its terrorist campaign' (Watt 1999). In time this set in train a dialogue that resulted in the Northern Ireland peace process (a process Thatcher criticized, although she facilitated it). When the existence of this back channel was leaked, it caused considerable embarrassment to Thatcher. A former official involved in talks commented: 'It was rather ironic that it was Thatcher who gave the go-ahead, given her ferocious language at the time' (Watt 1999).

In his autobiography, John Major reveals that he also found it severely embarrassing when it was disclosed that (after he took over from Thatcher as prime minister) he continued to use the same back channel (Watt 1999). This sense of embarrassment is caused by the performative contradiction of using the minus Y-status label *terrorist* while negotiating, which suggests the positive Y-status authority function of *legitimate interlocutor*. So-called *back channels* are ways of talking without publicly conferring Y-status function. However, this only works if they remain back channels. Once disclosed, the choice is between acknowledging the positive Y-status function of the other conferred through the now-revealed back channel (now a front channel) or insisting on the negative status function of the other and so, implicitly, accepting for yourself the negative status function of someone who *appeases terrorists*.

To stick to principles or not to stick to principles?

When to stick to principles, and when not to do so, is always a contentious issue. This is a choice confronted by any group that contemplates desisting from 2-D conflict and accepting the structural confines of a 1-D conflict.

After 2017, the UK Conservative government led by Theresa May was supported in office by the Democratic Unionist Party (DUP) of Northern Ireland. In the Brexit referendum the DUP supported Brexit, while Sinn Féin took a pro-European stance. Potentially Brexit entails reintroducing a hard border between the Republic of Ireland and Northern Ireland because, once the United Kingdom leaves the EU, the Irish border constitutes an external border between the EU and a third state (the UK). As set out by the European Commission headed by negotiator Michel Barnier, the fallback position is for Northern Ireland to remain inside the EU customs union, thus in lockstep with the relevant commercial laws of the Republic of Ireland, while the rest of the UK leaves (Boffey and Rankin 2018). However, that would result in a customs border between Northern Ireland and the rest of the UK. Such an outcome would be anathema to the DUP, who perceive this as the thin end of the wedge to a united Ireland – an economic union paving the way for the political union of Ireland. Because of the DUP's power-to prop up the Conservative Party, the DUP had the power-over to dictate the official line of the government on this issue. Consequently, Prime Minister May issued a number of strongly worded statements to the effect that such an eventuality would be entirely unacceptable as such an arrangement would threaten the constitutional or institutional integrity of the UK (Boffey and Rankin 2018).

In this context, there was significant pressure, including from the Irish *taoiseach* (prime minister) Leo Varadkar, for Sinn Féin to take their seats in the Westminster Parliament, where they have seven seats, which they have not claimed. So, Sinn Féin are presented with a dilemma: do they use their seven seats to put forward the Irish nationalist position, which favours the EU Commission fall-back position? Or, do they let the DUP continue to use their ten seats in Westminster to block a move that could strengthen the links between Northern Ireland and the Republic of Ireland and, furthermore, create the potential for a hard border that would symbolically divide Ireland even more deeply?

Sinn Féin has a long history of participating in elections to Westminster, while abstaining from taking their seats, which dates back to before the division of Ireland into the Republic of Ireland and Northern Ireland. Getting elected is a way of obtaining the Y-status authority position of democratic representative, while not taking their seats is a way of not granting Westminster the Y-status position of a legitimate parliament with respect to the people living on the island of Ireland. It is an innovative way of claiming an elected politician Y-status position, while simultaneously destructuring the Y-status of the political system. So, even though it might be in the interests of Sinn Féin to take their seats, this would end a long-held policy of destructuring the legitimacy of the Y-status function of Westminster.

The Sinn Féin MP Paul Maskey explained their position as follows: 'For 100 years now, Irish republicans have refused to validate British sovereignty over the island of Ireland by sitting in the parliament of Westminster' (Maskey 2018). In other words, for 100 years Irish republicans have refused to recognize the Y-status function of Westminster. Maskey acknowledges that it may seem odd, especially to British people unfamiliar with the Irish situation, why someone would get elected but not take their seat. However, the point of getting elected is to demonstrate that they 'provide active representation for our constituents' (Maskey 2018). In other words, they claim their Y-status authority position as elected politicians. However, he continues: 'Westminster is not their parliament, and never will be' (Maskey 2018). Taking their seats could be interpreted as confirm-structuring that Westminster is *their* parliament, which it is not. Why can Westminster not represent Irish people? Because 'Westminster does not now act – and never has acted – other than in the interests of Britain' (Maskey 2018). Maskey further reinforces the negative Y-status of Westminster by stating that Westminster constitutes 'a parliament that facilitated and supported 50 years of anti-Irish *apartheid* and *supremacist sectarian* rule' (Maskey 2018; italics added). The use of the words *apartheid* and *supremacist sectarian* are current negative Y-status functions. For subalterns this status is the negative equivalent of *terrorist* in the language games of the powerful. In the BDS campaign against normalization of Israel, the negative Y-status designation *apartheid* is similarly used (BDS Movement 2018). It is a matter of principle not to confirm-structure the status function of legitimate interlocutor to anyone who practises *apartheid*. It should be noted that Sinn Féin are allies of the BDS movement, so would be familiar with their discursive strategies. In short, for Sinn Féin, reaching the goal of opposing the DUP in Westminster is not worth the sacrifice of longstanding principles and a carefully constructed negative Y-status authority other.

Making the sacrifice: moving from zero-sum to positive-sum

Prior to the peace process in South Africa the African National Congress (ANC) maintained a campaign of isolation and anti-normalization of the Apartheid regime. They orchestrated a worldwide campaign of boycotts to isolate the regime – a strategy which the BDS models itself upon with regard to Israel (BDS Movement 2018). In his autobiography *Long Walk to Freedom*, Nelson Mandela describes his risky decision in 1985, while still incarcerated, to begin secret talks with the National Party. This was a decision that he reached without the approval of the executive committee of the ANC (Read 2010: 317). The ANC was not in principle opposed to negotiation but only if certain preconditions were met and at that time none of those conditions had been met (Read 2010: 317). To be clear, the objective of the ANC was not minor change to an already-existing political system (1-D conflict plus moderate reform of 2-D bias). Their objective was fundamental structural change through overt 2-D structural conflict.

Given the depth of the conflict, discussion appeared to have a low probability of success. Consequently, up to that point the policy of the ANC had been significantly more confrontational. As has been convincingly argued by Read (2010), Mandela decided to embark upon talks because he considered the 2-D confrontation as zero-sum, with potential for only a zero-sum victor/vanquished outcome. Because there were perceived to be only winners and losers, the regime would fight bitterly. Consequently, even if the ANC might emerge victorious in the end, the cost in human suffering and death would be considerable. After all, the South African army was still a formidable force.

To see the good sense of 1-D structured negotiations both sides had to be persuaded that a positive-sum conflict, with all its compromises, was preferable to a zero-sum deep conflict. Essentially, for the white South African land-owning class, their trade-off was to relinquish the Apartheid political system in exchange for holding on to their considerable land holdings. For the followers of the ANC, the trade-off was the end of Apartheid and the start of political democracy but without the right to redistribute land without compensation (Terreblanche 2002: 417–24).[1]

To start with the talks were kept secret, just as in the case of the British government and the IRA. The move from 2-D destructuration to engagement

(1-D structured conflict) has the risk of recognizing the Y-status authority of other. In addition to secrecy, the ANC used Mandela's position in a manner that could allow them to remove Mandela's Y-status function as an ANC representative. He was in prison and so could be described as *out of touch*. Furthermore, his age could be used to dismiss him as *an old man* who didn't know what he was doing. If he failed, he could be cut loose as an individual without ANC authority Y-status; if he succeeded, he could be portrayed as the innovative leader who took the party in a new direction. Mandela writes:

> There are times when a leader must move out ahead of his flock, go off in a new direction, confident that he is leading his people in the right way. Finally, my isolation furnished my organisation with the excuse in case matters went awry: *the old man was alone and completely cut off, and his actions were taken by him as an individual, not as a representative of the ANC.*
> (Mandela 1994: 459, quoted in Read 2010: 318; italics added)

Mandela became the innovative leader, and began a long peace process, which gradually moved 2-D confrontation into 1-D structured conflict. Principles were held on to, as South Africa became a democracy, but there were also compromises, as left-wing promises of land and wealth redistribution were significantly compromised (Terreblanche 2002: 417–24). The goals of peaceful co-existence and compromise gradually won out over deep structural conflict. The idea of Mandela as either *an out-of-touch old man* or an *innovative leader* was a clever strategy to sidestep the dilemma posed by unofficial talks. In the case of failure the ANC could claim they were not negotiating or having talks and so not face the kind of embarrassment that Thatcher and Major felt when they were, so to speak, *found out*.

Israel used a similar strategy in the build-up to the Oslo talks. To begin with Israel was represented by two academics, Yair Hirschfeld and Ron Pundak, who secretly met and negotiated with PLO representative Abu Alan on the outskirts of Oslo, beginning 20 January 1993. In conversation, Peres jocularly referred to the negotiators as 'crackpots', yet the negotiations continued. Abu Alan sensed (or got word of) this attitude and asked the Norwegians to confirm the Israeli academics' Y-status authority. He was reassured that they actually had Y-status authority as official representatives (Morris 2001: 617). The use of academics, rather than politicians or civil servants, suggests the creative use of ambiguous Y-status, which can be withdrawn. The jocular reference to them as *crackpots* suggests a willingness to dissociate from them, if it suited. If the secret negotiations had gone awry, yet been discovered, the Israelis could have dissociated themselves from negotiating with the PLO, who had the negative Y-status of *terrorists* at that time.

Non-violent struggle

Mandela and Gandhi are often characterized as archetypal of what is variously known as passive resistance, non-violent resistance, non-violent struggle or non-violent revolution. This is not entirely correct with regard to Mandela, as he was willing to use violence (Read 2010: 232). However, as his negotiations developed, he became gradually more converted to non-violent resistance, followed by dialogue.

As theorized here, a revolutionary programme of non-violent resistance consists of continual destructuration in response to established authority structuration. While Mandela and Gandhi are the two most celebrated heroes of non-violent resistance or revolution, the man who wrote the most used *how-to* manuals of non-violent revolt is (or was – he died 28 January 2018) Gene Sharp. His best-known manual is *From Dictatorship to Democracy: A Conceptual Framework for Liberation* (Sharp 2010), which is available for free from his website, the Albert Einstein Institution (aeinstein. org), together with about 25 other books, translated into ten languages. His books are known to have inspired modern uprisings from Ukraine's Orange Revolution of 2004, to the Arab Spring, to the Occupy movement, and are read by resistance groups throughout the world, including BDS (Walters 2018).

Sharp opens *From Dictatorship to Democracy* by making clear that this is a manual for overthrowing dictatorships, replacing them with democracy. Sharp acknowledges that '[i]n some situations where no fundamental issues are at stake, and therefore a compromise is acceptable, negotiations can be an important means to settle conflict' (Sharp 2010: 10). In the conceptual framework used here, Sharp is saying that when there are no systemic structural issues at stake then it is acceptable to negotiate authority or economic conflict at the level of 1-D structured conflict. However, negotiated settlement is very different from overthrowing cruel dictatorships to replace them with freedom and democracy (Sharp 2010: 10), which entails deep structural change.

Negotiated compromise is 1-D power, in which social actors have different goals (higher wages versus higher profits), while overthrowing dictatorships entails 2-D conflict. In the latter, what is required is a shift in power structures, and 'such a shift will occur through struggle, not negotiations' (Sharp 2010: 10). Following this, Sharp explains how an opposition group may be tempted by negotiation with a dictator but that this temptation should be resisted, however appealing the offer (Sharp 2010: 10–11).

In other words, short-term episodic goals should not be allowed to override the longer-term aim of structural change, which promises a fundamental shift in dispositional power.

2-D conflict often leads to violence but Sharp rejects physical violence as a strategy. This is not on normative grounds, due to moral considerations, but because, as a social fact, violence is likely to be ineffective. Essentially, because dictators lack legitimacy, or a solid Y-status ring of reference, they always have well-honed and effective means of coercion at their disposal. So, violent opposition plays to their strength (Sharp 2010: 4–5). To return to the example of South Africa, the Apartheid regime was backed by the most effective military on the African continent.

In contrast to their military strength, dictatorships have vulnerabilities that can bring them crashing down. Sharp cites many examples of this phenomenon, including: the collapse of Communism in the Eastern bloc in 1989 and the 1979 fall of the Shah of Iran in the face of the Islamic revolution. The greatest vulnerability of dictators, backed by coercion, is the fact that they have a weak or incomplete validating authority ring of reference. In this context Sharp recounts a Chinese parable of the monkey master (Sharp 2010: 17–18), which hinges around an awakening among a bunch of enslaved monkeys to the fact that their cruel master was not intrinsically powerful but had power because they were collectively obedient to him. As stated by Sharp, one of the principles of authority is 'the belief among the people that the regime is legitimate, and that they have a moral duty to obey it' (Sharp 2010: 18). Using the conceptual tools of this language game, the Y-status of authority is constituted by a ring of reference that consists of the people who are willing to confirm-structure orders given.

Obedience to authority goes beyond validating Y-status as it also allows the mobilization of resources by the dominant. It gives the dominant access to the organization of human resources, including skills, which routine obedience demands (Sharp 2010: 19). If authority and these forms of obedience are withdrawn, the dictator becomes powerless. A cruel dictator is already weak in true authority. If those who deliver routine obedience to everyday tasks, those without a deep commitment to that authority, were to withdraw their obedience, the regime would become powerless. If those social actors who obey out of short-term pragmatic dominant ideology were to withdraw their confirm-structuration to the Y-status of regime officials, then the structures of authority, which are really simulacrum authority, not actual authority, would collapse.

To be successful, a non-violent struggle should be a complex form of struggle that takes place with regard to all the structures that sustain the despotic political system. The common error of non-violent struggle is to rely solely on one or two methods, such as strikes and mass demonstrations

(Sharp 2010: 30–1). In order to be really effective, destructuration must take place on many levels, including the psychological, social, economic and political. Sharp compiles a list of 198 ways of non-cooperation across these levels (Sharp 2010: 79–86). With system-wide destructuration the social structures that sustain the dictator are effectively immobilized.

When resisting it is important not to be tempted to use violence because violence, even of a low-level variety (such as throwing stones or burning tyres) creates the pretext for the despotic power to move the conflict onto the ground where the despot is at their strongest: violence and coercion (Sharp 2010: 32).

Sharp portrays non-violent struggle as a massive act of non-cooperation right across all aspects of society (Sharp 2010: 55–6). He advocates massive destructuration, thus 2-D structural conflict, with respect to most aspects of social structural reproduction. Obviously this will entail forgoing the everyday episodic power-to that comes from obedience, and routine reproduction of social structures.

Some methods of non-cooperation are overt and interrupt the flow of everyday life, such as sitting down in the street or going on hunger strike. Other methods of non-violent struggle include the apparent continuation of everyday life, while subtly subverting it. For instance, people may report for work, but then deliberately work slowly or become 'sick' in the middle of work (Sharp 2010: 32).

Sharp considers non-violent struggle as implicitly democratic because it entails a popular withdrawal of consent to the social structures that sustain despotism. He argues that to sustain this democratic impetus, the people must be democratic in their practice. That is to say, they should not be tempted to be secretive (Sharp 2010: 33–4). Openness suggests a strong ring of reference, so is conducive to effective resistance, while being closed suggests the same weakness as the despot: a lack of an authentic authority ring of reference.

Sharp's analysis draws our attention to how in extreme situations the best strategy for a subaltern can be 2-D conflict through destructuration across the board. The only qualification I would add to Sharp's position is that it underestimates the need for 2-D conflict to channel itself into structured conflict at some point in time.

When should 2-D become 1-D structured conflict?

Sharp is a trenchant advocate of the absence of compromise. However, there comes a moment when all 2-D conflict has to restructure into 1-D structured conflict. Otherwise, everyone is disempowered. So, when does that tipping point occur?

In his insistence upon the absence of dialogue with despots, there lies the danger that the absence of structure can become a way of life; the danger of popular revolt is followed by total social disintegration. To prevent this there must come a point where 2-D conflict becomes open to some form of peace process that can channel popular dissent into new practices of structured 1-D conflict. Constant revolution is not the road to freedom. It is the road to powerlessness.

When the more powerful are confronted with destructuration and so fail in the exercise of power-over, the more powerful have an incentive to restore routine structural reproduction, in order to regain their power-over. Yes, they can use coercion, but coercion is unstable, as the other remains a potentially rebellious subject. The more stable strategy is to change the incentive structure by making the situation positive-sum, by giving the subordinate actor more gain, dispositional power, or power-to out of confirm-structuration. If the subaltern gains more from compliance, she may move from a policy of resistance.

When confronted with this, the subaltern has to evaluate whether or not the betterment is purely in short-term goals or whether this actually entails a structural change that is permanent. If there is profound structural change then the 2-D conflict has achieved something real. If, on the other hand, this is temporary goal attainment, the subaltern may well have good reason to continue 2-D conflict.

In 2017 the airline Ryanair was hit by a number of pilot strikes that forced them to cancel a number of scheduled flights. The pilots demanded the right to form a trade union, which would be a structural change. At first the chief executive, Michael O'Leary, was unyielding. Then, after being forced to cancel numerous flights, he offered a €10,000 one-off payment (and other goodies) to each compliant pilot (Humphries 2017). In other words, O'Leary was destructuring the demand for union recognition, but offering a short-term goal – a significant sum of money – in its place. However, the pilots refused, and so destructured his offer. The money must have been tempting, but acceptance of it would have allowed for the structural reproduction (confirm-structuration) of the status quo, whereby there were no trade unions in Ryanair. The pilots would have gained goals (financial gain) but without a dispositional power increase. Finally, in response to a planned pre-Christmas strike, which would have seriously damaged the airline's reputation, O'Leary backed down, and recognized the union Impact as representative of the pilots (McLoughlin and Heffernan 2017). In so doing, O'Leary recognized, or confirm-structured, the authority status function of Impact. This was 2-D conflict in which the less powerful prevailed through collective action and destructuration. They were offered significant goal incentives in order to reproduce the status quo but refused.

The same juxtaposition of goals and structures applies in cases where the goal is authority. The Catalan independence vote was primarily an authority claim – an independent republic. However, there was also a secondary goal related to economic desires. Essentially, Catalonia is the most economically prosperous region in the Spanish federation and, consequently, contributes disproportionally more in federal taxes. The Spanish prime minister at the time, Mariano Rajoy, did everything in his power to destructure the independence referendum. He stated that the police, local councils and all other organs of government had an 'obligation to impede or paralyse' any effort to carry out the vote (Rajoy quoted in BBC 2017). However, having destructured and used coercion against the Catalans, Rajoy made it known that he would countenance greater regional fiscal autonomy, rather than independence (Boffey and Jones 2017). In other words, Rajoy was attempting to re-engage the Catalan independence movement by offering them a goal (a better fiscal situation), while still destructuring the idea of independence.

Of course, in making these types of distinctions (between goals and structures) it has to be acknowledged that, unlike the Ryanair pilot refusal of €10,000, what appears as a goal also has a structural element. Greater fiscal autonomy can also be conceived of not only as a financial but also a structural gain. Once a region is perceived to be financially autonomous there is the possibility that this is also a step along the road to political independence. So, while there is an element of accepting 2-D defeat on the Y-status function of a republic but a gain of greater dispositional authority Y-status function in the fiscal area, the latter may, over time, have implications for political authority. In other words, Y-status fiscal autonomy may well feed into creating better conditions of possibility for a Y-status republic.

When that tipping point should be followed, from 2-D conflict to 1-D, is complex. Learning from the mistakes of the Oslo Accords, the key weakness was a lack of structured process to prevent backsliding on commitments made. The Y-status of the Palestinian National Authority was conceived of as a temporary state of affairs, as was the continued occupation of areas B and C. With the benefit of hindsight, Palestine should have been recognized as a sovereign state at that time and the continual delay of full withdrawal from areas B and the majority of C should not have been possible, even if the exact division of the contentious parts of the border were unresolved. I do not think that the PLO or Israel were wrong to negotiate when they did, to move from 2-D conflict to a 1-D structured process, but I think the agreement itself was flawed by not being sufficiently structurally constrained. Obviously, events undermined the process. To mention a few: if Rabin had not been assassinated, if Hamas had not engaged in attacks against civilians, if Arafat had been more resolute (by not agreeing one thing in negotiations and then saying something else to please his home audience) and if Netanyahu had not consistently stirred Israelis against the peace process when in opposition (Gilbert 2008: 584–5) and worked against it when prime minister (Tharoor 2015; Levy 2013), perhaps the outcome might have been different. As always, contingent events played a part. However, what crucially undermined the process was that the populations, especially the average Palestinians, did not feel the immediate benefits of the compromises made. In other words, there was not a positive-sum dividend, which was palpable to all concerned.

A similar danger lurks in Northern Ireland if there is a return to a hard border with the Republic of Ireland. In that case, some Irish nationalists will feel that their compromises were in vain, thus a zero-sum loss, instead of positive-sum gain. Similarly, in South Africa there is growing discontent over the fact that political equality has not translated into greater economic equality.

As observed by the poet W. B. Yeats, quoting the Irish nationalist leader Charles S. Parnell, there is a problem if the average cheering revolutionary finds himself after the revolution 'still breaking stone' – 'Parnell came down the road, he said to a cheering man: "Ireland shall get her freedom and you will still break stone"' (Yeats 1933: 159). Post-revolutionary political systems can only remain stable if they deliver actual dispositional power to the majority (including many of the worst-off) supporters of the revolution. If a negotiated settlement does not deliver palpable power-to gain for the average resistance fighter, they will revert to 2-D conflict, or potentially so, with a subaltern ideology waiting for its opportunity. Within the latter, those who compromised will have the negative Y-status of *traitors* to the cause.

Note

1 At the time of writing, this compromise is unraveling. In response to rising anger at inequality, the ANC is moving towards amending the country's constitution to allow for the expropriation of lands without compensation (Kumwenda-Mtambo 2018).

4

The third dimension of power: Practical consciousness knowledge, consciousness-raising, the natural attitude and the social construction of reasonable/unreasonable

In its original formulation, Lukes analyzed the third dimension of power using the conceptual vocabulary of *false-consciousness* (Lukes 1974). This draws from a long Marxist tradition of explaining the non-revolutionary predispositions of the proletariat in terms of their inability to know what their *real interests* are. However, the concept of false-consciousness has the unfortunate connotation of positing a *true-consciousness* that represents the *real interests* of social actors, which the latter are incapable of discerning.

Relative to the Marxist tradition, privileging the perceptions of the Marxist thinker as real interests over the observed interests of social actors entails an implicit condescension towards the latter. This is a performative contradiction within a supposedly egalitarian theory (Clegg et al. 2006: 212–14; Haugaard 1997: 18–19).

Another issue is that the idea of false-consciousness suggests a link between the truth and the absence of domination. In everyday life social actors implicitly appeal to this idea when they use the expression *speaking truth to power*. However, in its simple form this perspective obscures the fact, which is much discussed by Foucault (for instance, 1980: 118 and 131), that truth claims are frequently used to reinforce relations of domination (analyzed in Chapter 6). In its unqualified form, *speaking truth to power* often assumes a language of truth that is absolute, which transcends social relations, as a view from nowhere. This is sociologically implausible and, as we shall see, often constitutes a premise that is used to legitimize domination. However, abandoning these presuppositions does not mean the phenomenon of 3-D power is unreal or unimportant, but we must start from different premises.

Social actors as interpretative beings: concepts

Let us begin from the sociological foundation of social order, which is *social action*. As Weber observes, what makes social action *social* is that interacting social actors attach meaning to their interaction (Weber 1978: 4). Social order is reproduced because social actors behave relatively predictably. That capacity derives from the fact that they are interpretative beings who place meaning upon the world. Social action has meaning, which comes from structure. All acts of structural reproduction are ordering practices that constitute acts of interpretation.

We are by nature interpretative beings that make sense of the world by imposing concepts upon incoming data. These concepts limit the data, and in so doing, give them meaning. When I see a chair as a *chair*, it is the consequence of a combination of sense data and the concepts I impose upon those data. The nature of this interpretative process is made manifest in our interpretation of gestalt pictures. Take the instance of a duck-rabbit picture (Figure 4.1). The incoming data are the lines on a page and the concepts triggered in the brain are either a *duck* or a *rabbit*. Notice that it is *either* the *duck* or the *rabbit*; when it is a *duck*, there is nothing *rabbit-like* about and or vice versa. The reason is that the brain has to choose between the two concepts, which makes it either one thing or the other. In the case of this picture, there are equal data available for two concepts, which is the unusual quality that gestalt pictures have. Jokes often have this quality too.

In everyday life we can experience this ambiguity of meaning when it is twilight. That moment between night and day, as dusk descends, the world becomes ambiguous, and things appear at first as one thing and then as another. Imagine that it is dusk as you walk along a country road. In the distance you catch sight of a person but, as you approach, you perceive that it's a shovel with coat hung over it. The moment the perceived object switches from being *a person* to being a *shovel-coat* all personhood is lost, just as there is nothing *rabbity* about the duck-rabbit picture when interpreted as a *duck*.

Figure 4.1 Duck-rabbit

Sightings of ghosts are usually momentary glimpses of this kind; the light is not good, confused data are coming in. The mind tries the concept of person and then decides there are not enough data to support the concept of person; consequently, the concept is rejected. However, we experience this as a human presence that just disappeared into thin air – a ghost!

Imagine you are in crowd and see someone in the distance you think you recognize; you think, *Oh, that's Paul*. You try to get close enough to greet Paul, only to discover that he looks nothing like your friend Paul and you are left wondering, *how could I have thought that?* Again, the image of your friend Paul constitutes a concept, which is momentarily triggered by weak data. However, the moment you have more data, the person in question ceases to look anything like Paul. However, to you it appears that someone who looked like Paul has now morphed into someone different.

We generate concepts that we impose upon the world relative to an interpretative horizon, which is the consequence of socialization. This knowledge is largely tacit and constitutes what is often referred to as our *second nature*. Our first nature refers to our biological capacities, which are overlaid by programming from our experience of the world.

Language as first and second nature

In his linguistic theories, Noam Chomsky argues that, as the human brain develops, the growth of brain neurons enables certain concepts and linguistic structures to be generated (Chomsky 2002 and 2006; see Pinker 1995 as an introduction). These concepts are semi-innate, in the sense that they have a physical basis in the brain structure. However, in order to constitute part of the human capacity for language, they must also be exposed to external stimulus.

In the case of language acquisition, the majority of these processes take place before the age of seven. Moving beyond language, other capacities, including mathematical capacities, are acquired later as the brain develops and is exposed to the relevant experience. When the development of the brain and the priming external stimulus correspond in a felicitous way, children can acquire words through surprisingly limited exposure, often with as little as a single instance. Conversely, if stimulus and brain development are not in synchronicity, then the child fails to acquire those concepts. If a child is too young for a concept, repeated exposure will not enable her to acquire it – similarly, it is impossible to teach multiplication to a child of four. When the optimum time has passed, exposure will fail to inscribe the brain. It is for this reason that feral or imprisoned children, without linguistic exposure before the age of seven, never develop full linguistic competence.

The particular linguistic capacity that children acquire is their *generative grammar* or *mental grammar*, while the *universal grammar* is their general innate potentiality (Pinker 1995: 110–12, 236–40 and 285–8). In the language game used here, the universal grammar corresponds to our *first nature*, while our generative grammar is our *second nature*.

Sociologists tend to shy away from Chomsky's linguistic theories because the concept of a universal grammar is interpreted as suggesting biological determinism that precludes conceptual space for socialization. This read of Chomsky is mistaken as it is quite clear that exposure is required for language acquisition. The same would apply for socialization in general. The idea of a generative grammar, which is primed through exposure, gives us insight into our second nature, consonant with the sociologist's emphasis upon nurture over nature. We (I and hopefully also the reader) were exposed to both the concept of *rabbit* and *duck* during childhood second-nature cognitive formation, which is why we are able to see the above gestalt picture as a *duck* or as a *rabbit*. However, if we had not had that exposure (or indeed the exposure to cartoon drawings), we would be unable to see the duck-rabbit picture as a duck-rabbit picture.

Put simply, Chomsky's position is similar to arguing that our capacity to ride a bicycle is based upon biological capacities, including a sense of balance, while simultaneously recognizing that acquiring the capacity to ride a bicycle entails a significant amount of learning, which we internalize as second-nature.

Practical consciousness knowledge

The term *habitus* was coined by Elias (1995) and has been popularized by Bourdieu (1977: 78 and 1990: 52–65). *Habitus* refers to both physical-emotional disposition of habit and the epistemic knowledge that sustains our second nature. In theorizing the four dimensions of power I wish to analytically distinguish between the epistemic and the ontological because they correspond with two different dimensions of power: 3-D and 4-D respectively. Therefore, I wish to split this use of the concept of habitus into two. This is for analytic purposes only. In actual social life the two aspects are linked, as are the various dimensions of power.

With reference to the epistemic aspect, social theorist Anthony Giddens uses the term *practical consciousness knowledge* (Giddens 1984). We will follow his lead, referring to practical consciousness or practical knowledge. The word *practical* describes the everyday practical problem-solving aspect of this knowledge, which has resonances of Wittgenstein (1967). In Giddens' theory there are three aspects to our knowledge of social life. *Discursive consciousness* is the knowledge we readily put into words, and practical consciousness is a tacit knowledge that enables social actors *to go on* in life (Giddens 1984). In addition to these two forms of consciousness there is also the *unconscious*, the suppression of which is necessary for ontological security, which we will discuss further in the context of 4-D.

Practical consciousness is not the equivalent of the unconscious, as is sometimes suggested in the literature, even by Bourdieu (1977: 77 and 1990: 56). In Giddens (1984), practical consciousness is not unconscious in any sense that suggests suppression. There is a free flow between discursive and practical consciousness. At any time social actors have the discursive capacity to penetrate their practical consciousness knowledge and bring it to discursive consciousness. However, they do not do so routinely because the amount of knowledge that exists at the level of practical consciousness is vast in its extent. To be efficient, social actors focus their discursive consciousness on immediate goals, while relying on practical consciousness for the majority of structural reproduction. (Right now I am explaining social theory, holding that at discursive consciousness, while I draw upon my use of the English language as practical consciousness knowledge.)

Theoretically, this flow is important because it enables social actors to step back from the practical consciousness, and evaluate it. This facilitates reflective agency with regard to their practical consciousness knowledge. In Bourdieu's account of habitus there is a tendency to be over-determinist, for instance, when he refers to the habitus as 'immanent law', or '*lex insita*' (Bourdieu 1990: 59; see more generally 1990: 52–65). In Giddens' account of practical and discursive consciousness, there is more conceptual space for reflexivity and innovation. That said, I do not want to exaggerate the significance of discursive consciousness reflection. In everyday routine interaction, there is indeed a high level of predictability based around the taken-for-granted nature of practical consciousness knowledge. Because practical consciousness is so complicated, the discursive representation can never cover every aspect of interaction. It is for this reason that grammars and dictionaries never really capture the complexity of language use adequately.

In perceiving the world we usually have a sense of purpose, adopting an intentional stance towards it. In order to do this efficiently, we focus our discursive knowledge upon our desired goal outcomes, ignoring the reproduction of social structure. When I purchase a pound of sugar, I do not wonder about the convention of weights and measurements, why currency has the value it has, how I know that the cash desk is the cash desk; I just know *how to go on* (Wittgenstein 1967: § 208). Consequently, I keep this kind of knowledge at a lower level of consciousness, at practical consciousness.

However, when in a foreign country, we are often forced to reflect upon these taken-for-granted realities.

Knowledge moves between practical and discursive consciousness and back. Possibly the best example of transferring practical into discursive consciousness is the teaching of your native language. The students constantly ask questions, such as: *when do you use 'less', rather than 'fewer'? If it's fewer in the sentence, 'give me fewer bananas', why is it 'give me less milk?' Why not 'fewer milks'?* In response, the native speaker teacher has to reflect upon practical consciousness knowledge of their native language and then slowly translate it into discursive consciousness as they explain. While the teacher is busy transferring knowledge from practical into discursive consciousness, as the student learns, she does the reverse. As she learns to become a competent speaker, she begins to speak from practical consciousness knowledge.

I am sure many have had the experience of going to a foreign country with school knowledge of a language, which is largely discursive, and not being able to speak properly. Then, with enough exposure, they find themselves constructing sentences without having to think discursively. Suddenly they have the sensation of speaking the language. They have an *I-know-how-to-go-on* feeling. However, if they pause and ask themselves *how did I know how to go on?*, that discursive self-consciousness makes them hesitate and quite likely falter and stumble. Converting practical consciousness into discursive consciousness impedes their capacity for social action because speaking at a normal pace requires massive levels of practical knowledge, which exceeds the capacity and speed of discursive knowledge.

Practical consciousness as 'for-the-sake-of-us' knowledge

Practical consciousness knowledge is knowledge that we experience as immediate, as part of everyday social action. Objects are interpreted as meaning given, relative to our practical intentions in the world. Our capacity to go on has a solipsistic aspect; meaning relates to how things exist *for us*. When I enter a dining room and see a table set for dinner, I see a table, with forks, knives, spoons, plates and glasses, all of which represent use-function for me. I do not stand there and discursively think through what it means for a *table* to be a *table*, or a *fork* a *fork*. Nor do I think discursively along the lines: *it is customary to use wide flat bits of timber, with four legs (although there could be fewer or more) to support them, as tables*. Neither do I see the *forks* in terms of their metallic *atomic structure*, as a scientist might, if they were to use them as part of a chemical experiment. I simply see the table for-the-sake-of-me, as an object that exists because of *the use that I want to make of it.* We do not reflect on this solipsism; we just *go on* in this situation.

The natural attitude

When we go on unreflectively, we approach the world with what the phenomenologist Alfred Schutz (1967) called the *natural attitude*. To be able to eat our dinner, or get out of bed in the morning, we constantly impose meanings upon the world that appear to us just as part of *the natural-order-of-things*, which is the *natural attitude*.

The natural attitude is suspended if something unfamiliar happens. Our practical consciousness becomes inadequate and we use discursive consciousness to get us through. Imagine a cutlery setting is part of a formal elaborate place setting with several forks, knives and spoons, which you are not accustomed to, as you live more simply. In this case, you do not see the cutlery with a natural attitude and you may feel unsure how *to go on*. Discursive consciousness takes over. You will watch what *other people do* and imitate, to make your actions felicitous in the eyes of others.

This discursive consciousness use of cutlery will, most likely, distract you from *ease in conversation* because eating should be second-nature practical knowledge. Instead, it is taking up part of your discursive consciousness, leaving less of your discursive knowledge for making conversation. In these situations, social actors are likely to utter phatic communion banalities, which do not require significant discursive reflection. These may come thick and fast, as the person is insecure. However, once the knowledge of cutlery use becomes practical consciousness, they can adopt the natural attitude towards it, and their entire discursive consciousness can be used to focus upon conversation. Similarly, when individuals start a new job, they do not consider the norms of their new place of work as part of the natural-order-of-things. So, they are reflexively monitoring interaction, in order to be felicitous. Quickly they become socialized into the local norms, which become practical knowledge.

Natural attitude and multiple interpretative horizons

When we adopt the natural attitude we assume the meanings of things exist out there, as a prose-of-the-world. This is despite the fact that these meanings shift depending upon context. The latter, in fact, should tell us that the meaning is socially constructed, not just out-there. When expecting to eat our dinner, we see the *fork* as a *fork*. However, if the fork is antique, in the natural-order-of-things of an antique dealer it loses meaning as an eating tool and instead is interpreted as an item of rarity or exchange value.

As Marx observes in *Das Capital* (1976: 132), a coat has a dual existence: as a garment to keep us warm (use value) and as a commodity with exchange value. This is similar to the gestalt duck-rabbit picture. The same things, be they *lines on a page, objects, such as the structure of a fork, or a coat,* can be one thing or the other depending upon which concept we place upon them. The X shifts to Y1 or Y2 in different local language games, which constitute alternative circumstances C.

In the case of each these meanings, there is incommensurability of meaning because they are part of different systems. For instance, *use value* and *exchange value* of any object are not just singular meanings on their own or taken singly. Rather, they are part of a system of meaning, which makes sense systemically. The exchange value belongs to an economic system, while the use value is part of the life-world of everyday problem-solving.

While the meaning of the world-out-there is a reflection of our interpretative horizon, it appears external to us. At the core of our natural attitude is *misrecognition* of the source of meaning (Bourdieu 1990: 68). The natural attitude suggests that the world-out-there comes with its meaning already imprinted upon it, while in fact that meaning is a reflection of our second-nature practical consciousness. As argued by Heidegger (1962), the world appears out-there but is, in fact, as far as meaning is concerned, a reflection of our being-in-the-world. Our being-in-the-world and the world-out-there-full-of-meaning are not two separate facts but are mutually constitutive; the world has meaning for us, only as part of our subjective being-in-the-world, which is where 3-D connects to 4-D.

If we dig up a perfectly preserved archaeological artifact but *we do not know what it is,* the interpretative horizon that imposed a concept upon it has been lost, and in so doing the object itself has lost its meaning, even if its materiality endures. The object's meaning does not lie in its materiality or form but derives from the ring of reference that imposes concepts upon it. Its existence as, say, a Neolithic *funeral urn,* is inextricably bound up with the being-in-the-world of the Neolithic people who saw it as a *funeral urn.* Hence, its meaning is not intrinsic but in fact structural and systemic. Neolithic society structured and confirm-structured it as having a Y-status function funeral urn. If we, in contemporary society, do not see it as a funeral urn, that meaning is no longer confirm-structured. If we confirm-structure it as something different (a storage jar), then the meaning of the material object has changed. The latter is significant for agency, because even though an individual social actor intends a certain meaning by structuration, they do not have the power to be sure that their intended meaning will be the one that is actually reproduced. The speaker does not have the agency power to define meaning; it is the respondent who does. This applies both to external objects and to Y-status of self.

We are complex interpretative beings who impose concepts upon incoming data incredibly fast, nearly instantaneously. And we do so differently, depending upon context. One moment a piece of bread is food; the next it can be the sacred body of Christ in a Christian ceremony. As Giddens emphasizes, even though we do not consciously reflect upon our practical consciousness knowledge, the knowledge is vast in its extent, immensely complex, and continually dependent upon a reflexive assessment of the contextuality of social life (Giddens 1984: 26). While it has a reflex quality, it is neither trivial nor shallow.

Practical consciousness as default and local language game

Practical consciousness is made up of local language games that constitute interpretive horizons, which are particular to context. Marx famously observed that in communist society a person would no longer be defined by their actions within the sphere of economic activity. Rather, in communism a person can hunt in the morning, fish in the afternoon, rear cattle in the evening and criticize after dinner (Marx 1974: 82). In fact, the complexity of advanced modern society entails the capacity to switch from one interpretative to the next in a matter of split seconds. It is possible to be fisherman and critic or secular and religious within seconds of each other as the world switches gestalt quality depending upon which interpretative horizon is imposed.

An experiment was conducted upon physics students at well-regarded US universities, including Johns Hopkins and MIT, in which they were asked in a non-academic context, in a pub or similar location, to explain the physics of the flipping of a coin. To the surprise of the cognitive psychologists carrying out the experiment, the majority of students responded with everyday explanations, which they should have known to be false in term of physics (Gardener 1991: 3). This can be interpreted as some kind of learning failure whereby there is a tendency for practical knowledge to override discursive knowledge, as a default. Their knowledge of physics had not properly penetrated practical consciousness knowledge. Consequently, they reverted to unschooled practical consciousness when off-guard (Gardiner 1991: 4–7).

While social actors exhibit this tendency because practical knowledge is foundational to the personality, there is also something else going on in this experiment. The students were both young *scientists* and *competent social actors*. Relative to the latter interpretative horizon they understood that an appropriate explanation for an everyday situation and a science lab were two different things. As part of their practical knowledge, they would have monitored the context of their social actions and then applied the appropriate interpretative horizon to that context. Going back to the gestalt of the duck-rabbit picture, the analogy would be that coin-flipping is analogous to a *duck* in everyday life and to a *rabbit* in the laboratory (or is the right answer the other way around?).

Practical knowledge as enabling

Shared practical consciousness knowledge empowers social actors. This applies both to material resources and authority resources. As argued at length by Barnes (1988) and Searle (1996 and 2007), the fact that a cup is a cup and that a paper note with '50 euro' printed on it (an X) is a *€50 note* (a Y) makes it possible for social actors to engage in interaction with respect to these objects, in a manner that delivers power-to. With regard to the capacity building shared knowledge, Barnes writes as follows.

> Any distribution of knowledge confers a generalized capacity for action upon those individuals who carry and constitute it, and that capacity for action is their social power, the power of the society they constitute by bearing and sharing the knowledge in question. *Social power is the added capacity for action that accrues to individuals through their constituting a distribution of knowledge and thereby a society.*
>
> (Barnes 1988: 57; italics added)

Barnes' definition of power, in terms of social knowledge, brings to the fore the significance of practical consciousness knowledge in constituting the symbolic content of both authority and economic resources.[1]

Because social actors tend to approach the world external to them with the *natural attitude* there is tendency for them to assume that these meanings adhere in the objects, which is not the case. What makes an *ounce of gold* a valuable item (thus an economic resource in capitalism, or suitable for making sacred objects in many religions of antiquity, while profane in others (Islam)) is the fact that we routinely interact with other social actors who similarly confer the status function upon the yellow metal. The fact that others view this metal in a similar way creates a confirm-structuring ring of reference, which is a reflection of a historically contingent system of knowledge.

The same applies to status functions. If an X is to count as a Y in circumstances C, part of the circumstances C is shared meaning between the social actors. The natural attitude shapes what authority dispositional powers that a person (an X) who counts as a Y (authority position) has. It appears as part of the natural-order-of-things that a *university professor* has the power-over students to set essay topics, deadlines and grade those essays. The latter may well have a significant impact upon the life chances of the students, so this resource becomes a significant power-to, -with and -over in the lives.

In a position of authority a social actor becomes a Y, and so it appears part of the natural-order-of-things that they can have certain resources but not others. Take a father–daughter relationship as an instance of social power. In contemporary Western society it is considered entirely appropriate and natural that a father has authority with regard to what a child-daughter eats and to ensure that she gets an education. However, in some traditional societies a father's authority would additionally extend beyond childhood to include the dispositional power resource to determine the daughter's future marriage partner. In situations where a family moves from the latter society to the former, or where education changes the interpretative horizon of the younger generation, huge conflict arises between these interpretative horizons.

In the film *Sand Storm* (Zexer 2016), a Palestinian-Israeli film, we see the conflict between a university-educated Bedouin wanting to marry for love-choice, and her family, who consider it entirely inappropriate that she should wish to choose her marriage partner. The father thinks that he is expressing love and care for his daughter, while she experiences his actions as constraining domination. The rest of the family, including the female members, all back the traditional way. Thus they constitute the ring of reference that renders the father's actions felicitous and reasonable, while the daughter is constituted as infelicitous and unreasonable.

The only ring of reference that validates her love-oriented interpretative horizon is her boyfriend, and whatever social contacts she has at the university. Invariably the daughter is confronted with a stark choice: either she must leave the family for good, by moving to a local metropolis with her partner, where their actions would be felicitous, or stay with the family whom she cares about, give up the person she loves and marry whomsoever her father chooses for her. As this choice entails two whole systems of meaning tied to her whole being-in-the-world, this constitutes a deep existential choice. In the end, she chooses to comply with her father's authority, and marries someone for whom she has no love. Following Gardener above, there is a tendency for the interpretative horizon that she has from childhood to override the newer one.

Her behaviour is felicitous, the (so-called) 'right choice', relative to the local family interpretative horizon, in which she was socialized. The film ends with her being deliberately spiteful, in small symbolic ways, to the marriage partner chosen by her family. He is nonplussed by these attacks. In this instance, she is showing the kind of subaltern resistance described by Scott (1990). She is discursively, and overtly, buying into the dominant ideology of her family but deep inside there is another interpretative horizon that rejects what she has done. The jibes at her nonplussed husband are a symbolic act of destructuration to the dominant ideology.

In this example we can see how enablement shades into 3-D conflict and domination. In what sense does she *choose* to comply? She is not overtly coerced with physical threats. Yet, she goes against some of her own deepest desires. She knows that making the choice she desires violates the system of meaning, the authority and, consequently, the honor of her family. Making *her own choice* in these circumstances is, relative to the inter-pretative framework of her family upbringing, *selfish and unreasonable*. So, she makes the *altruistic* (relative to the family interpretative horizon) choice and is 'reasonable'. However, this (so-called) *choice* is more a consequence of constraint than freedom. Yet, she could have chosen otherwise (she nearly does), so she is not a cultural dupe either.

Practical consciousness as *the reasonable*

Authority hinges around a felicity-versus-infelicity dichotomy. If I, with the Y-status function of *university professor*, were to order the students *to take showers*, or walk around the parking lot with a notebook *issuing parking tickets*, that would be infelicitous. It would *not just be wrong*, or mis-taken action; it would be unreasonable. It would not be like thinking that $3 \times 45 = 125$, when in fact the correct answer is 135. This is qualitatively different in that it is incorrect but not unreasonable. If I were to command the students *to take showers* or issue *parking tickets*, I would be deemed not simply incorrect but beyond reason altogether (see Jenkins and Lukes 2017). To use everyday language, I would be deemed *crazy*.

In the article 'Noumenal Power' (Forst 2015), Forst argues that political power is a noumenal phenomenon in the sense that it entails a cognitive event, which entails reason giving. He writes: '*to have and to exercise power means to be able – in different degrees – to influence, use, determine, occupy, or even seal off the space of reasons for others*' (Forst 2015: 116 and 2017: 42). This theoretical position inspired a special issue and further debate in the *Journal of Political Power* 2018 (mainly issue 1, with an article in issue 2 and Forst's reply in issue 3) in which prominent power theorists criticized his position. A number of thinkers, including Lukes (2018), Gilabert (2018) and Kettner (2018), criticize Forst for suggesting that all power presupposes reason. Lukes also argued that Forst overestimates reason, as against emotion – social actors can have emotional reasons for compliance. I will not reproduce the broad claim that *all power* is noumenal (I am sidestepping this argument) but a more moderate version of it, as follows: any power structure that presupposes the claim that X counts as Y in circumstances C constitutes a cognitive event that must be considered reasonable to be successfully reproduced. Maybe the word *reason* is misleading as it suggests scientific reason, as in 3 x 45 = 135. However, the more accurate conceptual tool is *reasonable*, as measured by the felicity-versus-infelicity response that is involved. This is Forst's intended meaning. He is not arguing that social actors are constantly driven by some abstract higher reason, as in Enlightenment reason. Rather, that actors have reasons that guide their action, which means their action is reasonable. In this sense the fanatic is guided by reason, although his process of reasoning may be objectionable, relative to standard opinion.

Among the forces that bind social actors to accept authority or symbolic economic resources (of the form X counts as Y in circumstances C) is meaning. To contradict meaning is infelicitous. The meaning of *traffic police* includes the power of issuing parking tickets, while the meaning of *university professor* includes marking essays. It is reasonable for university professors to grade essays, but unreasonable for them to attempt to issue parking tickets. What counts as reasonable, of course, varies from society to society, and from interpretative horizon to interpretative horizon.

At the fundamental core of symbolic authoritative and economic resources is a sense of the reasonable. What this amounts to is a sense of non-contradiction. If an X is a Y, that Y-ness defines the conditions of possibility. A *university professor* is Y1-status and *traffic police* is Y2-status. If a university professor goes around the car park issuing parking tickets he is not behaving as a Y1, rather he is behaving like Y2. Y1 does not equal Y2; they are different things. Behaving as if they were the same constitutes a cognitive failure of meaning. It entails misunderstanding the difference between two concepts, Y1 and Y2, which is unreasonable.

Constraint and reasonableness

The desire to be reasonable constitutes an extraordinarily constraining force in everyday interaction. This is particularly evident in 1-D where social structures override goals. If we vote in an election, our ballot is a piece of paper, an X, which counts as Y, *a vote*, in circumstances C, *an election*. In a well-established democracy the act of voting, confirm-structuring the Y-status function of a ballot, has an implicit logic to it, which is compelling. If our party gets fewer votes than another political party it is part of the (supposed) natural-order-of-things to admit defeat, even though this is entirely contrary to our desire to proclaim that our party has won. To vote, obtain fewer votes, and then proclaim victory is unreasonable because it constitutes a *performative contradiction* of what it means to vote. Voting means one thing, while not accepting the authority of those votes means its opposite; they are contradictory acts, and therefore unreasonable. In everyday life, the knowledge that a given action would appear unreasonable is a powerful bond upon social actors, which constrains them into routine felicitous structural reproduction. Of course, this constraint is not determinate, which provides conceptual space for innovative or radical counter-hegemonic agency.

The unreasonable as akin to a private language act

The concepts of *marriage for love* versus *arranged marriage* confer incommensurable Y-status. Parents and children with different interpretative horizons in this regard will consider the other unreasonable. This unreasonableness is very different from reason in science. It is about felicity and infelicity. Systems of thought presuppose certain meanings that render the other either reasonable or unreasonable.

As we saw in the discussion of so-called *terrorists*, to be deemed unreasonable carries with it the serious cost of exclusion. Part of this type of 2-D exclusion entails the judgement that the other is unreasonable. Once the other is outside the felicitous they lose their status of full personhood.

Wittgenstein famously argued that there is no such thing as a private language (Wittgenstein 1967). He did not mean that individuals are incapable of constructing a private language for themselves, as children often do in play. Rather, that a private language is not a real language in the sense of being a social system of meaning because it does not have a public element (Wittgenstein 1967: § 258–64). If a person were to speak such an artificially created language there could be no external justification of meaning (Wittgenstein 1967: para. 261). She could never be wrong about meaning, and in that sense it would not be a public language (Wittgenstein 1967: para. 269). I do not wish to disagree with Wittgenstein on this point. In fact, my insistence that meaning is reproduced only through confirm-structuration is consistent with Wittgenstein's argument. However, I would like to add a qualification to this that infelicitous acts of structuration, which are deemed unreasonable by the ring of reference, constitute a kind of private language *act*. It is not a private *language*; the point is that the destructuring other has rendered the initial act of structuration infelicitous, unreasonable and, therefore, not part of the system. Destructuration constitutes an act of exclusion, which deems the act of structuration unworthy of becoming part of a publicly shared language. The act of structuration, which is thwarted, renders what was intended as a public language a private act. The failed action is not systemic but may continue to be meaningful to the initiator.

Private language acts can only become a shared public language, or real language, if others can be found who are willing to confirm-structure. When initiating social change, the only way this can happen is through a form of consensus-building, which is the foundation of structural change.

The concept of *gay marriage* was until fairly recently infelicitous relative to the majority interpretative horizon. To successfully change a society there must be a subculture that constitutes a local ring of reference where the concept is felicitous. Once that subculture exists, what was once a private act becomes a public language, although only for a minority. Within this community the concept meets with felicity. However, in order for the law or other major public institutions to be changed, this minority language has to become a majority position. Marches and public events are arranged, which are a way for the minority community to reproduce structure publicly. Increasing numbers participating in public demonstrations demonstrate the existence of a significant ring of reference willing to confirm-structure gay marriage as reasonable.

High Y-status confirm-structuration will add felicity to a new ring of reference. Similarly, and inversely, the loss of status will weaken a ring of reference. In Ireland, on 22 May 2015, a referendum was held to change the constitution in order to allow gay marriage. The proposed change was passed by 66%, which would have been unthinkable not that many years earlier. Central to this was the combination of high-status endorsement, combined with the low status of the Catholic Church's opposition. The constitutional change was important to the young and popular *taoiseach* (Irish prime minister) Leo Varadkar, who is openly gay. This combined with the Catholic Church's loss of authority. In the past the Catholic Church had a 'moral monopoly' (Inglis 1998), which was subsequently seriously dented by a succession of scandals. This change of mood was summed up by Varadkar: 'In the past the Catholic Church had too much dominance in our society' (Varadkar quoted in Bashir 2018). This meant a shift in the conditions of possibility, which made gay marriage reasonable, thus possible.

Practical consciousness and discursive consciousness: consciousness-raising

While practical consciousness is enabling (power-to), its tacit nature has the potential to legitimize 2-D structural bias. Because social actors reproduce the majority of social structures from practical consciousness knowledge, they are often discursively unaware of the extent to which they reproduce 2-D structural biases. In this case, we are not dealing with *false-consciousness* but tacit knowledge that is not, as yet, subject to discursive examination. It is a dominant ideology without, as yet, subaltern counter-discourse.

An insightful account of raising practical to discursive consciousness is found in Simone de Beauvoir's account of writing *The Second Sex* (2010). The book started as a confession concerning her personal life. Thinking about the project, she decided to begin by asking the following question:

> 'What has it meant to me to be a woman?' At first she thought of this as a formality, as a preliminary exercise to get into the real work: 'I never had any feeling of inferiority, no-one had ever said to me, "You think that way because you are a woman"; my femaleness had never bothered me in any way. "In my case" I said to Sartre, "it hasn't really mattered."' Sartre urged her to think again: 'But still, you weren't brought up in the same way as a boy: you should take a closer look.' She did, and was amazed: 'It was a revelation. This was a masculine world, my childhood was nourished by myths concocted by men, and I hadn't reacted to them in the same way I should have if I had been a boy. I became so interested I gave up the personal confession in order to focus on women's condition in general.'
>
> (Moi 2010; quotation marks refer to de Beauvoir's words)

The revelation that de Beauvoir experienced was awareness of converting practical into discursive consciousness. As a body, an X, she was defined as a woman with a certain Y-status. As such, she knew at the level of practical consciousness how to perform gender – it was part of her natural-order-of-things. However, in response to Sartre's prompting, she began to raise that knowledge to discursive consciousness. As a consequence, she became consciously aware of the extent to which the structuring of social life is centred upon male social norms, that her female Y-status was less than male Y-status

While *The Second Sex* concerns the position of women in general, de Beauvoir uses herself as the underlying case study (Moi 2010). She uses her practical consciousness of her own socialization, and performance of gender, to discursively describe the social construction of *femininity*. Women who read the book use their practical consciousness as a sounding board. The book was an instant best-seller because it resonated with the practical consciousness of other women. The success of the book made a local interpretative horizon felicitous: feminism became mainstream.

The success of *The Second Sex* is not attributable to the fact that de Beauvoir revealed some hidden Truth (with a capital T), or that she exposed *false*-consciousness using *true*-consciousness. Rather, she used her practical consciousness knowledge of how to *go on* with the performance of

everyday life as the basis for a discursive description of the social construction of gender. In so doing she became discursively aware, or self-conscious,
of the implicit 2-D male bias of everyday life.

Awareness of 2-D bias makes overt 2-D conflict likely, but not inevitable.
The self-aware feminist may decide to let short-term goals override her
awareness, and sense of injustice; for instance, she may use her skills as
a female to flatter men to gain advantage. Or, she be aware of the 2-D bias
and somehow consider it inevitable because of reification, which we will
come to in the next two chapters.

Social change as resonance

The idea of consciousness-raising does not reproduce the false-versus-true-
consciousness dichotomy, yet it covers some of the same underlying intellectual territory. There is no foundational truth claim here. The *#MeToo*
movement has not found an irrefutable Truth. Rather, a number of social
actors have discursively articulated their experiences and created a new
ring of reference with others who have had similar experiences. These
experiences were ones that for a long time they felt would be regarded as
infelicitous but some event triggered discursive articulation, and in so doing
created a ring of reference. In this case, validation can be characterized as
resonance – a conceptual tool coined by Rosa (2017).

The women of the *#MeToo* movement discursively articulated an interpretation of the world that found *resonance within the practical consciousness* of other women. The latter created a ring of reference that constituted
an epistemic ring of reference that rendered their testimony felicitous. The
#MeToo movement was initiated by Tarana Burke in 2006. However, in the
aftermath of the Harvey Weinstein scandal, which broke in October 2017,
Alyssa Milano encouraged tweeting as part of an awareness campaign. It
was a combination of events: the scandal over the behaviour of movie pro-
ducer Weinstein and the brazenly misogynistic behaviour of Trump that
combined with the mass technology of the internet to create the conditions
of possibility for global resonance.

In response to *#MeToo*, *The Washington Post* and ABC News conducted
a poll in the USA concerning women's experiences of unwanted sexual
advances or sexual harassment. A majority of 54% had received unwanted
sexual advances, and 79% said they had experienced sexual harassment
at work. Of the latter, 52% found the experience humiliating, 64% were
intimidated and 83% were angry. Asked if men who sexually harass
women at work get away with it, 65% said they usually get away with it,
as against 29% who said they get punished (*The Washington Post* 2017).
In other words, this was an experience that was relatively common and

not inconsequential for the women involved. Yet the expectation was that it would go unpunished. So, it is pointless to complain.

In short, this was a shared experience, which was waiting to be articulated. Consequently, the moment it was articulated by women who already had high Y-status, it met with huge resonance. Over half the female population had practical consciousness knowledge of harassment and over three-quarters of women had experienced this at work.

The #*MeToo* movement's discursive articulation resonated with practical consciousness knowledge. The #*MeToo* movement created the conditions of possibility for women to speak out concerning gender-dominating experiences and be heard. *Being heard* means is not literally what these words mean – rather, being perceived of as reasonable. The latter is not the same as some claim of absolute Truth. It is being deemed reasonable within the language game of felicity. It means having the citizen's authority to be heard.

If we return to the example of Hillary Clinton in debate with Donald Trump (discussed in Chapter 2), Clinton found his presence overpowering, intimidating and creepy. She writes:

> We were on a small stage and no matter where I walked, he followed me closely, staring at me, making faces. It was incredibly uncomfortable. He was literally breathing down my neck. My skin crawled.
>
> It was one of those moments where you wish *you could hit pause and ask everybody watching: 'Well, what would you do?'*
>
> (Clinton 2017: 136; italics added)

The significance of hitting the pause button and asking everybody *Well, what would you do?* is a request for a ring of resonance. Clinton wants to know how the audience would react if she were to say: '*Back up, you creep. Get away from me. I know you love to intimidate women but you can't intimidate me, so back up.*' At that time, she was unsure how her audience would interpret such a statement. It might be interpreted as symptomatic of a (supposed) female inability to control her emotions, thus infelicitous. In the absence of the capacity to measure for resonance Clinton took the conservative option of staying calm and saying nothing.

This exchange took place a year *before* the #*MeToo* movement act of resonance. If the same exchange had happened a year later, Clinton would have known that the *back up, you creep* reaction would be felicitous. So, her reaction would have been different. With regard to constraint, Clinton would have been freer to say *back up, you creep* if the same debate had taken place a year later.

Consciousness-raising has a certain intrinsic bias against it. Performing social life, or structuring and confirm-structuring, without radical doubt is more comfortable and makes the performance more convincing. The natural attitude makes the performance of social life unproblematic. Once actors know the practical consciousness script of *femininity*, they just *go on*. As observed by Clinton, it means not being thrown off by harassment, taking it and going on as if nothing has happened. That script gives women immediate agency, even if that agency may be less than male agency, thus reproducing 2-D gender bias.

In examining the complicity of the less powerful in their own domination it is important to understand that power is rarely all-or-nothing. Clinton's stoicism, or fortitude, in the face of Trump probably played well with some watchers of the debate. Her choice was not categorically mistaken in terms of episodic power, although it may have been the wrong decision in terms of her self-esteem and relative to a longer-term feminist agenda to increase the comparative structural dispositional power of women.

Note

1 While Barnes' analysis has much to recommend it, it is too focused upon power-to and power-with. So, domination disappears from view (Haugaard 1997: 23–40). The same comment can be made with regard to Searle's essay on power (Searle 2007). However, these views constitute a significant counter-balance to the propensity of most thinkers, for instance, Foucault (1980) and Flyvbjerg (1998), to over-emphasize the normatively undesirable aspects of power-knowledge. As we shall see, the dominating aspects of power-knowledge are the flipside of Janus-faced duality, consisting of enablement/domination.

5

The third dimension continued: Conventions, reification, the sacred and essentialism

In the previous chapter we saw that 3-D entails practical knowledge of structuration practices. This knowledge can be raised to discursive knowledge and subjected to critique. It was argued that consciousness-raising is a necessary, though not sufficient, condition for social change that challenges domination.

The overall question that interests power theorists is the following: why do the less powerful more often than not confirm-structure structural bias, thus acquiesce in dominating power-over? We have already seen a number of answers to that question: coercion, goals override structures, episodic power-to overrides hypothetical dispositional empowerment, dominant ideology, fear of being infelicitous, fear of being unreasonable, the natural attitude, having practical consciousness knowledge but not discursive consciousness, awareness of social structures (absence of consciousness-raising), uncertainty as to whether there exists a sphere of resonance that would accept the change.

In addition to these forces reinforcing the status quo, in this chapter we look at other 3-D epistemic ways in which stability is maintained, in particular through reification. Reification entails obscuring the conventional nature of social structures in order to prevent social actors from considering them as socially constructed, therefore potentially possible to structure differently. However, let us first of all examine a pervasive misperception concerning the link between conventionality and arbitrariness, which is core to the justification of reification.

Does conventional equate with arbitrary?

Most social and political power, other than coercion, presupposes the formula *X counts as Y in circumstances C*. The underlying problem of social order is, of course, that the Y designation is entirely conventional. Once social actors think of social structures as conventional, they tend to assume that this entails that they are also *arbitrary*. The assumption that conventional equates with arbitrary is even pervasive in sociological theory, including Bourdieu (see, for instance, Bourdieu 1990: 67). The justification for reification is often premised upon the idea that conventional is equivalent to arbitrary. Reification works as a block upon social disintegration. It is assumed that once the conventionality becomes apparent, social structures lose their justificatory force. Contrary to this, in the theoretical position developed here, acknowledging the socially constructed nature of social structures does not undermine their relative justificatory worth. They can be justified relative to their use as sources of empowerment. This is significant both sociologically and normatively.

In 1917 when Marcel Duchamp sent a *urinal* to be exhibited as a work of *fine art*, Duchamp was critiquing the art world by pointing out that the conventions of fine art were conventional, therefore arbitrary. It is conventional that the Mona Lisa is a work of fine art but that a urinal is not. In everyday discourse a urinal is usually considered the opposite of art: as a purely functional object that is aesthetically displeasing both in appearance and association. A couple of years after the urinal intervention Duchamp attached a moustache on a cheap copy of the Mona Lisa in order to make the point again. He vandalized, and thus made profane, what was by *convention* considered one of the greatest works of fine art.

The ideas of exhibiting a urinal as fine art and defacing the Mona Lisa were considered brilliant interventions and were foundational to the Dadaist art movement. While there is some dispute over the meaning of *Dada*, in my interpretation the obvious inference is that the sound *dada* is one of the commonest sounds that an infant makes when they are pre-linguistic, therefore pre-conventional. Dadaism signals the abandonment of all convention as arbitrary social construction. Exhibiting the urinal as art and defacing a copy of the Mona Lisa were ways of inverting convention, thus highlighting its arbitrariness. This intervention has been hugely influential upon postmodernism and twentieth-century conceptual or radical art movements.

The idea that the conventional social construction of everyday life renders it arbitrary and therefore meaningless is core to existentialism, which was emerging during this same period. In Sartre's *Nausea* (2000 [1938]) the main character, Roquentin, is in a deep existentialist crisis. Part of that crisis entails a hyper-awareness of the contingency of all acts of signification. Roquentin places his posterior on a *seat* and realizes that the *seat* 'could just as well be a *dead donkey* ... Things have broken free from their names. They are there, grotesque, stubborn, gigantic, and it seems ridiculous to call them *seats* ...' (Sartre 2000 [1938]: 180; italics added).

This realization of the conventionality of *seat* gives rise to a feeling of the contingency of all things, which leads to a deep sense of meaninglessness, culminating in nausea.

It is one of the ironies of history that Duchamp devoted the later years of his life to playing chess, which is the paradigmatic embodiment of the *falsity* of the idea that *conventional equates to arbitrary*. I think that Duchamp intuited that the conventions of chess were far from arbitrary. Consequently, he interpreted chess as the highest form of art.

It is entirely *conventional* that a *knight* or any of the other pieces move as they do. The pieces embody a complex set of Y-status conventions. However, these conventions constitute the conditions of possibility for one of the most exciting games ever invented. These conventions are entirely socially constructed, yet they are not arbitrary.

To explain this there are two issues. First, if chess players were to arbitrarily change the conventions of the game as they went along, they would be unable to play. To a skilled chess player, the exact Y-status qualities of each piece are key to strategic play that enables him to prevail over an opponent. Without being bound by the constraints of the Y-status of each piece, the players would be unable to play.

Second, the combination of pieces constitutes a system of conventions that works better or worse. Even though the rules of the game are conventional, it is possible to evaluate them normatively, using pragmatic criteria. This would not be the case if they were arbitrary. Take the convention of *checkmate*. Let us imagine that this convention were replaced with a different convention, say, that the game is played until there is only one piece left, which would signal the winner. Imagine, further, that this new convention was combined with abolition of the existing convention that a pawn can become a queen when it reaches the other end of the board. The result would be that the game would become significantly longer and most games would never end as a few, and especially two, pieces could chase each other around the board indefinitely. This change in convention would be an outcome that would make this reformed game, call it chess2, inferior to original chess (with the checkmate ending). If two conventions are arbitrary, they are equal. In essence Duchamp was claiming that the urinal was equal to widely recognized works of fine art, within the language game of art, because of the arbitrariness of meaning. In contrast, if one convention can be shown to be better than another, the second convention is no longer an arbitrary social construction.

The normative designation *better* is not relative to some transcendental aim but, rather, to a pragmatist consequential mode of justification relative to use-function within a specific field or language game.

Let us consider a couple more examples. Numbers are conventions but they are not arbitrary. First, we can only use these conventions to carry out complex calculations if we are constrained by them. If we were to change those conventions at will, we could not do mathematics. In short, the empowerment of these conventions is premised upon constraint.

Second, some numerical conventions are better than others. The Arabic numeral system constitutes a better set of conventions than the Roman number conventions because large numbers represented in Roman-style are more complex than the equivalent Arabic numbers. Multiplication of big numbers using the Roman numeral convention is virtually impossible. If one of the *uses* of the field, or language game, of numbers is multiplication, then it follows that Arabic numeral conventions are better than the Roman ones. Consequently, a preference for Arabic number conventions over Roman numeral conventions is not an arbitrary choice.

The Ogham alphabet is an early Irish phonetic alphabet that used the convention of representing sounds through lines in complex patters. In terms of simple one-word inscriptions on rock, Ogham is useful. However, in terms of reading full sentences on paper, the Roman alphabet is significantly less complex. If the use of an alphabet is to express words discursively in books, then it follows that the Roman alphabet constitutes a better set of conventions than Ogham. It is not arbitrary that this book is written using the Roman alphabet, not Ogham.

In response to Sartre's characterization of the existential crisis, it is correct that a *seat* could be called a *dead donkey*. However, once the convention has been established that the signifier *seat* refers to a piece of furniture, if we were to suddenly call that referent a *dead donkey* this change of convention would be entirely disempowering to communication. In this regard, it is worthy of note that at the height of the cultural revolution (1966) the Chinese reversed the traffic convention that red means stop and green means go. This switch didn't last because the result was chaos (*The Economist* 2013).

Words are, to echo Wittgenstein (1967), *conceptual tools*. They are simply more or less useful practical things that enable us to get a job done. If carpenters were to use screwdrivers as chisels, and chisels as screwdrivers, they would produce poorer-quality work. The joints made with a blunt screwdriver would be loose and the sharp edge of the chisel makes for an inadequate screwdriver. If such a carpenter were asked why they used the screwdriver as a chisel and the chisel as a screwdriver and they were to respond that *it is purely conventional, therefore arbitrary, that chisels are chisels and screwdrivers are screwdrivers*, the inferior quality of their work would be used as proof of the fact that it is actually a better convention to use *chisels to shape wood* and *screwdrivers to fasten screws.* In other words, there is nothing arbitrary about that convention.

As we shall see in greater detail later, in the discussion of cultural capital, the ability to devise efficient and clever conventions is part of the art of inventing new cultural capital. In the case of the carpenter who decides to reverse the conventions of chisels and screwdrivers, she depletes her resources. Her power-to capacity to make wooden constructions (chairs) with firm joints is undermined. The typical use of chairs entails that a chair made with loose joints, which collapses when you sit on it, is not as useful as a sturdy chair, which can support body weight. This normative judgement is not linked to a foundational claim about the essence of chairness, as in reification.

To return to Duchamp, this leads us to two points: the urinal as art constitutes a category error. It is like Serena Williams turning up with her tennis racket to a chess championship. Or, it is like entering a saucepan in a competition for a sailing yacht designs.

The second aspect concerns the use function. Does a urinal serve the use function of art better than the Mona Lisa? I would say no, it does not. Obviously, fine art is not my specialism, so I do not think it is my place to defend what I consider the use function of fine art. However, so that the reader can understand how such an argument might work, I will give *fine art* a use function, which I find convincing. The use function of fine art is consciousness-raising (from practical to representational consciousness) with respect to aesthetic perceptions. Just as the female readers of *The Second Sex* recognize their practical consciousness knowledge of gender construction in the text, the viewer of a painting similarly has a moment of epiphany where she recognizes some aesthetic quality represented on canvas. To take an example, relative to my practical consciousness of the sea, built up over years of sailing, a Turner seascape captures the nuance of the aesthetic quality of clouds and the sea. In contrast, a urinal captures my urine but not my practical consciousness of aesthetics. Hence, I can say that as fine art, the urinal misses the point entirely. Furthermore, Turner's seascapes capture the essence of the aesthetic quality of the clouds and sea better than, say, those painted by gifted amateurs.

To be clear: I am not attempting to rigidly fix Art (with a capital A) as a reified thing-in-itself. There are other art forms or fields of art, which is why I use the qualifier *fine* art, to indicate a particular artistic field with its own language game and use function. For instance, artists can create their own sub-field of *political* art, which has the function of consciousness-raising with respect to domination. Within that field, Turner's seascapes have low use function, whereas Picasso's *Guernica* would rate as a masterpiece.

A qualified version of Duchamp's critique of art might be that the conventions of art have become reified and, as a consequence, a restraint upon creativity. This point brings us back to our main argument.

Reification

While it is erroneous to equate conventional with arbitrary, this is a not simply a Dadaist or existentialist error but reflects an assumption that is taken for granted in everyday social life. It is generally assumed that once actors perceive that social structures are *mere conventions* then anarchy reigns. Relative to this assumption, reification is the process whereby the conventional nature of social structures is obscured and social stability created.

As we have seen, according to the natural attitude it appears that the world-out-there consists of things-in-themselves. This constitutes the foundation of reification as essentialism, whereby the world-out-there comes with meaning which is intrinsic to it. The natural attitude renders reification plausible. Social actors simply assume that things out there have meaning that transcends their act of interpretation. With the natural attitude the social construction, thus conventionality, of social structures is lost as an interpretative event. However, with consciousness-raising that conventionality has the potential to become apparent.

Reification is a process of misrecognition whereby social structures are stripped of their conventionality, thus social construction becomes obscured. Once social structures appear as non-conventional, they appear beyond critique. When 2-D structural bias occurs, the less powerful have a significant interest in social change, while the more powerful have an interest in the status quo. So, in general, reification is a form of misrecognition that is in the interests of the more powerful. However, counter-intuitively, it is often the case that the less powerful have deep symbolic attachment to these reifications, often greater than the more powerful. For instance, the reifications of religious belief are highly attractive to the poor, as they give meaning to a life of poverty.

Writing about his role as an intellectual, Foucault wrote that he considered his task 'to describe that-which-is by making it appear as something that might not be, or that might not be as it is' (Foucault 1988: 36). He then went on to argue that his genealogical method was an attempt 'to show how that which-is has not always been' (Foucault 1988: 37). The objective of this form of critique is to show 'that since these things have been made, they can be unmade, as long as we know how it was made' (Foucault 1988: 37). Foucault demonstrates how the social structures of society are social constructions, which have been made in some point in time, often as the result of petty confrontations and contingent events. By demonstrating this Foucault showed the fragility of social structures, rendering them open to contestation.

Reification is the opposite of the processes advocated by Foucault. Reification is a misrecognition whereby that-which-is *must* be because *it was never made*. In that sense reification is a way of *sealing off* social structures from critical justification (see Forst 2017: 42) by claiming they cannot be unmade.

There are many processes whereby reification is accomplished, and we do not have space to cover them all. However, the commonest are as follows: *the sacred, charismatic authority, teleology, Truth* (with a capital T), *nature-based-essentialism* and *bureaucratic-based-essentialism*. Again, the caveat remains that these are ideal types that are rarely found in the pure form.

Reification through the sacred

One of the central hypotheses of Durkheim's *Elementary Forms of Religious Life* (2008 [1915]) is that, from a sociological perspective, religion is a way for society to worship its own social norms by creating a sacred sphere. Thereby, society takes the moral essence of society beyond the everyday.

Typically, the sacred is profoundly moralizing and is claimed to be beyond *mere convention*. In contrast, the profane is that which social actors are willing to acknowledge was made and therefore can be unmade. Aspects of food production, construction and cooking are cases in point. Most traditional societies understand that farmers, hunters and builders have to adapt to circumstance. A society without any profane sphere would be too rigid to survive.

Conversely, in order for social norms to have rigidity with respect to authority and morality, the *sacred* is created. The sacred is surrounded by ritual to ensure that everyone knows that this is something extraordinary. It is tied to some force that is transcendental, thus linking it to a sphere that appears external to society. The transcendental makes plausible the claim that the sacred is *not* social, therefore *not* made, thus *cannot* be unmade.

In monotheism the transcendental force is a singular being: God, who is socially constructed in man's image. However, to give this external force a transcendental quality, this act of creation is presented as if it were the other way around, as if God created man. This imagined entity embodies the infinite, which cannot be changed. The use of the male pronoun, *He*, is deliberate, as the three Abrahamic monotheistic religions are patriarchal. Thus, for all three faiths, patriarchy is sacred and cannot be unmade.

In monotheism, the quality of infinity creates the illusion of immutability. Going back to Plato (2007), the infinite belongs to the sphere of the unchanging, while change is seen as a sign of imperfection, finite, ultimate death and nothingness. Plato did not posit the infinite in a deity but in ideas that transcended visible reality.

In contrast to monotheism, polytheism posits several gods who are finite and, typically, often embody frailties and imperfections. As a consequence, polytheism tends to be less rigid, which makes it less effective for the purposes of reification. In Japan, Shinto is entirely tolerant of Buddhism and Christianity. Animism posits the transcendental source of the sacred in animals or the landscape. In so doing, it can have the effect of reifying important societal balances with nature, necessary for the survival of a community. As we shall see, reification is not intrinsically normatively negative.

The discursive sacred

Possibly the paradigmatic monotheistic account of creating sacred social norms is the account of the Ten Commandments. The Jews had been enslaved in Egypt and miraculously escaped, which included the parting of the waters so they could walk across the seabed. After these events, they made camp at the base of Mount Sinai, where thunder, lightning and trumpeting sounds raged overhead. The stage was set for the Lord to come down upon Mount Sinai. The people were terrified and in awe but Moses spoke to them and told them not to fear. Moses ascended the mountain and disappeared into the swirling cloud and mist. After 40 days he returned, but during his absence they had lost faith, and were worshipping a golden calf. Moses became enraged and smashed the tablets of stone the Lord had given him. God then gave Moses a second pair of stone tablets identical to the first.

The point of the miraculous escape followed by thunder and lightning was to inspire in people a sense of the extraordinary. Let us not forget these people were migrants, previously enslaved (or of low status), who, quite likely, had a weak sense of collective identity. This was a moment when their society was recreated anew. This event could not be a mundane or profane event – hence thunder, lightning and trumpets. To create a collective entity, a society, which was more than a collection of random individuals who had escaped slavery, this moment of foundation had to be something extraordinary, which could never be unmade.

The lexical order of the Ten Commandments is revealing. Unfortunately, the numerical order is not entirely consistent in the various manifestations of Judeo-Christian monotheism but overall priority is similar. I will follow the Jewish order here, as I am speaking about their foundational moment. The first tells the Jewish people who their God is. The second that there is only one God and that they should not worship graven images. The third that they should not take the name of God in vain. The fourth that they should keep the Sabbath. The fifth commands that they honour their father and mother. The sixth that they should not kill. The seventh that they should not commit adultery. The eighth that they should not steal. The ninth that they should not bear false witness against their neighbour. The tenth that they should not covet their neighbour's house, wife, servants, animals or anything else.

The first four commandments concern the unitary transcendental nature of the sacred foundation of society. It is only with the fifth commandment that we come to authority, which concerns the authority of the household. The household was significant because traditional societies are patrimonial (Weber 1978: 226–37), which means that politics is considered an extension of the household, headed by the patriarch. In the sixth (fifth, in Christianity) commandment we have a specific moral precept concerning the norms of interaction, which is a prohibition upon murder. The rest then follows a functional logic directed at creating social order. The prohibition upon adultery reinforces the family structure. The prohibition upon stealing makes possible the creation of economic resources. The prohibition upon bearing false witness makes law possible.

Taken in lexical order, first comes the sacred, then authority and finally all the various moral precepts that are required to structure that society. It is fundamental that the community is directly linked to God. In order to be a member of the community of Jews you must believe in God. It is God who made the community and gave it its structuring principles. These structuring principles are indivisible from the presence of the infinite, thus immutable. These structures were *not made* by Moses, but handed down by an infinite being, and therefore *cannot be unmade*. They are not social conventions and they are certainly not arbitrary. Why should we not kill, or commit adultery, or steal or bear false witness or covet our neighbour's possessions? Because these are the laws of God, and there is only one God (forget finding a different law from some other God), and that God is the God our community. If you are who you are, as a member of this community, following these laws is part of who you are. Not to follow them, and to be who you are, is unreasonable. In essence, the Y-status function of membership of this community, and all the obligations and conditions of possibility that follow from that, are rendered sacred, thus never to be unmade. Social integration and systemic stability are tied in an indissoluble knot.

Notice that these structures are not presented as desirable because of the beneficial consequences they bring. In other words, these conventions could be defended as non-arbitrary based upon their beneficial consequences, which is the strategy we will follow in Chapter 9. It would have been relatively simple for Moses to explain, based upon consequential reason, that a society requires authority, based upon the family, and that a complex political entity requires prohibition upon murder, theft and so on in order to create an economy and polity. However, this would have required argumentation and justification. In order to pre-empt justification, these laws are not open for discussion because anyone who presumes to challenge them is challenging the word of God, an infinite being, in whose presence a mere temporal human should be overawed and obedient. These structures are *sealed off* from discussion and debate characterized as a profanation of the sacred. Anyone who presumes to evaluate these laws is unreasonable. Thus reification is complete.

In a society where theocratic justification is the norm, there may well be tolerance of different religions but this is usually coupled with the rejection of any attempts to challenge the process of foundational reification itself. To make this point I include an abbreviated transcript from a debate on Egyptian television between an atheist, a clerical personage and the chair of the programme. I have removed the names and identification to make this anonymous. Egypt has a long history of cohabitation of all three monotheistic faiths but atheism seems a particular challenge. The atheist began by explaining that he did not believe in God and that he did not require religious belief in order to be a moral person. He was challenged to account for his existence and the creation of the universe and, in response, began to explain the Big Bang theory. However, the TV presenter interrupted the atheist and the exchange concluded as follows.

TV Presenter: You are confused and unreliable. You deny the existence of God and reject our religion and principles ...

Atheist: Is that so bad?

TV Presenter: Of course, you come here to talk about a certain idea, but have nothing to offer. You offer atheism! You offer heresy! I apologize to the viewers ... you cannot stay with us on the show ...

Clerical personage: Look, dear M., you need psychiatric treatment. Many young people suffer from mental illness, due to material or mental circumstances ...

TV Presenter: It's like ... [he] says. Have you seen a psychiatrist? ... I advise you to leave the studio and go straight to a psychiatric hospital. You shouldn't be here. Unfortunately, I cannot let you be here any more ...

(M.E.M.R.I. TV videos 2018)

The point of this excerpt is to highlight the connection between the denial of reification, infelicity and madness. For a believer for whom religion is rooted in the literal word of God, there cannot be debate concerning the existence of the source of the reification. Justification beyond the sacred elicits the response of unreasonable. The sacred is not subject to justification: it just *is*. Therefore any debate with the sacred constitutes a form of unreasonableness or, in this case, madness.

Notice the combination of commanding the atheist to leave the studio combined with the patronizing concern for his mental health. In terms of power, the atheist has no authority to speak. He is the *abject unreasonable* who invites destructuration on all fronts, except admission of his own madness.

This is another instance of the absence of authority to speak discussed in Chapter 2. Reification is a way of *sealing off* the other, of creating a maximally unequal speech situation. In a theocracy, or semi-theocracy in this case, contesting the premises of reification is the route to powerlessness, to exclusion and unreasonable infelicity. Hence, the social order remains stable, beyond foundational contestation.

To qualify the above, this is not a blanket assertion concerning all monotheism or monotheists. Several versions of the monotheist religions have become less foundational concerning the nature and source of religious belief, and do not interpret scripture literally. Rather, they interpret these texts hermeneutically, often as metaphor or allegory. In that case the faithful are not as defensive of the reifying foundation. As a consequence, they would not necessarily view atheism as unreasonable, or as a form of mental illness, as in the case above. Recently, the current pope, Francis, has engaged in dialogue with Eugenio Scalfari, who is a known atheist (Giuffrida 2018), which suggests a less reified viewpoint.

Normative evaluation of sacred reification

I prefer to keep the normative analysis separate but in order to clarify any potential misunderstanding let us deal with one specific normative issue at this point. I asserted that the presentation of the Ten Commandments was based upon reification. As reification is normally portrayed as normatively undesirable it would not be unreasonable for the reader to infer that I am suggesting that the Ten Commandments are, therefore, normatively undesirable.

It is important to understand that in the power-based normative framework used here, normative evaluation is not binary. Something is not either normatively desirable or normatively undesirable. Rather, normative judgements are consequential and on a scale. Reification is a way of fore-closing debate. Once a norm or structure is reified, debate ends. In the long run, the greater the openness to justification, the greater the likelihood that all social actors will find norms that reflect their collective interests in a positive-sum relationship (this will be examined further in Chapter 9). As reification limits justification, it is clearly an impediment to open-ended justification, thus not normatively desirable. However, against that, the use of the transcendental to reify norms can have positive consequences. If the consequence of creating an all-powerful God to reify the commandment *thou shalt not kill* is that the murder rate becomes lower, this is a normatively desirable outcome.

3-D through reification creates social stability. The alternative to reified social stability is often crude 1-D coercive power. While these reifications may entail misperception, it should be acknowledged that, in consequential terms, living with such reifications is better than living in a society that is entirely based upon 1-D coercion. It is true that reification through monotheism leads to a certain pacification of society, which may be preferable to constant civil war of each against all. This is similar to the argument put forward by Socrates in favour of a 'magnificent myth', which would serve as a 'fairy story' to stabilize social order in the Republic (Plato 2007: 3.3 414). To echo Hobbes (1914), reification is preferable to a state of war of each against all.

Furthermore, as I have already suggested, several of the commandments are justifiable pragmatically in terms of use function. The prohibitions upon murder, theft and lying constitute a condition of possibility for law, and following that polity and economy. So, these conventional commands do not require reification, as they can be justified in consequentialist terms.

Charismatic authority

Weber considered charismatic authority as linked to the person and to the sacred. For Weber, the prophet, exemplified by Moses, was the archetypal charismatic leader. The charismatic leader is someone who is extraordinary, who has superhuman and often supernatural qualities. Weber writes as follows.

> The term charisma will be applied to a certain quality of an individual personality by virtue of which he is considered extraordinary and treated as endowed with supernatural, superhuman, or at least specifically exceptional powers or qualities. These are such as are not accessible to the ordinary person, but are regarded as of divine origin or as exemplary, and on the basis of them the individual concerned is treated as a 'leader'. In primitive

circumstances this peculiar kind of quality is thought of as resting on magical powers, whether of prophets, persons with a reputation for therapeutic or legal wisdom, leaders in hunt, or heroes in war.

(Weber 1978: 241)

Weber argues that while the person endowed with charismatic authority thinks of themselves and God as the origin of their authority, in fact, it 'is *recognition* on the part of those subject to authority which is decisive for the validity of charisma' (Weber 1978: 242; italics added). The idea that this authority rests upon recognition is theoretically consistent with the position defended here, that authority ultimately presupposes confirm-structuration by a ring of reference that confirm-structures Y-status function. When recognition is withdrawn, the charismatic leader and his followers attribute this to being deserted by God, or having somehow lost his magical or heroic powers (Weber 1978: 242).

Weber saw charismatic authority as opposed to instrumentally rational and traditional authority because charisma entails reference to extraordinary powers (Weber 1978: 244). Charisma is irrational relative to the rule-governed rationality of bureaucratic administration. Because it is extraordinary, it is also at variance with the routine of traditional action. Weber views charismatic authority as an essentially unstable form of political order, which does not last over time. For those in authority achieving stability entails a slow progression from charisma to tradition and/or bureaucratic instrumental authority. While modern society is characterized by a tendency towards legal instrumental bureaucratic authority, charismatic leaders interrupt this process and initiate social change. However, over time, there is a move back to instrumental bureaucratic authority.

Weber overestimated the secular rationality of modernity. The history of the twentieth century and what we have seen of the twenty-first century demonstrates that charisma is absolutely part of the everyday of advanced modern, globalizing, high-modern or postmodern societies. The practical consciousness of social actors does not consist of a singular continuous logically consistent interpretative horizon. Rather, the typical practical consciousness constitutes a fragmented set of interpretative horizons, which constitute local language games that are used in different contexts. It is a mistake to assume that an individual who works with scientific reason all day will continue to think the same way about her politics. In 'Why Are There So Many Engineers among Islamic Radicals?' Gambetta and Hertog (2009) demonstrate a correlation between the academic socialization of engineers and predisposition towards political radicalism of a highly sacred-cum-charismatic type. This is not a direct relationship, but an elective affinity, akin to the elective affinity between Calvinism (which is other-worldly) and early capitalism (which is worldly) (Weber 1976).

Even if we do accept the elective affinity argument, the article confirms the view defended here that social actors routinely act from a multiplicity of interpretative horizons that are mutually incommensurable. Engineers are perfectly capable of being scientific one moment and religious another. With modernity, scientific interpretative horizons advance but we should not infer from this that magical sacred interpretative horizons decline correspondingly.

Everyday practical consciousness sacred social practice

The story of Moses and the Ten Commandments is a dramatic rendering of the establishment of the sacred. The commandments are a discursive consciousness set of rules, as are the sacred texts of monotheism. It was part of Durkheim's (2008) theory that the distinction between the sacred and profane structures everyday life. In theocracies these discursive texts loom large. However, the sacred applies not only discursively but also to practical consciousness. Everyday interaction is frequently structured relative to practical consciousness knowledge of the sacred-versus-profane opposition.

Alexander convincingly argues that the principles of sacred and profane structure contemporary societies in lots of subtle ways, which go beyond the manifestly discursively sacred. As in the theory propounded here, Alexander argues that authority is performative (Alexander 2011). He argues that the most felicitous performances are the ones that cast those in authority as somehow linked to the sacred, while their opponents are tied to the profane (Alexander 2009: 66–7). The successful use of the tension between sacred and profane lies at the core of charismatic authority in everyday life. Contrary to Weber, charismatic authority should not be thought of as a disruptive exception. Rather, charismatic authority is a norm, which social actors continually use to gain high Y-status.

Alexander analyzes the US presidential campaign of Obama versus McCain (see Alexander 2009, 2010 and 2011; Alexander and Jaworski 2014) and demonstrates how Obama's success hinges around his capacity to occupy the realm of the sacred. In his first post-primary acceptance speech on 4 June 2008 Obama declares that he stands for a bright, golden future, whereas McCain represents the failed past of the Bush presidency. As things stand 'America has fallen on tough times, the Dream lies in tatters. The nation has fallen off the hill' (Alexander 2009: 75). In essence, America has become profaned but Obama, who comes from a group that was erroneously despised, will redeem the future. Obama identifies himself with a future that overcomes this profanation. After securing the nomination he says: 'Generations from now, we will be able to look back and tell our children that this was the moment when we began to provide care for the sick and good jobs for the jobless; this was the moment when the rise of the Oceans began to slow and our planet began to heal' (Alexander 2009: 75). The echoes of Genesis and Exodus are implicit in this declaration. 'The next day, the Times ran a large photo depicting Obama as a Jesus-like figure offering salvation. He is elevated above a teeming crowd, with hundreds of hands stretching out to touch him. He has become a charismatic vessel, filled with the sacred promise of repair' (Alexander 2009: 75).

The capacity to balance the sacred and the profane is not an easy task. At one point during the campaign, Politico.com revealed that campaign staff had removed two headscarf-wearing Muslim women from the background of an Obama photo op (Alexander 2009: 77). At the time an online campaign was suggesting that Obama was a covert Muslim, a group who were framed as the enemies of American freedom, and thus part of the profane. So, the removal was a way avoiding this profanation. However, *the act of removal* was in itself a profanation relative to the interpretative horizons of the liberal Left who were Obama's core base. In order to undo the latter contamination, staffers opened up a space between the candidate, Obama, and campaign staff. It was the latter who had made this mistake – while they were motivated by the desire to protect the candidate from the racist (profane) lies that were made about him (Alexander 2009: 77).

A similar difficult balancing act was displayed with regard to Obama's decision to appear on television with his children and let them be interviewed. A legacy of patrimonialism is a prevalent practical consciousness perception that the highest political office is patriarchal. A play was made to transfer Obama's sacred Y-status authority as actual *father* to the president as the patriarch. However, when journalists suggested that Obama was putting his children in harm's way and/or exploiting them for political gain, he ran the danger of profaning the sacred. Again, in response, a distinction was maintained between the actions of Obama and the campaign staff responsible for the television appearance (Alexander 2009: 77). Both cases show a complex balancing act whereby the sacred aspects of social action were attributed to Obama, while the inadvertent profanations were attributed to campaign staff.

Foucault (1979) characterizes the modern army as a disciplined, machine-like entity. While not denying that this constitutes a real part of the modern military model, Smith has convincingly argued that the modernization of contemporary armies is accompanied with strong elements of the sacred. In this regard, consider military uniforms, with their overpolished boots and buttons. These are the glitter of the sacred. Similarly, medals are rewarded as sacred tokens to those who accomplish extraordinary exploits (Smith 2008: 279).

Both Alexander and Smith are influenced by the work of anthropologist Robert N. Bellah (1967), who argued that American political life is characterized by significant elements of civil religion. Presidential speeches are littered with appeals to God and the inauguration process itself has elements of a coronation. The latter ceremony is a way of institutionalizing charisma, by imbuing the political office with the sacred.

Elections as a sacred process

The process of rendering political institutions sacred applies to the entire democratic process. Voting has a magical sacred quality. At the time of writing both the election of Donald Trump and the Brexit referendum have, respectively, been called into question by the Mueller investigation and the Commons investigation into the actions of Cambridge Analytica. When the Cambridge Analytica whistleblower, Christopher Wylie, was asked by the Commons select committee whether or not the Vote Leave infringements of the democratic process swayed the result of the EU referendum, he gave an interesting two-part answer. The first was that in Olympic contests when a gold-medalist is found doping there is no discussion of whether or not the doping allowed him to win, or when a student cheats in an exam whether the cheating enabled her attain the grade she did. In both cases the result is declared null and void, irrespective of the effect or advantage conferred by the infringement. The second part of his answer was to confirm that, indeed, cheating had made the crucial difference (Wylie 2018).

Currently, the attempt to hold a second Brexit referendum is an uphill struggle, despite the infringements and the additional fact that the majority of voters voted on the basis of false information. However, annulling the referendum altogether would appear to be outside the conditions of possibility. Similarly, while it is thinkable that Trump could be impeached, annulling the election is unthinkable, whatever the Mueller enquiry finds. So, the question remains: why are elections different from doping in the Olympics or cheating in examinations? The answer is that the election process itself has acquired a sacred aura surrounding it, which makes questioning the result politically infelicitous. Election and referenda have become a magical moment when *the will of the people* is revealed. It forms a type of collective union, not dissimilar to the collective union of a religious ceremony.

To be clear, I am not claiming that elections should not be considered important. As we will see in Chapter 9, there are sound normative consequential reasons for respecting the outcome of elections. However, if we were totally consequentially logical or pragmatist about this, we should respect results only to the extent that they fulfill their purpose as a measure of support for candidates or causes. An election should be viewed as analogous to a thermometer as a measure of temperature. If they fail to measure correctly, there should be no problem disregarding the result, in the same way as we would disregard the readings of a faulty thermometer. However, such a view is infelicitous relative to popular public opinion, which suggests that there is a surplus of meaning with sacred qualities.

Recently in Egypt, President Sissi was re-elected with 97% support. Prior to the election, plausible political rivals were arrested or put under considerable pressure to withdraw their candidacy. There was only a 40% turnout and that figure is comparatively high relative to the tradition of Egyptian strong-leader politics. During Mubarak's tenure the official turnout figure would be 35% to 40%, but the real figure was reputed to be in the region of 20% or less (Bar'el 2018).

The result is fairly obviously democratic in name only. It is not a result that anyone is expected to believe as accurately representative of support. So it constitutes a kind of simulacrum democracy. The question remains: what function does this kind of 'election' serve? The answer has to be that going through the process confers a sacred quality, which invests authority with institutionalized legitimacy. Elections have a consequential normative value as a measure of support. However, when you subtract that (as you can if the election is rigged) there is still a surplus left, which constitutes this sacred element.

Essentialism and nature as sources of reification

Essentialist thought goes back to an ancient teleological way of thinking. In explaining why an acorn became an oak, Aristotle claimed that it had the essence of *oakness* within it. This entailed that the final end, or objective, of an acorn is to become an oak, which explains its growth. To Aristotle the nature of a thing is defined by its essence, which gives it potentiality (Aristotle 1941 (Physics): 2.1–9 192b–200b). Teleology entails explaining the cause of an event from its final outcome.

This mode of explaining cause and effect is perfectly logical for interpreting the actions of thinking subjects: either persons or intelligent animals. For instance, if you see a person chopping wood, then taking the wood to light a fire, the teleological explanation for the wood-chopping behaviour is the person's desire for a fire. In the pre-modern world our interpretative horizons were relatively continuous, therefore there were not different explanations for different kinds of phenomena (Gellner 1989: 77–8). Thus, for instance, as is stated in the book of Genesis, the essence of the sun and moon is explained in terms of their usefulness to us: to give us light. Teleologically speaking, the sun and moon are analogous to street lamps.

In contrast, with regard to natural phenomena, modern scientists distinguish use from origin. The light of the sun is the consequence of a nuclear reaction, from hydrogen to helium, while the usefulness of this light is considered irrelevant to understanding why the sun is the way it is. The natural scientist has one gestalt interpretative horizon for making sense of physical phenomena and another for making sense of the actions of persons around them. This is symptomatic of a splitting of interpretative horizons, which is part of the cognitive revolution of modernity. In contrast, a religious worldview that includes *intelligent design* is precisely such a pre-modern teleological undifferentiated singular interpretative horizon. In this perspective the design of a car (which is an intelligent design) and the design of the universe are explained in exactly the same way.

In the pre-modern world, teleology was not simply a reflection of monotheism. Rather, the monotheistic faiths reflected a practical consciousness knowledge in which the world was singular. Because human behaviour can be explained in term of *telos*, it appeared reasonable to extend this way of thinking to the natural-order-of-things. Pre-modern thought tended to be continuous, with a singular interpretive horizon, for the whole of reality. Consequently, a holy personage or a sage could pronounce upon the order of the universe (what we would refer to as astronomy or physics) and dictate morality (Gellner 1989). In contemporary society an expert is expected to pronounce upon their respective field of expertise – although there are exceptions to this.

The teleological interpretation of the natural world has significant implications when extended normatively to the social world. Socially, the extension of this interpretative horizon makes it appear self-evident that different people have essences within them that define their final ends. In the context of this interpretative horizon, Aristotle asked himself whether slavery was justified (Aristotle 1941 (Politics): 1.2 1253b). Surprisingly, relative to our interpretative horizon, he defends the institution. He argued that different intelligences and character dispositions mean that some people are better able to define their own ends than others. Consequently, there were some whose essence was such that they should serve the *telos* of others.

Similarly, in the Republic, Plato argued that children should be socialized into the myth of metals (Plato 2007: 3.3 414). Essentially they should be taught that some are naturally born with an essence of gold, others of silver, bronze and iron. These essences should define the natural hierarchy of the republic. If someone has an essence of gold it is just, fair and reasonable that they should govern those of a lesser metal. Relative to that interpretative horizon, the democratic egalitarian ideal is an injustice because it treats *unequal* people as if they were equal. It would be like treating iron as if it were gold, which is unreasonable. Socrates builds a complex hierarchical society upon the (apparent) truism that 'no two of us are born exactly alike. We have different natural aptitudes, which fit us for different jobs' (Plato 2007: 2.2 57).

Essentialism was not an idiosyncratic peculiarity of the Ancient Greeks. Rather, the whole feudal system in Europe and the caste system in India were based upon it. In the feudal world, European elites spent vast fortunes in order to maintain a particular lifestyle, which led to their ultimate economic demise. While selling land to fund elaborate carriages might seem instrumentally irrational, it was entirely reasonable relative to the elite's objective of emphasizing their essential difference from commoners. They deliberately made themselves appear different from the ordinary rank-and-file as a demonstration of their different essence. Often, they made a point of speaking a different language from the majority. German, Scandinavian and Russian aristocracy used to converse amongst one another in French. If they spoke a different language, dressed differently and had different gestures, they *were* different. This is a bit along the lines of the everyday logic *if it walks like a duck, and quacks like a duck, it is a duck*. If elites behave and look different, they must be different.

In Kerala, India, higher castes used to go to great lengths to avoid the sun (Philips 2004), with the result that they appeared whiter than the rest of the population. This was not simply some disinterested aesthetic choice; it was part of structuring a belief system that they were a group who were essentially different from the rest of society. Because lower castes were darker (as people who worked outside tend to be), it was perceived as evidence that they had a natural essence that made it part of the natural-order-of-things that they were manual workers. In a circular logic, those who were white had the essence of higher caste, and those who worked outdoors had the essence of lower caste. As toiling outdoors under a baking sun made you brown, and remaining indoors in the shade kept you white, the visible facts of social life confirmed essentialist beliefs. Similarly, in many societies, having long fingernails suggests high class. Obviously manual workers cannot maintain long fingernails, so this creates a similarly reinforcing circle between empirical reality and essentialist belief systems.

Essentialism makes certain hierarchies reasonable. From the perspective of the less powerful that question their lesser Y-status, this is a way of foreclosing their 'space of reasons for others' (Forst 2015: 116). It is part of the essence of things that hierarchy should be as it is.

Essentialism has resonance with the natural attitude. People with different Y-status are simply out there, as part of the natural-order-of-things, in much the same way that sticks and stones are. Essentialism obscures the social construction of Y-status functions. It makes it appear unreasonable to contest inequality because the language game entails denying the essence of things. It makes it appear absurdly infelicitous, in the manner of someone basing an argument on premises that run counter to visible reality.

Reifying gender through essentialism

A paradigm instance of reification though essentialism is to be found in nineteenth- and early-twentieth-century social constructions of gender. These social constructions were presented as naturally occurring essential differences between men and women. In 1825, a widely read periodical women's magazine, *The Ladies Monthly Museum*, described these essential differences as follows.

> Man is strong – woman beautiful. Man is daring and confident – woman is diffident and unassuming. Man is great in action – woman in suffering. Man shines abroad – woman at home. Man talks to convince – woman to persuade and please. Man has a rugged heart – woman a soft and tender one. Man prevents misery – woman relieves it. Man has science – woman taste. Man has judgment – woman sensibility. Man is a being of justice – woman of mercy.
>
> (Quoted in Alexander 2006: 238)

Notice that this is phrased in such a manner that each sex appears to *complement* the other. Every male essential virtue is balanced with a female one. The author is deliberately trying to appear even-handed, while claiming that the two sexes are by nature essentially different. So, if they really are different in this way, it appears entirely fair and reasonable that women should not, for instance, participate in politics, as it runs counter to the essence of femininity.

These essential differences were constantly mobilized against the suffragette movement. These justifications were not expressed as domination. Rather, the reification of supposed natural differences made the exclusion of women from the political realm appear an act of concern. As one New York politician John Boyle O'Reilly commented in the mid-nineteenth century, 'It would be no more deplorable to see an angel harnessed to a machine than to see a woman voting politically' (quoted in Alexander 2006: 249). Note the equivalence between an *angel* and a *woman*. The exclusion of women from the vote is not domination; they are angels, which reflects their essence as part of the natural-order-of-things. Given their angelic essence, it would be a profanation of the sacred to see them work in industrial production (factories were often described as satanic mills). Women have a higher virtue, similar to angels, which would be profaned by the cut-and-thrust of politics.

This point of the equivalence between angels and women is a way to portray domination as a compliment, indeed as a privilege. As the early modern feminist Mary Wollstonecraft comments: '[w]omen are, in fact, so much degraded by mistaken notions of excellence ...' (Wollstonecraft 2014 [1792]: 33).

The intended audience of *The Ladies Monthly Museum* were women of status. The magazine was intended for 'ladies of established reputation in the literary circles' (quoted in Hughes 2015: 463). The reason for the positive (yet patronizing) tone was that women were meant to internalize these values and, to a significant extent, they probably did.

Writing in the late eighteenth century, Wollstonecraft describes how she constantly had to dismiss 'those pretty feminine phrases, which the men condescendingly use to soften our slavish dependence ...' (Wollstonecraft 2014 [1792]: 31). The central thrust of Mary Wollstonecraft's *Vindication of the Rights of Women* (2014 [1792]) was to deconstruct the idea that men and women were essentially different. She argued that any perceived differences were the product of socialization. This was not only a feminist normative tract but displayed a sociologically astute awareness of the social construction of gender. Yet, despite her political leanings and sociological perspicacity, Wollstonecraft admitted that she herself found it 'difficult to deny the central presumption her age, that women possess natures different from men' (Landes 1988: 13).

Wollstonecraft's practical consciousness was telling her, based upon her socialization, that men and women were by nature essentially different but, in her discursive consciousness, she understood that much of this perceived difference was the product of socialization. As practical consciousness is our taken-for-granted reality, it is a constant effort to make discursive consciousness override practical consciousness.

If it is part of the natural-order-of-things that different peoples have different essences, it is entirely reasonable that some should have power-over others or, at the very least, have differential access to resources. Different Xs are predisposed to different Y-status in circumstances C, each with different scopes of power. Within this language game, it would be entirely unreasonable for the two sexes to confound their power resources, in the same way as it would be crazy for the traffic police to hand out reading lists and professors to issue parking tickets. Scopes of power are complementary, not in competition. The (so-called) *natural talents* of women should be used to complement those of men, not compete with them. Once accepted, the 3-D essentialist reifications make 2-D bias appear entirely reasonable and so acquiescence is assured.

Essentialism and orientalism

This 3-D naturalization of (so-called) essential differences is found in numerous discourses of domination, including the justification of colonization. Again, as in the descriptions of the essential qualities of women, these accounts are presented in positive terms. To take an instance, Lord Balfour is highly complementary concerning the achievements of the Egyptians and 'orientals' more generally, while he considers them essentially incapable of self-government. As quoted by Edward Said (2003), Balfour writes as follows.

> Western nations as soon as they emerge into history show the beginnings of ... capacities for self-government. ... You may look through the whole history of the Orientals in what is called the East, and yet you never find traces of self-government. All their great centuries – and they have been very great – have been passed under despotism, under absolute government. All their great contribution to civilization – and they have been great – have been under that form of government. Conqueror has succeeded conqueror; one domination has followed another; but never in all the revolutions of fate and fortune have you seen one of those nations of its own motion establish what we, from a Western point of view, call self-government. *This is the fact.* It is *not a question of superiority and inferiority ...*
> Is it a good thing for these great nations – I admit their greatness – that this absolute government should be exercised by us? I think it a good thing.
> (Balfour quoted in Said 2003: 32–3; italics added)

Within what Said terms *orientalism* (Said 2003), government of the colonized is not presented as dominating superiority – 'It is *not a question of superiority and inferiority*'. There appears to be real concern with the other. We are presented with a *fact* concerning the essence of the colonized, which is that they have never been capable of self-government, although they have wonderful achievements. Of course, there is a subtle condescension implicit in the presumption to speak on behalf of the oriental (Said 2003: 34–5) but that is not discursively overt.

The tone of the compliments that Balfour pays to the oriental resonate with Wollstonecraft's observation that women are, 'in fact, so much degraded by mistaken notions of excellence...' (Wollstonecraft 2014 [1792]: 33) and her characterization of the 'pretty feminine phrases, which the men condescendingly use to soften our slavish dependence...' (Wollstonecraft 2014 [1792]: 31).

The use of compliments to mask domination is a way of making contestation of structures more difficult. If the more powerful actor portrays the essentialist description as a compliment, it appears ungrateful, churlish and impolite for the less powerful to contest it. So, there is a double-lock here: reification plus politeness-cum-gratitude, to cage the less powerful into felicitous confirm-structuration relative to the structural bias.

Rationalization: a borderline case of reification

In the above, the objective is to create a form of reification that stabilizes social order by making it appear legitimate to *both* the more and less powerful – to the structurer and to the confirm-structurer. However, a different phenomenon also exists where the other is essentialized in a manner that entirely denigrates the less powerful. In that case we can surmise that the intended audience is only the more powerful. I refer to this phenomenon as a *rationalization*, which was a concept used by Pareto (1935) to refer to the rationality that elites use to justify their actions. These types of reifications are for home consumption among the elites and, as such, should be distinguished from the above account of essentialism.

Rationalizations make no effort to persuade the subaltern. The racist discourses associated with many fascist and alt-right positions take the form of rationalizations. As the audience is composed of fellow racists, these discourses are overtly derogatory. In rationalizations of this kind there is no (condescending) flattery or compliments to entice the subaltern. This difference is evident in Howard Odum's doctoral dissertation, from Columbia University in 1910, which became an influential book with the telling title *Social and Mental Traits of the Negro*. The following is a quotation.

> The Negro has little home conscience or love of home, no local attachments of the better sort ... He has no pride of ancestry, and he is not influenced by the lives of great men ... He has little conception of the meaning of virtue, truth, honour, manhood, integrity ... He does not know the value of his word ... Their moral natures are miserably perverted.
>
> (Quoted in Alexander 2006: 272)

The intended readership of *The Mental Traits of the Negro* is not people of colour; the target is other white supremacists. The objective of the book is to provide the dominant with justification for institutionalized racism, without any attempt to gain epistemic buy-in from the dominated.

The primary reason elites produce rationalizations is for reasons of ontological security, which ties into 4-D power. One of the primary social ties of social integration is the belief in the self as reasonable and rational. Thus far we have emphasized how the dominant convince the less powerful that domination is reasonable. Here the issue is that the dominant have the desire to validate a self-perception as reasonable. It is rare to find a dominating elite, however tyrannical, who are willing to admit that they are entirely self-serving, unreasonable, ruthless dominators. Consequently, social actors will go to considerable lengths to convince *themselves* that what they do is entirely reasonable and justifiable. Generally speaking, they will justify the indefensible, if structuring the indefensible is part of their everyday social practice.

Elite rationalizations are different from the condescending compliments that Wollstonecraft refers to and are exemplified in the quotation from *The Lady's Monthly Museum* or Balfour's characterization of Egyptians. If the woman accepts this praise, she buys into a discourse of complimentary and complementary essential virtues. The ultimate end of that discourse is simpering and fawning females reciprocated by flowers and condescension. In contrast, the end of the rationalizations is coercion, exclusion or even death.

When confronted with rationalizations, the subaltern may pay tribute to the discourses of rationalization but they do so out of fear of coercion. It was (is?) a common theme of US racism against blacks that they were less intelligent than whites, more akin to animals. Blacks were well aware of this racism. They often scripted their actions accordingly for fear of coercion. This is observed by Nat Shaw, a poor black Alabama sharecropper, in the following quotation.

> I've joked with white people, in a nice way. I've had to *play dumb* sometimes – I knowed not to go too far and *let them know that I knowed*, because they taken exception of it too quick. *I had to humble-down and play shut-mouthed in many cases to get along*, I've done it all – they didn't know what it was all about, it's just plain fact ... And *I would go to 'em a heap of times for a favour and get it* ... They'd give you a good name if you was obedient to 'em, *acted nice when you met 'em and didn't question 'em about what they said they had against you. You begin to cry about your rights and the mistreatin' of you and they'd murder you.*
>
> (Quoted in Scott 1990: 34; italics added)

Shaw is fully aware that he is dominated and considered less intelligent. In order to obtain favours, Shaw does not challenge these negative perceptions. However, Shaw has not internalized the 3-D reifications concerning his race, which the oppressors use to justify their domination. Notice that the use of the concept of *favours* suggests the absence of citizens' rights.

The apparent compliance of the subaltern is cognitively significant for the dominators, as it validates their worldview. By paying tribute to the indefensible, the subaltern eases any feelings of cognitive dissonance among the dominators. Therefore, such deference is gratefully received, while the shattering of the illusion provokes anger (*they'd murder you*). The latter reveals the coercive source of domination and it can reasonably be conjectured that the anger also constitutes a reflection of the fact that, deep down, the powerful know these arguments are not convincing. This unacknowledged awareness creates the need for repression of self-reflection, resulting in an inner tension that is released in anger, when challenged.

Rationalizations constitute a form of reification, as they essentialize the less powerful. However, the source of compliance does not lie in the essentialism but in fear of coercion. So, in that sense, this phenomenon is really an extension of 1-D coercive power, as it is not the 3-D reification that is the source of compliance. Thus rationalizations are a borderline case of 3-D and 1-D coercive power.

6

The third dimension continued: Descartes' error, reification of truth and fallible truth

In the everyday forms of critique inspired by the Marxist and Enlightenment traditions, social actors conceive of themselves as engaged in an unmasking of ideology, where truth is distorted by power. As we have seen, this perspective is summed up in the everyday perception of critique as *speaking truth to power*. However, as observed by Nietzsche, the 'will to truth' is not disinterested, rather a desire for mastery or power (Nietzsche 2006: 312–15). Following Nietzsche, Foucault argues that truth and power are inextricably intertwined (Foucault 1980 and 1988).

From a sociological perspective, I endorse the Foucault/Nietzsche scepticism concerning the idea of knowledge without power. However, as has been argued by Habermas (1990), the Nietzsche-cum-Foucault position appears prone to performative contradiction or self-exception. The claim that all truth claims constitute a will to power is itself a truth claim, which appears to be self-refuting. It is analogous to the Epimenides paradox, which runs as follows: *Epimenides is from Crete, and he claims 'All Cretans are liars'*. For it to be true that all Cretans are liars, Epimenides is an exception to his own assertion. Similarly, without qualification, the truth claim that all truth is a will to power would appear to make an exception of itself. Self-exception has resonances of false-consciousness claims in the Marxist tradition – others are suffering from false-consciousness while we (Marxists) have the key to true consciousness.

In this chapter I will follow Nietzsche and Foucault by arguing that power/knowledge/truth are inextricably linked. However, I avoid the implicit performative contradiction or self-exception, through qualification, by carefully distinguishing Truth (with a capital letter), which is a form of reified usage, from truth (with a small t), which is a fallible claim.

We begin with a discussion of Truth and truth, followed by an account of knowledge, emphasizing struggles between fields of knowledge.

Descartes and Nietzsche: in search for truth/Truth

In Foucault's work the big philosophical question of truth is described as Descartes' problem, while the *use of truth* is characterized as Nietzsche's problem. Foucault writes as follows.

> It is true that Western philosophy, since Descartes at least, has always been involved with the problem of knowledge. This is not something one can escape. If someone wanted to be a philosopher but didn't ask himself the question, 'What is knowledge?' or, 'What is truth?' ... in that sense could one say he was a philosopher? ... Since Nietzsche this question of truth has been transformed. It is no longer, 'What is the surest path to Truth?' but, 'What is the hazardous career that Truth has followed?' That was Nietzsche's question.
>
> (Foucault 1980: 66 – use of both lower case and capitals for Truth are original)

In the above paragraph Foucault distinguishes Descartes' search for philosophical truth from Nietzsche's perception that truth is used to perpetuate relations of domination. Analyzing the question *What is the hazardous career that Truth has followed?* entails making sense of the way that Truth has been socially constructed and then used to legitimize 2-D structural bias, which is a sociological quest.

As we shall see, Descartes' philosophical quest is a paradigmatic instance of a view of Truth that is reifying and quasi-sacred. In pursuing (what he considered) the pure philosophical (actually sacred) quest for truth, Descartes performed an archetypical act of reification. Let us use Descartes' account of truth as paradigmatic of the reification of Truth. As we shall see later, this reified view is prevalent in everyday life and is key to understanding the relationship between Truth and power as a sociological (but not philosophical) phenomenon.

As framed by Descartes, the problem of truth is to find a foundation that transcends the local and contingent. Within this paradigm, Truth (with a capital letter) is something that no one can doubt. It is with a capital T because the absence of doubt already points towards reification. The argument *I think, therefore I am* constitutes an attempt to find an absolute, transcendental foundation that goes beyond social construction. Descartes writes as follows.

> as I observed that this truth *I think, therefore I am*, was so certain and of such evidence, that no ground of doubt, however extravagant, could be alleged by the sceptics capable of shaking it, I concluded that I might, without scruple, accept it as the first principle of the philosophy of which I was in search.
>
> (Descartes 1912: 25; italics original, underlining added)

In the words 'so certain and of such evidence' and 'capable of shaking it' Descartes makes it clear that he is looking for a ground that is so solid that no sceptics, whatever their arguments, would be able to question this foundation. Hence, *I think, therefore I am* should constitute the ultimate self-evident claim.

Tellingly, upon further reflection, Descartes finds this foundation inadequate because at the core of the thinking subject is a finite being that is imperfect and susceptible to illusion. The existence of dreams demonstrates that the mind can be momentarily convinced by illusion. In the end, in order to achieve an unambiguous foundation, Descartes postulates a *perfect being* in place of the imperfect thinking subject (Descartes 1912: 28 and 31). The attributes of the latter equate to God. Truth presupposes a perfect being who is 'infinite, eternal, immutable, omniscient, all-powerful, and, in fine, has ... all the perfections which I would recognise in a God' (Descartes 1912: 28). So, Descartes concludes that it is impossible for anyone to remove all sceptical doubt 'unless they presuppose the existence of God' (Descartes 1912: 31).

For Descartes the only way to remove all doubt is to presuppose a *perfect being* that is infinite and therefore transcends any form of human activity. Once deified, this foundation has all traces of social construction removed. While the search for the absence of doubt made Descartes' quest an implicitly reifying exercise, it becomes explicitly reifying when Descartes resorts to the Perfect Being. In social theory terms, Descartes creates a foundation that is beyond social construction by making it sacred. It is ironic that the philosophical quest turns into a performance of Truth as theological reification.

When Foucault refers to Nietzsche's question *What is the hazardous career that Truth has followed?* he is looking at the *use* of Truth by social actors. Foucault stated that following Nietzsche's approach means understanding why it is 'in our societies, "the truth" has been given such value, thus placing us absolutely under its thrall?' (Foucault 1988: 107).

Following Foucault-cum-Nietzsche means analyzing the use of Truth as a reifying function. The Cartesian view of Truth is theocratic, not philosophical, as claimed. When Descartes argues that a foundation requires a Perfect Being, this effectively gives the game away. However, this kind of foundational and transcendental view of Truth has huge *use value* in social interaction. Once social conventions are linked to so-called 'secure foundations' they are no longer socially constructed. These foundations are then built upon through induction, and a whole edifice of social structure is placed beyond critical evaluation. Disagreement with Truth becomes unreasonable; the speaker of these infelicitous utterances has negative Y-status.

When Nietzsche proclaimed the death of God, in *The Gay Science* paras 125 and 343, or in the prologue to *Thus Spoke Zarathustra* (both Nietzsche 2006), this is not a theological claim in favour of atheism, although Nietzsche was an atheist. 'The real problem, Nietzsche argued, was not that God has ceased to be believable, but – given the way science seamlessly slotted into the same foundational space – nobody had really noticed the significance of the event' (Grimwood 2011). For Nietzsche, freedom lay in the recognition that, with the absence of God as a foundation for know-ledge, there was the potential for liberation from the quest for absolute foundations. In contrast to this freedom, the majority of secularized social actors replace God with scientific Truth. As theorized here, Truth is reified, analogous to the sacred, as an attempt to disguise its social construction. Through reification a freedom is lost, which is the realization that social structures are indeed social constructions, thus have been made, and therefore can be unmade.

Later in the chapter we examine how fields of knowledge are built around battles of Truth. However, before that I wish to demonstrate that this argument does not invalidate the idea that there is such a phenom-enon as truth, with a small t.

Truth with a small t

This argument has two parts, as follows. First of all we will show that the philosophy of science does not actually suggest a reified concept of Truth – quite the contrary. To make this point we will use Karl Popper's account as an exemplar of a mainstream account of the search for scientific truth, which will be followed by an exemplar from actual science. The second part of the argument concerns what socially constructed fallible truth looks like, which will be based upon William James' pragmatism, Kuhn and Wittgenstein.

According to Popper the objective of science is not a search for a tran-scendental claim that is immune from falsification. That search is a form of pseudoscience (Popper 1976: 40–2). Popper writes; 'Now I hold that sci-entific theories are *never fully justifiable or verifiable*, but that they are never-theless testable' (Popper 2002: 22; italics added). Because the truth is *never fully justifiable*, truth is beset by doubt, not certainty.

For Descartes, absence of doubt is everything. To quote, again: 'this truth … was so certain and of such evidence, that no ground of doubt, … could be alleged …' (Descartes 1912: 25). In contrast, Popper acknowledges doubt as inherent to any truth claim, which means the absence of a secure foundation.

Descartes wanted an unshakeable Truth foundation from which he could inductively build more unshakeable Truths. Induction is a process where you move from an unshakable foundation to a wider theory, while holding on to the secure foundation. In contrast, Popper argues that this use of *induction* will invariably fail, because there are no such foundations ever to be found. Popper argues that there is no *problem* of induction (suggested by Hume) because induction is not the path to scientific discovery (Popper 2002: 6–7 and 14).

Descartes wants to get beyond social construction, while Popper accepts that science is made up of *'conventions'*, which constitute *'the game of science'* (Popper 2002: 32; italics added). As suggested by Kuhn's account of paradigms and scientific revolution (1970 and 1977), Popper does not go far enough in recognizing the social aspect of science, which is a point we will come back to. However, for the moment, Popper goes far enough (for the purposes of this argument) to demonstrate that there is a significant difference between the pursuit of Truth and the pursuit of truth.

Popper argues that scientists begin from general hypotheses, which constitute *'irrational creative intuition'* (Popper 2002: 8; italics added). There can be hardly anything further from an unshakeable foundation than an *irrational creative intuition*. To check the plausibility of the intuition the scientist looks for statements that accord with this intuition and those that would falsify it. If the latter set is inherently empty – in other words, if there is no potential for falsification, thus no room for doubt – then the statement does not qualify as science (Popper 2002: 17, 65–6). This means that the premises that Descartes was looking for are not part of the language game of science.

For Popper the search for truth entails the use of a theory that is *never fully justifiable or verifiable* and begins from an *intuited guess*. What makes this science is that the theory must be falsifiable. The scientist looks for instances of falsification and if they are not found, for the moment, the theory has proved its mettle or is true. So, the best we can ever say is that a theory is true until it is falsified by a counter-example (Popper 1976: 146). This in-built uncertainty and fallibility precludes reification of truth. Thus, it is unlike Truth.

As we shall see later, in actual practice scientists fall well short of this ideal, because there is always the temptation to make Truth claims, in order to foreclose debate. However, this is not the essence of sound research.

What is truth?

The philosophical viewpoint that aligns most closely with the social theory propounded here is pragmatism. Pragmatism is a theory of action, which is oriented towards results, use and purpose. It is oriented towards power, as the capacity for action. Within this tradition *truth* constitutes a *term of commendation*. William James writes as follows.

> Let me now say only this, that the truth *is one species of good*, and not as is usually supposed, a category distinct from good, and co-ordinate with it. *The true is the name of whatever proves itself to be good in the way of belief, and good, too, for definite, assignable reasons.*
>
> (James 1981: 37; italics original)

The term *truth* is not some transcendental quality but a term of commendation that is gauged relative to the objectives of a field of knowledge. As theorized here, a field of knowledge should be considered a set of conceptual tools that enables its practitioners to get something done. Following Kuhn, this field constitutes a realm of practice and perception. Within this framework *truth* is a term of recommendation reserved for the practices and perceptions that are the best conceptual tools.

Fields of knowledge consist of social structures, which are conventional, but not arbitrary. Rather, these structures are oriented towards some kind of goal. The structures that do this better than others deserve the recommendation of being called *truth*. Essentially a theory or paradigm is a set of conceptual tools that is better oriented towards the aims of that field of knowledge than any other set of conceptual tools. To take an example, the field of evolutionary biology is a field of research oriented towards understanding how it is that biological organisms have evolved and exist in their great variety. Relative to contemporary knowledge of this field, Charles Darwin is the first person to provide conceptual tools to answer this question in a manner that deserves the term of recommendation of the signifier *truth* (see Dawkins 2006: 1; de Saussure 1960).

In his introduction to *The Origin of the Species*, Darwin opens by stating that his observations on board HMS *Beagle* 'seemed to me to thro some light on the origin of the species...' and that after five years he 'allowed himself to speculate on the subject' and to 'sketch' conclusions that 'seemed to me probable' (Darwin 1998: 3). The words 'thro some light', 'speculate', 'sketch' and 'probable' are as tentative as Popper suggests scientific truth should be. There is no reification here. The theory he propounded gave those interested in this subject a set of conceptual tools that delivers power-to answers to relevant questions relative to the goals of their scientific field, rather than some immutable Truth. Put simply, if you wish to understand the slow emergence of biological variety, as evidenced by fossils, or how the difference between closely related species living in different environments (such as finches on different islands) came about, the theory of evolution provides a set conceptual tools that is useful, thus deserves to be recommended as truth.

Conceptual tools that are true are not reified, thus they evolve. While Dawkins greatly admires Darwin, he introduced another conceptual tool into the field of evolutionary biology. Observing coral reefs and jellyfish, Dawkins rethought the meaning of *biological organisms*. In Darwin biological organisms are presumed as singular entities, which is a perception that accords with the natural attitude. Dawkins suggests as a conceptual tool that organisms should be reconceptualized as giant survival machines for replicators of molecules, called DNA. Within this paradigm biological organisms are interpreted as analogous to complex mutually interdependent colonies of cells (Dawkins 2006: 21). Dawkins does not claim that he has discovered the singular Truth that will never be superseded. Nor does he claim that he has proven Darwin 'wrong'. The obsession with proving others wrong (unfortunately, so characteristic of much academic debate) is a legacy of a binary worldview of Truth versus error. For Dawkins the *replicators-of-DNA* description constitutes a useful conceptual tool for furthering our understanding of variation among the species. This concept is added to the conceptual toolbox of evolutionary theory, and both are *useful*. What makes this *truth* is a normative evaluation to the effect that, at this point in time, this concept is a useful conceptual tool, relative to the objectives of evolutionary biology.

In classic Newtonian physics the underlying assumption concerning matter was that there is a given reality in which things present themselves as either one thing or the other. The world was made up of sortal concepts whereby something is *this* or *that* (as you would sort apples or oranges). Again, this is a worldview that is in accordance with the natural attitude of practical consciousness. However, it has been observed that in certain experiments particular features of physical phenomena can be made manifest at the expense of others. It was this insight that led Werner Heisenberg to formulate the uncertainty principle, whereby the intervention of the observer becomes part of the data. However, Niels Bohr interpreted this phenomenon slightly differently. At the time physicists were particularly concerned about the fact that light showed signs of being both waves and particles. For Bohr the point is not interference by the observer, as for Heisenberg. Bohr argued that the results of these experiments showed a form of wave–particle duality of light. Thus, 'evidence obtained under different experimental conditions cannot be comprehended within a single picture, but must be regarded as *complementary* in the sense that only the totality of the phenomena exhausts the possible information about the objects' (Bohr 1949). The particle and the wave description are not mutually excluding descriptions, thus a difficulty to be overcome with better experiments. For Bohr the world of science is not a binary one of right and wrong. Rather, the two perceptions constitute complementary descriptions of light, or a complementary duality. In essence, Bohr argues that these experiments are different physical tools to make visible different gestalt qualities, or conceptual tool qualities, of light within the field of physics. Again, this constitutes a use-function account of experiments that moves away from any reified notions of Truth-in-itself. In this case the physical tools have an analogous function to conceptual tools that deserved the recommendation of truth. Furthermore, the theory itself constitutes a set of conceptual tools that is useful, thus can be recommended as truth.

Relative to this view, an expensive piece of experimental machinery, such as the CERN Large Hadron Collider, is a tool for showing us different properties of particles relative to various theories that are to be tested. However, there is no expectation that the Truth of particles, in their pure essence, will be revealed once and for all. In that sense, experiments are an accompaniment to conceptual tools. The experiments make visible the gestalt qualities of various social constructions of truth within a field of knowledge.

Experiments and concepts are analogous to the chisels, saws and other tools of a carpenter's chest. If certain tools are useful they should be accorded the positive normative endorsement of the signifier *truth*. Of course, that is only for now, until we *construct* better tools, which then deserve the term of commendation, *truth*.

Deep and shallow conflicts over knowledge

From a sociological perspective, power/knowledge/Truth/truth falls within the logic of 1-D and 2-D conflictual power. On the one hand there are contests of power-knowledge that reproduce epistemic regimes, which are comparatively shallow 1-D conflicts. There are also deep epistemic 2-D structural conflicts where regimes of knowledge fight for dominance.

Foucault opens *The Order of Things* with a bizarre and puzzling passage, which is a quotation from Borges, where the latter quotes from an ancient Chinese encyclopaedia where it is written that

> Animals are divided into: a) belonging to the emperor, b) embalmed, c) tame, d) suckling pigs, f) fabulous, g) stray dogs, h) included in the present classification, i) frenzied, j) innumerable, k) drawn with a fine camel-hair brush, l) et cetera, m) having just broken the water pitcher, n) that from a long way off look like flies.
>
> (Foucault 1970: xv)

This passage strikes us as an impossible list, which makes us laugh because of the impossibility of thinking in this way (Foucault 1970: xvi–xvii). Foucault argues that the reason for this is that the *tabula*, or *historical a priori* is missing (Foucault 1989: 127). We do not understand what it means to think in this manner. To our interpretative horizon this appears as disorder, or as a form of dystopia.

The laughter also comes from the juxtaposition of this apparently arbitrary list with the information that it is supposed to be an encyclopaedia. Moving beyond Foucault's interpretation, relative to our everyday interpretative horizon, the signifier *encyclopaedia* conjures up a reference work, which has high Y-status authority. In the past, pre-internet age, most literate homes had *the Encyclopaedia*, which was considered a repository of Truth. Discussions over the table dinner would be resolved by consulting *the Encyclopaedia*, which contained the definitive answer. How can a random list be part of such a repository of Truth?

One way that this list could make sense to our ears is that it is an inventory of the animals that the particular compiler happened, entirely contingently, to have had contact with leading up to the moment she wrote the entry. For instance, maybe she had just completed a painting of animals using a fine camel-hair brush. In the scene there were animals in the distance that were indistinct (like flies). While she was painting, her cat knocked over the water pitcher and so on. We could easily embellish this story to cover all the above categories. However, if this is the explanation, relative to the modern interpretative horizon, this account fails the test of Truth, suggested by the word encyclopaedia. Truth is not some *contingent* experience. Rather, Truth represents something of universal application. For instance, Linnaeus' taxonomy of natural organisms claims to be universal. That taxonomy is unconnected with Linnaeus' personal life – what he contingently happened to be doing in the run-up to the creation of the taxonomy.

There are two ways in which this encyclopaedia disconcerts. First, we cannot make sense of the interpretative horizon or system of knowledge that saw this as order and/or, second, we cannot make sense of the implicit Truth claim suggested by the word *encyclopaedia*. This distinction is important for understanding the nature of deep 3-D epistemic conflicts.

Knowledge

At the most general level, *knowledge* refers to social actors' general interpretative horizon that gives them a certain gestalt perception of things-in-the-world. However, not all interpretative horizons have equal authority status. Some are considered unreasonable. Like truth, the signifier *knowledge* has an evaluative component that suggests that the interpretative horizon is desirable.

Western philosophy is driven by an obsession to reassure us that our perceptions are knowledge, not arbitrary imaginings. Going back to Plato, are we really seeing reality or are we in a cave watching shadows? How do we know that the knowledge we use to make sense of the world actually gives access to a true picture of reality-out-there?

Kant argued that the observer brings *a priori* knowledge to interpretation (Kant 2003). This knowledge is an ordering device that the mind imposes upon the world. This includes time, space and causality. Kant considered these to be transcendental, in the sense of transcending the particularities of any social order. By virtue of that quality they give True access to the world-out-there. In contrast to Kant, by referring to *historical a priori* (Foucault 1970: xxvi and 1989: 127), Foucault signals that the ordering practices of systems of thought are social constructions that reflect a particular historical conjuncture. These constitute local socially constructed interpretative horizons. Unlike Kant's characterization of *a priori* knowledge, this is not universal, and therefore does not confer the status of Truth.

Durkheim made a similar argument to Foucault's in his *Elementary Forms of Religious Life* (Durkheim 2008 [1915]), which was also an implicit critique of Kant, on sociological grounds. Essentially, anthropology teaches us that what passes for knowledge is radically different across space. A difference between Durkheim and Foucault is that Durkheim accepted that Kant's categories were universal in the highly qualified sense of always present in the human mind. However, Durkheim argued that these categories of thought are different in substance depending upon culture. All aboriginal societies had concepts of time and space but the social construction of these concepts was different from that of Western society. Hence, while ordering along the categories of time and space may be a universal attribute of cognition, the actual qualities of these orderings are widely different. For instance, Western industrial society is premised upon a linear clock-time, while most traditional societies typically use circular time, measured around the seasons and religious rituals (Durkheim 2008: 353–4). So, even if we concede to Kant that all societies have a concept of time, the specifics of these categories are not universal. Durkheim's idea that certain categories recur in societies but are variable depending upon social context accords with Chomsky's distinction between universal and generative grammar. It is part of universal grammar to have a concept of time, while the generative content is different depending upon context. Hence, the differences in historical *a priori* are as different as the differences between actual spoken languages, which, while different, still share certain underlying characteristics.

The bar for knowledge is lower than that for truth. What qualifies as knowledge is a system of thought that is considered reasonable. While truth claims tend to be singular, knowledge refers to the wider local language, system of thought (Foucault) or paradigm (Kuhn).

Systems of thought or paradigms presuppose meaning wholism (which I write with a w, as the referent are wholes, not holes). Meaning derives from the relationship between elements within a system (Haugaard 1997: 46–53). This is influenced by de Saussure's linguistic theory where the meaning of each word is relationally constituted through difference from every other word (de Saussure 1960: 120). Possibly the easiest way of explaining meaning wholism is by using chess as an exemplar of a micro-language (see de Saussure 1960: 110). Does a *knight* have any meaning in itself? Certainly not – outside the game of chess it has no meaning whatsoever; the meaning of the *knight* is defined by membership of the game of chess. Is it possible for someone to understand the meaning of knight without understanding the meaning of the other pieces, including *bishop*, *pawn*, *queen* and so on? The answer is no, because the significance of the knight can only be appreciated relative to the other pieces.

In the essay 'Second Thoughts on Paradigms', Kuhn uses a thought experiment to explain this phenomenon (Kuhn 1977: 309–12). Imagine a father and young child walking along the shore of a lake. The child sees a white bird and says *bird*. Wishing to expand her vocabulary, the father says: *It's a swan*. They see some more *swans*, which the child identifies correctly. They come another somewhat different white bird, which she also identifies as a *swan*, but the father corrects her: *It is a goose*. Later she sees a smaller white bird, which she identifies as a *goose*, but she is corrected again: *It's a duck*. At the end of the walk the child is identifying *swans*, *geese* and *ducks* flawlessly. When the child first learns the word *swan*, but cannot distinguish it from a *goose* or *duck*, does she truly understand the signifier *swan*? The answer is *not really*; true understanding comes from learning the meaning of a signifier in relationship to a series of differences and similarities within a linguistic whole.

Meaning wholism entails that each linguistic system is self-contained with concepts unique to it, which suggests incommensurability because meaning is relational. It is for this reason that translation from one language to another is so deeply problematic, as there can never be exact equivalence between two systems. Knowledge constitutes relational concepts within incommensurable local language games.

Due to incommensurability, movement from one system of thought to another is abrupt. It is analogous to moving from chess to tennis. In Kuhn science is characterized by scientific revolutions and in Foucault there is discontinuity between epistemes. In his archaeological phase Foucault

(1970 and 1989) argued that the last 500 years have been characterized by three systems of thought: the Renaissance (1500–1650), the Classical Period (1650–1800) and the Modern period (1800 to 1980; the present at Foucault's time of writing).

In the Renaissance period resemblances were the key to knowledge. The human face resembles the sky, with the intellect resembling God's wisdom, the eyes analogous to the sun and the moon and the mouth to the planet Venus, as the mouth gives passage to kisses in expressions of love (Foucault 1970: 19). Within this system of thought, Truth and falsity were decided by the local rules of the game. Renaissance debate concerned how precisely a typical flowering plant (think of a sunflower or a daisy) resembles the human body. Is the face analogous to the flower, as they look alike? Or, is the human face equivalent to the roots, as the mouth is used to absorb food (Foucault 1970: 24)?

These two possible perceptions of resemblance gave rise to a debate between the plant upside-downers and the plant right-side-uppers. For the sake of argument, let us imagine that the right-side-uppers won the debate for Truth. However, while the plant-upside-downers were wrong, their claim still lay within the conditions of possibility. It was still possible to observe that *a plant is an upside-down human* and be deemed reasonable, although mistaken. While not Truth, their ideas still qualified as *knowledge*. As a thought experiment, imagine a contemporary biology conference and someone delivering a paper to the effect that a plant is right-side-up (or upside-down) person. This would be greeted with stunned silence, as the person would be deemed entirely unreasonable. The Renaissance debate is simply outside the conditions of possibility of modern science. It is beyond true versus false; *it is not knowledge.*

Kuhn's paradigms have the same quality of discontinuity, with attached conditions of impossibility. Kuhn began to develop the idea of science as paradigmatic when asked to deliver a series of lectures on the history of physics. He was a PhD student at the time, and started his preparation by reading Aristotle's *Physics*. At first he approached the text assuming that Aristotle would have a worldview that corresponded to a primitive version of Newtonian mechanics. Interpreted in this manner, Aristotle's text appeared as full of apparent absurdities. How could this famous thinker have said all these absurd things (Kuhn 1977: xi)? Of course, the answer was that the absurdity was a consequence of interpreting Aristotle through the lens of Newtonian physics. Aristotle made sense of the world through an entirely different system of knowledge. For instance, when Aristotle saw a ball rolling down a hill it appeared self-evident that ball on the top of the hill and the ball on bottom of the hill were qualitatively different balls, as the action of rolling removed vital qualities, including energy, from the ball.

Once Kuhn understood the underlying interpretative horizon, Aristotle's physics became sophisticated. Kuhn understood the system of knowledge that informed Aristotle's statements.

Systems of thought and conflict

For both Foucault and Kuhn, knowledge conflicts take place at two levels. Certain conflicts over truth arise within systems of thought, which reproduce the local conditions of systemic possibility. These we can term shallow conflicts and they constitute a form of 1-D structured conflict. These take place within a system of knowledge. These would be analogous to democratic conflicts, where a shared sense of felicity around structuration and confirm-structuration are structuring the conditions of possibility. In contrast, 2-D deep epistemic conflicts also occur and are fought over the systems of knowledge. In such a conflict the stakes are much higher because being wrong is not simply being mistaken, but means being outside the conditions of possibility altogether. Being wrong means infelicity and unreasonableness. This entails a significantly more negative Y-status than simply being wrong.

Foucault asserted that the conflict between Marx and the bourgeois economists was a storm in a child's paddling pool (Foucault 1970: 262). By this he meant that it was a shallow conflict because both reproduced the same system of knowledge. For instance, both Marx and his adversaries accepted that the average value of commodities equated to embodied labour power, according to the labour theory of value. Marx and the bourgeois economists were engaged in a 1-D conflict of statements within the same system of knowledge.

In a recent essay, Jenkins and Lukes have discussed the distinction between deep and shallow epistemic conflict in terms of different levels of being mistaken. Jenkins and Lukes open with the following line: 'To be right is one thing, but to be told that what one says or believes is "not even wrong" is an even harder pill to swallow' (Jenkins and Lukes 2017: 6). If one is not even wrong, one is essentially 'trafficking in nonsense' (Jenkins and Lukes 2017: 6). Jenkins and Lukes give an example of such nonsense based upon Douglas Adams' *The Hitchhiker's Guide to the Galaxy*. The supercomputer Deep Thought is asked to answer 'the Ultimate Question of Life, the Universe, and Everything'. After processing this question for 7.5 million years the computer answers that the meaning of 'Life, the Universe, and Everything' is 42 (Adams 1995: 111). Whatever the answer might be, this answer is entirely meaningless. Whatever the correct answer is, we know that it cannot be an integer. This is not simply wrong; it is nonsense (Jenkins and Lukes 2017: 7). In other words, this answer lies outside the conditions of possibility of anything we can take seriously as knowledge.

Following Ryle (2009: 6–13), Jenkins and Lukes argue that these types of answers constitute a *category mistake*, which is an error that shows a misunderstanding of the concepts involved. Systems of knowledge create a context of felicity or infelicity that create the conditions of possibility for meaningful commensurable 1-D conflict. If social actors use widely different interpretative horizons, then statements constitute category mistakes relative to the other. This will either be experienced as 2-D exclusion or, if the structurer insists upon the validity of their interpretative framework, this descends into full 2-D conflict between knowledge systems.

Contested knowledge

Foucault's account of systems of thought, or *epistemes*, describes all-embracing interpretative horizons, which are discontinuous from one another (Foucault 1989). There is a radical incommensurability between the Renaissance and Modern systems of thought. Similarly, in Kuhn's account of paradigm shifts (1970 and 1977) there is radical incommensurability. However, paradigms are not as wide as *epistemes*. In Foucault, the disciplinary subdivisions are discourse formations (Foucault 1989), which have certain differences from one another but, in the larger scheme of things, it is wider epistemic differences that really count in terms of incommensurability. In Kuhn's account, one paradigm knocks out the other to become the only game in town. For both Kuhn and Foucault incommensurability suggests a radical shift where one system of thought replaces another. Once the Renaissance system of thought is replaced, it is over. Similarly, for Kuhn, once a scientific revolution takes place, the old paradigm ceases.

The Kuhn-cum-Foucault image of scientific revolutions and epistemic shifts is overdrawn. When Foucault introduces the Chinese encyclopaedia entry, he convincingly presents us with a system of thought that is both incommensurable and which is displaced, or vanished, presumably because it was vanquished in the battle for Truth. It is for these reasons that we are no longer sure how to interpret the text. However, in contrast to the encyclopaedia (which is probably a fiction made up by Borges; see Cseresnyesi 1996), when I first read Foucault's description of the Renaissance episteme I understood it instantly. It was *unlike* the Chinese encyclopaedia; I was *not* visiting an alien world. The interpretative horizon of the Renaissance was immediately intelligible because *it is far from dead*. Anyone with familiarity with the alternative therapies of hippy culture (which I am, from my teenage years growing up among artists and bohemians in the West of Ireland) understands what is going on.

The Renaissance interpretative horizon underpins the thinking of contemporary astrology and homeopathy. Astrology is based upon resemblances between astronomical formations, personality traits and future prediction. Similarly, homeopathy is based upon the principle of *similia similibus curentur* (Hahnemann 1833: 48–9) or the belief that like cures like. This doctrine of resemblances-cum-similarities dates back to Hippocrates (400 bc), which suggests that it is much older than the Renaissance. The underlying principle of homeopathy is that a sick person can be cured by the administration of the substances that would induce similar symptoms in a healthy person. This idea is similar to the everyday folk belief that *like cures like*, for instance, the cure for snakebites is to eat the head of the snake that bit you.

To this is added the somewhat bizarre twist (relative to the knowledge system of modern science) that these so-called medical substances should be diluted and re-diluted in water. It is believed that the greater the dilution, the greater the potency. This is referred to as the *memory of water*. This idea constitutes anthropomorphism relative to modern natural science, thus is infelicitous. However, the scientific taboo on anthropomorphic thinking is of recent origin in Western thought, emerging only in the nineteenth century.

The originator of homeopathy, Samuel Hahnemann, was a German medical doctor of the late eighteenth century. At the time of publication his magnum opus, *The Homoeopathic Medical Doctrine* (1833 [1796]), would have been taken as a felicitous intervention within mainstream medical knowledge. Although, the anthropomorphism of the 'memory of water' would, quite possibly, have been considered old-fashioned but not unreasonable.

Today the underlying principles of homeopathy confer low Y-status authority relative to the interpretative horizon of conventional medicine. The latter argues that the efficacy of homeopathy is similar to the placebo effect (Grimes 2012). However, in contrast to this low status, sales of homeopathic remedies are surging, with US consumers spending about $1.2 billion on homeopathic drugs in 2014 (*The Washington Post* 2015). So, the paradigm has not died at all. It co-exists alongside conventional medical knowledge but it has lost significant authority status.

If you visit the website of the British Homeopathic Association (britishhomeopathic.org), you find a page that resembles the websites of conventional medical associations in most respects. However, there is one difference – at the time of writing their top news stories ('Save Homeopathy and Herbal Medicines from the NHS' and 'BHA Challenges Flawed NHS

Consultation') both concern the issue of recognition by the British National Health Service, or confirm-structuration, as medicine by the NHS. This is typical of contested knowledge; while there is confirm-structuration from consumers, recognition from the state still has to be fought over.

Bourdieu observes that the modern state has a monopoly on authority (Bourdieu 2000: 172). This is somewhat of an exaggeration, as the state is in competition with other sources of authority, including religious institutions, multi-national companies and international organizations, including the UN, and, of course, sages among the general public. However, recognition as knowledge by the state is extremely important, as the state occupies a pivotal position in contemporary society.

We can also see this shift in Y-status authority with regard to astrology. Back in the late sixteenth century the Danish astronomer Tycho Brahe was awarded, by King Frederick II of Denmark, an entire island and a budget equivalent to 1% of royal revenues in order to build the most advanced observatory in the world (Thoren and Christianson 1990: 188). Uraniborg and Stjerneborg were observatories that housed the most sophisticated astronomical instruments of their day. They were the seventeenth-century equivalent of the Hubble Space Telescope today. Brahe was obsessed with creating an accurate map of the heavens. Seventeenth-century astronomers, including Kepler, had the utmost respect for the accuracy of the results from Brahe's observations (Christianson 2000: 304). This is an aspect of Brahe's work that is still recognized by historians of astronomy as genuine knowledge. Less emphasized is the fact that, at the time, the main justification for funding this magnificent observatory was that Brahe was expected to use the accurate mapping of the heavens to provide state-of-the-art astrological predictions, which would be used by the Danish state as an aid to government (Christianson 2000: 88–9, 103, 257–8, 265, 273 and 287).

As a thought experiment, imagine that NASA's application for the Hubble Space Telescope had included the justification that the results could provide *cutting-edge astrological predictions*. The idea is entirely laughable. Yet astrology has *not* receded from Western consciousness. At more or less the same time that NASA sought funding for the Hubble Space Telescope, Nancy Reagan employed the services of astrologer Joan Quigley to advise her and President Reagan. The extent of the advice is hard to ascertain for certain but Quigley claimed that it covered important matters of state, including foreign policy. In her defence, Nancy suggested that the advice simply concerned Reagan's safety (*Los Angeles Times* 2016). It is of note, however, that Nancy Reagan paid the astrologer through a third party in order to conceal the services. When the news broke that the First Family was employing an astrologer, this was met with a barrage of criticism that took the form of jokes and mockery. The *New York Post* ran with a headline 'Astrologer Runs the White House' and contained the jocose suggestion that the administration should include a cabinet post for voodoo (*Los Angeles Times* 2016).

This secrecy followed by mockery is symptomatic of the fact that astrology has gained negative Y-status function. Relative to the state, it no longer qualifies as knowledge. What has changed since the sixteenth century is relative Y-status authority function. Yet, the rise of infelicity is not absolute. It is only from a certain perspective and relative to certain functions, such as government. Many ordinary citizens still view astro-logical prediction as a form of knowledge. According to a YouGov survey (2015) conducted in the US (sample size 999), when asked the question *Do you believe that star signs can tell you something about yourself or another person?*, the results were: Yes = 30%, No = 51% and Not Sure = 19%. To the question *Do you believe that horoscopes can tell you something about what will happen in the future?*, the results were: Yes = 14%, No = 65% and Not Sure = 20%. Given the negative status of astrological belief, these fig-ures may well be under-representative (as we noted, Nancy Reagan was busy downplaying the role of the astrologer and hiding the payments). It is quite likely that qualitative research of actual behaviour would give much higher results (see Campion 2017). However, even if these figures do not under-represent, a significant section of the population considers astrology knowledge.

The Renaissance system of thought lives on through homeopathy and astrology. What has changed since the sixteenth century is *not* that resemblance has disappeared, as suggested by Foucault and Kuhn, but that its Y-status authority as knowledge is lower than it was at that time. In short, what has changed is this system of knowledge's relationship to power.

Creating a knowledge community

Being an interlocutor who is regarded as *reasonable* constitutes a Y-status function. In the case of Primo Levi we saw a social actor with no status authority by virtue of his race. A person who is deemed to speak category errors is in an analogous situation, from the perspective of knowledge authority. Because they are speaking from an interpretative horizon that does not qualify as knowledge, they are deemed unworthy of reasoned interaction. In Austin's example of naming ships, his lack of authority to name ships was tied to the judgement that his attempt to do so was infeli-citous and unreasonable. However, unlike Austin, highly esoteric minority positions can create felicity among the like-minded.

In 2018 the Flat Earth Convention was held in Birmingham. While most scientists would regard the idea that the earth is flat as entirely ludicrous, apparently there are those for whom this belief is not entirely absurd. Someone who believes that the earth is flat has a place where they can converge and be considered reasonable. However, a conference hosted by the Flat Earth Society will have lower Y-status authority than one hosted by the Max Planck Institute for Astrophysics (to put it mildly). The latter has authority to speak and be taken seriously by a wide field of resonance, including the state. The former only has its own sub-group as a ring of felicity.

If you visit the Flat Earth Society website, you will read the following news flash: 'Physicist Finally on Stage at the First Flat Earth UK Convention' (Flat Earth 2018). The question is: why is it so important that a physicist should address the Flat Earth Convention? The answer is that flat-earthers crave recognition by physicists because they have high Y-status authority functions.

In the event there were two physics PhD candidates at the convention, who were suitably critical of the flat earth hypothesis (Marshall 2018). The physicists did not in any way endorse the truth-claim that the earth is flat. However, from the point of view of the Flat Earth Society, the very fact that these PhD candidates turned up at the convention meant that, for a moment, they were considered worthy of being dialogic interlocutors with someone from the world of physics. This was a moment when 2-D exclusion gave way to 1-D discussion, even if their flat earth claims were considered false. The Flat Earth Society moved briefly from the status of infelicitous/unreasonable to the field of plausible knowledge, even if it was not accorded the status of truth. However, as a qualification, it is worthy of note that the physicists were PhD *candidates*. The completion of a PhD is the conventional certification required to be a recognized having the Y-status of full academic authority. These interlocutors actually had the authority Y-status function of *nearly physicists*. So, the status claim made by the Flat Earth Convention was, in fact, a borderline case of knowledge recognition.

Fields of knowledge on a scale

In the case of astrology we have an interpretative horizon that persists over time, yet which has lost status function among certain groups. We should think of knowledge as made up of local *fields* that are governed by certain conventions and modes of interpretation, which members of the field take seriously. Sociologically, *knowledge* is a status function conferred upon a local paradigm as reasonable. Epistemic fields have wider and lesser recognition as *knowledge*.

In terms of status authority, these fields can be approximately ranked on a scale. At the far end, with no status and pure unreasonableness, are individuals deemed to hold crazy beliefs, which are not validated as knowledge at all, thus are analogous to a private language. Moving a small step towards higher status, a small group, such as the Flat Earth Society, creates an epistemic field that is validated by its members as knowledge but by no one else. At a higher level of status are fields with significant membership but that fail to be recognized as knowledge with high status outside the knowledge community. The field of astrology is a complex one, with nuanced debates within the field, which has resonance with a significant segment of the population. For the latter, the pronouncements of certain famous astrologers have high authority value. However, astrology fails to qualify as knowledge among the natural sciences or to be recognized in academic institutions validated by the state. At a higher status level are epistemic fields with wide popular recognition but contested state recognition. The field of homeopathy has a significant area of resonance with the general population, but is highly contested relative to the fields of biology, medicine and state-run departments of health. At certain times homeopathy gains Y-status authority and can exchange views with biologists. Moving further up the status scale we come to fields such as the social sciences that are considered knowledge by a significant section of the population (I hope) and also by the state. However, within the social sciences the more quantitative disciplines, those that most resemble the natural sciences, have a higher status. Governments are more likely to seek the advice of economists than sociologists. Higher again are the natural sciences, which are widely regarded as repositories of either Truth (reified) or truth (fallibilism). Recently, due to growing scepticism around the interests of Big Pharma, medicine has lost some status authority among the general public, but relative to state institutions the field of medicine is still as high as ever.

Fields of knowledge

To place Bourdieu and Kuhn in dialogue, *fields* of knowledge are disciplinary *paradigms* where certain ways of looking at the world, or certain gestalts and modes of interpretation, are shared (Kuhn 1977: 293–319). As described by Kuhn, natural scientists share a common socialization, which makes them part of the discipline (Kuhn 1970: 47). This applies not only to natural science; it applies to all fields of knowledge to a greater or lesser extent. In its inception, a field of knowledge tends to be relatively unstructured but over time it becomes more disciplined, which means that the rules of the game become increasingly complex.

Being part of a local field of knowledge presupposes sharing what Bourdieu refers to as *ilusio* (Bourdieu 1990: 66–7). The word *ilusio* suggests *illusion*, which has the connotation of being *false*. That is not quite what is meant. To take an analogous use of terminology, the sociologist Benedict Anderson wrote a monograph on nationalism entitled *Imagined Communities* (Anderson 1983). The point of the word *imagined* in this case did not suggest *imaginary*. Rather, it was to suggest a process of imagination. It takes an act of imagination to believe that one is a member of a nation and, as such, one shares some essential qualities with a large group of persons, most of whom one has never met. *Ilusio* is a shared act of imagination, or world creation, whereby a group tacitly agree (practical consciousness knowledge) to treat an epistemic field as knowledge.

The *discipline* of a field of knowledge signals shared self-restraint. Members are reliable structurers and confirm-structurers relative to one another. In each field a disciplined person is someone who treats the conventions of the field seriously. When presented with what is considered hard evidence they respond, or confirm-structure, appropriately because they take the justifications of the field seriously. Thus the structures of the local knowledge system are reproduced in a manner that is relatively predictable and routine.

Shared *ilusio* and discipline entail that members of a specific knowledge community will be structurally constrained by shared rules of justification. In a 1-D conflict within the rules of the game, if one person shows reasonable justification for a particular position, other members of that knowledge community will engage. As they share concepts and modes of argumentation, they will be persuaded by what is considered, according to the rules of that particular field, better reason (see Forst 2017).

We have previously looked at democratic contests as instances of 1-D conflicts. If you stand for election, it is reasonable that you accept that whoever obtains the most votes wins political office. From a sociological perspective, the democratic game is paradigmatic of 1-D conflict. It would be self-contradictory to stand for election, and then proclaim victory with the fewest votes. Similarly, knowledge communities have rules pertaining to their field that count as reasonable justification. *Ilusio* and discipline entail that they never say, *that is a good justification, but I don't care, I won't accept that conclusion, because these ways of thinking are arbitrary social conventions.* These shared constraints constitute the conditions of possibility for power-over, power-to and power-with, relative to the objectives of the field.

Y-status within a knowledge community

What counts as knowledge for an epistemic community entails the conferral of a status function as a serious utterance. A statement within that community that conforms to the norms of that community may be discovered to be false but will, nonetheless, be taken seriously. Knowledge itself has authority, in the sense that members of a field will confer authority status upon a text, or experiment, which they consider paradigmatic within the field (see Alasuutari 2018). Within the community there is also Y-status hierarchy. Those social actors who are deemed to have internalized the interpretative horizon of that epistemic knowledge community are considered to have authority to speak for the field. As observed by Foucault:

> Medical statements cannot come from anybody: their value, efficacy, even their therapeutic powers, and, generally speaking, their existence as medical statements cannot be dissociated from the statutorily defined person who has the right to make them.
>
> (Foucault 1989: 51)

This applies not only to medical statements; it pertains equally to any field of knowledge that constitutes itself as a discipline. In the field of homeopathy, becoming a qualified homeopath entails a four-year course of professional training in the knowledge, *ilusio* and discipline. To take the Irish School of Homeopathy as an instance, their webpage tells us that 'At the Irish School of Homeopathy we provide a range of courses from complete beginners through to our postgraduate programme' (Irish School of Homeopathy 2018). What we see here is a hierarchy of status function relative to a system of knowledge. A beginner, with a one-year qualification, has some status, but high status function comes from a postgraduate qualification. We learn that 'Our *professional training course* [a link to the course is included] is a fully accredited course and leads to professional qualification and registration for those who wish to pursue a career as a homeopathic practitioner' (Irish School of Homeopathy 2018). The attainment of a professional qualification and registration means that you become *a homeopath*. This is a Y-status function that empowers the person to speak on behalf of this field of knowledge.

Once a member of the knowledge community goes through their four-year professional training to attain the Y-status of homeopath, they gain an authority status that forms a resource. The accreditation and registration is a certified document that is publicly registered somewhere, in much the same way that a title deed to a property is certified and registered.

There is a significant difference between certificates that are recognized by the state and those that are not. The state has a monopoly of accrediting certificates with legal standing. Some schools and universities are state-accredited while others are not. The latter have a kind of simulacrum

Y-status authority, where they typically imitate the state-accredited institutions but they are not considered authentic. Typically, a PhD from a non-recognized university does not confer authority status to speak the Truth/truth for a discipline. So, the value of the latter is significantly lower. Just as central banks validate paper currency, the state has a unique power to validate educational qualifications. Metaphorically speaking, the state equates to the currency reserve of fields of knowledge.

Fighting for knowledge capital through Truth

When Foucault was researching the history of the prison system (Foucault 1979), he came across a particularly notable case, which he edited and published separately as *I, Pierre Riviére, Having Slaughtered My Mother, My Sister, and My Brother: A Case of Parricide in the Nineteenth Century* (Foucault 1975). What puzzled Foucault about the case was the fact that there was so much documentation, by medical experts, surrounding this case. Significantly, and counter-intuitively, this evidence was not necessary for the conviction of Pierre Riviére. He had run out into the street brandishing a bloodied axe, proclaiming that he had killed his mother, sister and brother. So his guilt was beyond doubt. Furthermore, as cases of parricide were relatively common at the time, the case was not in any way a 'notable crime' (Foucault 1975: viii).

The reason that medical practitioners were so attracted to the case, and wrote incessantly about it, was that a new field of knowledge was being established. The field of *criminal psychiatry* was in its infancy. In the persona of Pierre Riviére there was a person who was obviously guilty and mentally ill. So, this was the perfect opportunity to use Pierre Riviére as an indisputable referent for the new signifiers of the discipline, many of which were still being socially constructed. For instance, at the time the concept of *monomania*, advanced by Esquirol in 1808, was still considered a dubious term (Foucault 1975: ix). In other words, *monomania* did not yet have the authority status of a Truth. It was still not a scientific fact-out-there. Consequently, it would have appeared as a socially constructed concept. The diagnosis might elicit a *so what?* response, because the designation could be considered arbitrary. However, the behaviour of Pierre Riviere, who was already publicly recognized as insane, provided the ideal opportunity to establish the signifier *monomania* with reference to something that everybody might agree was *real*. In other words, the concept might move from the status of social construction to that of Truth-out-there.

The would-be criminal psychiatrists were fighting for the existence of *monomania* as part of the furniture of the world. According to the natural attitude, the world-out-there is not socially constructed. Things exist out there to be 'discovered'. And when 'discovered', they are the Truth of the matter. In documenting the case these experts were transforming an epistemic field into knowledge.

In the act of claiming knowledge status for a field, the practitioners of that field also gain Y-status. Anyone who gains the Y-status as an expert within the field of criminal psychiatry has epistemic authority based upon a link to Truth. From then on, when the courts require expertise upon the criminally insane, a comparatively small group of experts hold the monopoly of Y-status authority to speak upon this subject.

Going back, say, to the sixteenth century, the behaviour that Pierre Riviére engaged in would, quite likely, have been interpreted as possession by Evil Spirits. In that case the person most qualified with the Y-status authority to pronounce upon that situation would have been a priest.

Fighting for Y-status

There are hierarchies between knowledge communities. If a knowledge community has a lower status than another comparable knowledge community, then a common method of increasing authority status value is to imitate the knowledge of a higher field. The objective is to create *equivalence* (see Glynos and Howarth 2007: 143–5 and 150–1) with a high status field that already claims Truth in the popular imagination.

Again, homeopathy is a field that is visibly fighting for its status authority. If we go to the webpage entitled 'The Faculty of Homeopathy' (2018), we find something quite similar to that of any webpage of a medical faculty at a university, which constitutes high status equivalence. Visually, we are confronted with a banner in dark blue, with *Faculty of Homeopathy* in white letters. This sits next to a crest with a convincing resemblance to a university crest – equivalence to a university is suggested. Underneath we see a photo of a group of serious individuals. We see what appears as a bespectacled professor, and three students all focussed upon something that suggests a laboratory experiment – again, equivalence to natural science. We do not know precisely what the experiment is because across the picture is another dark-navy-and-white banner, which states 'We ensure the highest standards in homeopathic education and practice' (The Faculty of Homeopathy 2018). In other words, the suggestion is that the students and professor are concentrating upon an experiment according to the *highest standards in homeopathic education and practice*. As a backdrop to all this, we see library bookshelves. Books are the artefacts of epistemic authority. The archetypal posed photo for an academic is against a background of books. The bookshelves suggest equivalence to an academic discipline. On the webpage we also find links to the *Homeopathy Journal*, and the next Congress, both of which confer status authority by suggesting academic equivalence. All these elements, taken collectively, constitute impression management for the purposes of creating equivalence to a medical faculty webpage.

However, there is one significant difference from a medical faculty webpage, which is a link called 'The Evidence'. Conventional medicine no longer needs to furnish 'The Evidence'. If we click that link, we are told the following.

> Homeopathy is more than 200 years old, used by tens of thousands of physicians and over 500 million people worldwide, making it one of the most popular forms of integrated medicine (1).
>
> (The Faculty of Homeopathy 2018)

The reference (1) is the following.

> Bell IR, Schwart GE. 'Adaptive network nanomedicine: an integrated model of homeopathic medicine'. (Scholar ed.) *Frontiers in Bioscience.* 2013: 5: 685–708.

We are told that the discipline is long established, which is an appeal to traditional authority. The 'tens of thousands' and '500 million' inform us that a huge epistemic community routinely confirm-structures this as a field of knowledge. The footnote refers to an academic article with *nano-technology* in the title, which suggests equivalence between homeopathy and cutting-edge natural science. The words in brackets (Scholar ed.) are unusual in a reference (I am not sure what they mean) but the suggestion is clearly that this is a scholarly article. The impression management of the scientific cutting edge is further reinforced by the title of the journal *Frontiers in Bioscience.* If the reader clicks this, they learn that this journal is listed in PubMed, the US National Library of Medicine, which again reinforces equivalence to conventional medicine.

As we read further, the problematic issue of the repeated dilution of the medicines is dealt with head-on. 'The Evidence' states:

> Scientific scepticism about homeopathy arises from its use of highly dilute medicines. There is a substantial body of research on this issue: a recent review of basic research on highly dilute homeopathic medicines found 98 replicated experiments, over 70% of replications were positive. Methods used to prepare homeopathic medicines are remarkably similar to some used in cutting-edge nanotechnology and there is growing evidence that nanoparticles play a crucial role in the action of homeopathic medicines.
>
> (The Faculty of Homeopathy 2018)

The reference to replicated experiments informs us that this discipline follows the norms of the natural sciences, while the suggested explanation for the efficacy of extreme dilution is couched in terms of nanoparticles. Again, the latter is the cutting edge of medicine. Interestingly, this introductory page does not explicitly refer to the *memory of water*, which is the conceptual tool used by homeopathic practitioners among themselves. This concept is anthropomorphic and therefore infelicitous in the natural sciences – so, best avoided in public front-stage impression management (see Goffman 1971 on impression management).

In 1988 the highly respected science journal *Nature* published an article on the subject of the memory of water. However, the title, 'Human Basophil Degranulation Triggered by Very Dilute Antiserum Against IgE' (Davenas et al. 1988), does not replicate the infelicitous words *memory of water*, although that is what it is about. At the time of publication, the decision to publish the article was considered controversial (Langone 1988). Consequently, the article was accompanied by an editorial that noted that 'There are good reasons why prudent people should, for the time being, suspend judgement' (Maddox 1988) and it stated that research went against the laws of physics and chemistry. Following publication of the article, some members of the editorial team replicated the experiments, under strenuous conditions, and concluded that there was no substantial basis to support the findings reported in the article (Maddox and Randi 1988). In terms of academic publishing this is really quite extraordinary: to publish an article, cast doubt upon the findings in the editorial and then disprove the article.

Even if the findings were ultimately proven false, the very act of publication in *Nature* was a major victory in terms of credibility for homeopathy – a point that was observed at the time (Langone 1988). The very fact of falsification (not truth) constitutes an engagement with homeopathy as a legitimate field of knowledge. After all, nobody bothers to falsify something that is totally unreasonable.

The influence of experts

The way the use of Truth infiltrates and structures society may be extremely subtle. In contemporary society extraordinary policy convergence among developed Western states has often been noted. Some of this can be explained in terms of the power of coercive institutions, such as the European Central Bank, but there is significantly more policy convergence than one might expect. Alasuutari and Rasimus (2009) analyze how Finnish parliamentarians use OECD scientific reports to justify policy decisions. These reports have no coercive force but are constantly referred to for justification of policy.

When justifying new social policy, politicians use these reports as a body of expertise that constitutes a neutral scientific grounding (Alasuutari and Rasimus 2009: 96–9). Once this science is used, innovative policies are not viewed as arbitrary, because they are backed by justifications that must be taken seriously as knowledge (Alasuutari and Rasimus 2009: 100). Justification relative to scientific reports is *evidence-based* policy, and becomes synonymous with what it means to implement *best practice* (Alasuutari and Rasimus 2009: 103). Everyone confirm-structures *best practice*. Only the unreasonable would destructure best practice.

When an expert report is referred to as justification for policy, even if the report is full of caveats and admissions of shortcomings (thus couched as fallible truth claims), there is always the temptation for the policy-maker to claim the results/advice of the reports were absolute and unambiguous. In other words, for the purposes of justification, Truth has more appeal than truth. Once all doubt is removed, disagreement is silenced as unreasonable.

Truth versus truth in practice

Characterizing fields of knowledge in terms of competition for status power runs the risk of suggesting the nihilist claim that truth is simply the will of the most powerful, thus always Truth. Here we must distinguish two aspects of power: the Y-status authority power of those who speak for the field, and the authority power-to potential of the field itself.

There is a distinction between rhetoric and the genuine attempt at truth-telling.[1] Rhetoric constitutes an orientation or strategy that refers solely to the objectives and interests of the speaker. Speakers with a rhetorical orientation will appeal to Truth (not truth) because such a foundation confers upon them greatest authority. The most extreme form of rhetoric is what Harry Frankfurt calls *bullshit* (Frankfurt 2005), which is totally instrumental action oriented towards manipulation of the other.

In contrast to rhetoric, the individual genuinely searching for local truth within a discipline will keep the power-to interests of the field (not her personal interests) to the fore. A field that operates with fallible truth will constantly self-correct and will therefore become more effective. Over a longer period of time, the pursuit of truth has more use value than the pursuit of Truth. Relative to the history of science, truth has evolutionary advantage over Truth. Because True presupposes reification, such a field of knowledge is inflexible. In contrast, because truth is more flexible than Truth, a field that is characterized by truth is highly effective at producing solutions to problems. Over time that will give it higher status authority, and this will create a positive feedback loop to the Y-status of its experts. Over time, a convergence emerges between enlightened self-interest in authority power and the power of the field itself. This is analogous to the distinction between short-term episodic interests and long-term dispositional interests in the democratic process.

In the pursuit of fallible truth the capacity to admit mistakes is considered a desirable quality. However, against that (and to qualify the above), in everyday practice, when a Y-status authority admits a mistake, there is a tendency to characterize this as failure. To take an example, when the neurosurgeon Henry Marsh decided to give a lecture entitled 'All My Worst Mistakes' to a prominent neurosurgical department in the USA, he did so under the understanding that everyone makes mistakes and that they learn from them, which is a position consistent with truth claims. When Marsh delivered the lecture to his American colleagues, 'it was met by a stunned silence and no questions were asked' (Marsh 2014: 154). Stunned silence and an absence of questions are both signs of infelicity. The audience essentially refused to engage – destructuring what he was saying. The lecture itself is an elegant example of the quest for truth, through the admission of error. However, the reaction suggests an audience more accustomed to the pursuit of Truth.

While there are sophisticated authority figures within fields of knowledge that hold fallible truth, such as Marsh above, this attitude is at variance with the social practices of everyday life. Based upon Gardner (1991), social actors act by default from their practical consciousness, as laid down in childhood socialization. As we observed, although Wollstonecraft was discursively clear that gender differences were socially constructed, she found it difficult to overcome essentialist accounts of gender. As children we are socialized into a binary view of truth. When a child is asked, *did you steal X?* the answer is binary: a Truth or a lie. In an everyday interaction, if we are asked, *is it raining?* the felicitous answer is similarly binary: *it is either raining* or *no, it is sunny*. This binary Yes/No or True/False aspect of everyday experience reinforces the natural attitude of practical knowledge, whereby even complex truth claims are presumed to be binary. According to this everyday understanding, the world is divided into absolutely *True* and absolutely *False* statements.[2] This understanding is, unfortunately, analogous to the Cartesian reified view of Truth.

While binary attitudes to Truth characterize natural attitude reasoning, it is not the case for scientific and more complex contested knowledge, where the socially constructed nature of concepts comes to the fore. Is it true that light consists of waves? As we have seen, a *yes* or *no* answer does not cover the truth of this matter. Light has characteristics of waves and particles. To take another example, when Galileo pointed his telescope towards Jupiter he saw four bright objects next to it, and decided they were *moons*. This was a revolutionary knowledge gestalt switch because it suggested that the physics of the earth and the heavens were the same (Kuhn 1985: 222). The perception of these bright objects as moons was a socially constructed judgement. Was it true that Jupiter had four moons? Well, yes, at that time this was the case. Now there are over 70, according to some counts. However, that is the simple answer. There are lots of objects orbiting Jupiter, which many scientists argue are not *really moons* but captured asteroids. The latter have irregular and retrograde orbits, which (so-called) proper moons do not. What makes a moon a moon is a matter of socially constructed interpretation.

For a long time Pluto was considered the ninth planet of the solar system. Recently the International Astronomical Union (which has Y-status authority as the official professional association of astronomers) demoted Pluto from the status of planet to dwarf planet. These judgements are temporary gestalts that reflect the development of a particular disciplinary field at any given point in time. The representatives of these fields have varying capacity to pronounce upon the truth, depending upon the Y-status authority of the field.

In contrast to the indeterminate view of truth, the binary true/false view of the world receives massive reinforcement from the prevalence of monotheism, which is entirely binary. There is the Truth of God, and the moral binary of sacred and profane. Secular societies are only of recent date, so we should not be surprised that the binaries of monotheism are a kind of default position for practical consciousness, with roots in a collective consciousness that goes back more than a millennium.

The natural attitude reinforces the foundational conception of Truth in another way. In everyday life social actors do not consider themselves as interpretative beings imposing concepts upon the world. The natural attitude entails the mistaken assumption that the world is made up of things-in-themselves. So it appears self-evident that the Truth of the matter entails finding the correct correspondence between mind-concepts and the essence of the things-in-themselves. Finding this correspondence entails a final vocabulary of Truth that describes the essence of these things-in-themselves.

Even within scientific communities, the perceived need for reification is especially strong when a field is contested, in its early stages. When fighting for the knowledge status of a new epistemic field it is very tempting for social actors to claim that their field of knowledge has discovered things-in-themselves. It takes extraordinary confidence to admit that this new field you are creating is comprised of conventions, which serve as conceptual tools that are (merely) vindicated by their usefulness at problem-solving. Once the reification of Truth becomes habit, it is very difficult to admit fallibility, and make more modest truth claims. (Well, that is the truth of the matter, for now...)

Notes

1 I have avoided calling this parrhesia as I do not wish to be sidetracked into a debate concerning what the Ancient Greeks and Foucault (2010) meant by parrhesia, and how this differs and converges with truth in modern science. For an excellent article on parrhesia, see Palacios (2018).
2 For Habermas on yes-no truth validity claims in interaction, see Habermas (1984: 273–337) and Cook (1994).

7

The fourth dimension of power:
The making of the social subject

The fourth dimension of power concerns the creation of the social ontology of social subjects. As social subjects, agents have certain predispositions, which make them more likely to structure and confirm-structure in a felicitous manner than others. Like the other dimensions of power, the fourth dimension is not inherently dominating or conducive to empowerment. Rather, it has elements of both, often as a duality. In this chapter we will focus more on the enabling and constitutive aspects. In Chapter 8, we will look at extreme forms of 4-D domination. We begin with an account of the concept of ontological security, which underpins the phenomenon of 4-D power, and then develop a historical sociological account of subject social ontology based upon Erikson, Elias, Gellner and Foucault, among others.

Ontological security

The being-in-the-world of social subjects is not given. Rather, it is constructed through the process of socialization. The being-in-the world of social subjects is inextricably tied to their practical consciousness, which creates second-nature expectations that create security in the social subject. However, when these fundamental ordering expectations are thwarted this causes a flooding through of emotions, including anxiety, shame and anger (Giddens 1984: 51–64).

Based upon the psychology of Erik Erikson, the foundation of ontological security is the establishment of routine, which begins with the infant's relationship with its primary carer. When the child is an infant, she experiences anxiety at letting go of the mother's breast, as she has no idea if it will return. Her first achievement in subject formation is the establishment of confidence in the return of the breast, which empowers her to let go of the breast without undue anxiety. In the words of Erikson: 'The infant's first social achievement, then, is his willingness to let the mother out of sight without undue anxiety or rage, because she has become *an inner certainty* as well as *outer predictability*' (Erikson 1995: 222; italics added).

The confluence between inner certainty and outer predictability is central to ontological security. As interpretative beings, our being-in-the-world is tied to our capacity to link together expectation with external occurrence. One of the favourite games of infants concerns object permanence. When an object is held in front of the child, entirely visible, and then passed behind something larger (for instance, a pillow) and returns to sight, the child expresses endless delight in the reinforcement of the increasing certainty that the momentary disappearance of an object does not mean its dissolution. She develops practical knowledge that objects may be out of sight but do not vanish into thin air. The foundation of ontological security is an inner certainty concerning the continued existence of the world-out-there, both social and material.

Our existence relative to the world-out-there entails the continual monitoring and making present of external reality. This is tied into our capacity to link memory with experience. The child has a memory of the breast disappearing but always returning. Learning object permanence is both an act of interpretation and memory. When the infant closes her eyes, her memory enables her to retain confidence in the fact that the world-out-there will still be there when she opens them again. This trust in the world-out-there is the inner certainty fundamental to ontological security (Giddens 1984: 53). In some instances, through separation at an early age, this process is disturbed and the person is left with a deep existential anxiety. This feeling of inner certainty can be broken later in life, with catastrophic results (Chapter 8).

The use of the past to order the present-flowing-into-the-future entails a capacity to order time and space. While the generalized capacity to order time and space is a universal property of cognition, as in Kant, the actual form that this ordering of time-space takes is variable relative to the society in question, as argued by Durkheim (2008). In highly ritualized societies, time and space are usually cyclical, while in modern Western societies time and space are predominantly linear. In the former societies, ontological security was associated with routine repetition of events with a sacred quality, while in modernity the future and space are predominantly ordered according to linear measured time and space.

The pre-linguistic child does not discursively construct a theory concerning the absence or presence of her mother's breast, nor about object permanence. Rather, this knowledge is part of her taken-for-granted reality. This inner certainty constitutes a default natural attitude, which defines the ontological predispositions: who we are. It is second-nature, which actors experience as internal to themselves, thus as if it were their first nature.

While the natural attitude suggests that the world-out-there comes ready-made with concepts attached, in fact, that naming-of-the-world is reflective of the person. Following Husserl (1991: 111), external reality is inseparable from a transcendental ego that organizes the world in a particular manner through interpretation. In some respects, this ego can be compared to a hinge (Guenther 2013) that ties together external reality with internal acts of interpretation. As we shall see in Chapter 8, in solitary confinement this link between external and internal personality can be broken, with devastating consequences for the personality structure. That hinge is constituted and reinforced by felicitous interaction, and avoidance of infelicitous interaction. Consequently, the self develops a *psychic attachment*, to borrow Butler's (1997: 8) phrase, to its practical knowledge and being-in-the-world.

Our practical consciousness knowledge of the world is inseparable from our being-in-the-world. In many instances these interpretative acts that order the world are a source of great emotional commitment. This is most obvious with regard to sacred objects. The person who believes that Jerusalem is sacred does not have this as knowledge separate from their being-in-the-world. However, to them, it appears as an external fact about Jerusalem for which they are willing to die. This emotional commitment constitutes an inescapable part of their disposition as a social agent.

The predispositions that come from social ontology also apply to many acts of ordering, including time and space. The fact that social actors of the early modern period started seeing the world in terms of measured time and space had important consequences. In the pre-modern feudal world, political power was largely based upon the robin principle. Essentially, robin-space is circular, becoming of less and less significance, the farther the robin flies from the nest. To translate this into measured-space ways of thinking: a metre of space near the nest is equal to the next two metres, which is then equal to the next four metres, and so on, until the space loses equivalence altogether, as it becomes valueless. In the feudal world, the human equivalent of the robin's nest was a castle, fortified city and sacred site. In a pre-modern world of city-states, and feudal fiefdoms, the lands far from the centre were not equivalent to the lands close to the main square. Their maps reflected this, with the scale growing smaller and smaller the farther the cartographer ventured from wherever they regarded as their centre of the world. Slowly, from the sixteenth onwards, space became measured space. One metre of land in the centre of Paris and one metre along the border with Spain became equivalent. Maps were drawn to scale, and wars were fought along measured borders. Cartographers mapped the world to an invariant measured scale. Once this appeared as the natural-order-of-things, social subjects were willing to give their lives for these borders.

From the perspective of 4-D, practical consciousness meaning is tied into the essence of the personality. A young child sees the human body analogously to the robin principle. Because it is the face that interacts with them (carries out communication), it is the centre of the body, with the limbs and extremities added on. Visually the face appears disproportionately larger than the extremities of body. In modern Western culture the child learns that this view of the human body is considered infelicitous when drawn by older children. This measured scale of the human body becomes a fact about the world-out-there.

The capacity of practical consciousness to enable ontological security constitutes an integral part of the personality. The level of inner certainty, and thus the level of ontological security, is not the same for all people. Some social actors have a strong sense of ontological security, which produces a highly secure personality type, while others are beset by anxiety and doubt. Insecurity occurs when the inner certainty and the world-out-there are out of synchronicity.

The reaction to undermining of inner certainty manifests itself also in ways to combat it, which include anger and denial. The young child expresses anger at the physical world-out-there that fails to conform to their inner certainty but, as they learn their powerlessness with respect to the world-out-there, they reserve that anger for the social-world-out-there, which they can influence. However, some adults retain the childlike quality of getting angry at the physical world when it does not conform. The condition of autism is a situation in which these predictive powers have somehow failed to establish themselves, so the world appears as virtually random, and this absence of order invokes frequent anger and frustration (Sinha et al. 2014).

The relationships with the natural-world-out-there and the social-world-out-there are significantly similar and different in a number of respects. The social world and the natural world are both predictable to some extent. The mother's breast disappearing and reappearing has an affinity with object permanence. However, the child learns that the laws of the social world and those of the natural world are not equally reliable. Part of successful socialization is learning to cope with the slight contingency around human behaviour. However, there are very real limits to this toleration for divergence. Unpredictability of interaction triggers ontological insecurity, followed by a display of frustration, anger or similar emotion.

In what Giddens terms *critical situations* the individual encounters moments where there is a radical disjuncture between inner certainty and outer predictability (Giddens 1984: 61). Such critical situations occur when others fail to behave in a predictable manner. Referring back to 3-D conflict, this is where interpretative horizons collide. There is significant difference between the depth of a conflict that takes place within shared structures (1-D) and conflicts that expose radical differences in structural reproduction (2-D conflict). In disagreement upon structural reproduction the inner certainties concerning the natural-order-of-things are not shared. Part of what makes these conflicts deeper and more intractable is that they create ontological insecurity. If a practical consciousness inner certainty is not shared, the perceived inappropriately structuring other is a fundamental threat to the natural-order-of-things and to the self. Deep conflicts have a deep emotional content (Heaney 2011) that creates a predisposition towards violence, as we saw with respect to 2-D conflict.

Language is public, and is reproduced collaboratively, through structuration and confirm-structuration. The transcendental ego's interpretative framework is a social-constructed *a priori*, constituted through interaction with others. While each person may feel individual, their interpretative framework is constituted by frames of reference that are public. Concepts and frames that do not find resonance with others are filtered out in response to infelicity. The transcendental ego is the product of interaction; while social subjects may feel individual, they are not monadic.

In the case of destructuration, or disconfirm-structuration, the response usually results in the demise of that social structure and reformation of the self. However, social actors have agency. They can create new collaborative spaces where they construct oppositional frames of reference. Such social actors will be perceived of as *deviant* relative to the majority but they may create a minority group that reproduces this different way of being-in-the-world. This results in a minority whose subculture constitutes a back region (Goffman 1971) where ontological security can be found, as resistance to dominant ideology. As we shall see later, the creation of such subfields of social practice is an integral part of coping with extreme domination. In such a context, resistance is about maintaining the right-to-be-in-the-world.

Ontological insecurity: breaching experiments

Ontological insecurity is a response to a disjuncture between inner certainty and outer reality. Breaching experiments performed by Garfinkel and by Milgram demonstrate how ontological security is implicated in everyday structural reproduction. They are artificial ways of creating *critical* situations and revealing the ontological foundations of 4-D power.

Garfinkel took everyday situations, which are usually unproblematic but have within them the seeds of gestalt ambiguity, and artificially made the process of structuration and confirm-structuration go awry (Heritage 1984). In everyday life the greeting *How are you?* is a form of phatic communion. Structuration of phatic communion entails ritualized communication where the literal meaning of the words is suspended in favour of renewing social bonds. Phatic communion constitutes an acknowledgement of someone as having authority status worthy of interaction, not simply a bodily presence or an extension of whatever job they are doing. In terms of outcomes, or immediate power-to, it is purposeless. It is a form of power-with, without immediate power-to.

In contrast to phatic communion, in some situations *How are you?* is a genuine request concerning someone else's wellbeing, especially if the interacting other is known to the speaker as unwell. In a medical consultation the objective of *How are you?* is directed at power-to cure of a malady.

In the phatic communion gestalt meaning of *How are you?* the correct confirm-structuration response is *Fine thanks, how are you?* However, in the second instance the response can be a complex one, detailing emotional, physical and other aspects of the person's present condition. To the competent social actor there is nothing incomprehensible about either interpretation. Yet, if the usage is incorrect, relative to context, the reaction is remarkably strong, indicating ontological insecurity.

As part of a breaching experiment Garfinkel instructed students to take the literal interpretation of *How are you?* in a context where the phatic communion interpretation is the correct one. The following is a sample dialogue.

> The victim waved his hand cheerily.
>> How are you?
>> How am I in regard to what? My health, my finances, my school work, my peace of mind, my...?
>> (Red in the face and suddenly out of control) Look! I was just trying to be polite. Frankly, I don't give a damn how you are.
>
> (Garfinkel 1984: 44)

The fact that the victim waves his hand cheerily alerts us to the fact that this is a casual encounter – phatic communion structuration. This is made explicit by the response, *Look! I was just trying to be polite.* The response, asking for criteria of wellbeing, is an act of destructuration to what should have been a statement/request that routinely is confirm-structured as phatic communion. The *Red in the face and suddenly out of control* complexion of the other expresses a sense of frustration and anger that inner certainty and outer predictability are out of synch.

Slippage of meaning often occurs when a response is unexpected. The initial structurer is free to accept the new meaning as valid. Typically, this happens when someone structures the phatic communion meaning but the other is manifestly unwell and decides to unburden problems. If accepted as valid, we remain at 1-D structured power-with. It is power-with because the purpose of phatic communion is the expression of solidarity. If the interaction also achieves something beyond that, such as help with the malady of the second actor, it is simultaneously power-to.

In some of these critical interactions the response was concern, coupled with a request about the other's wellbeing. However, this is not necessarily a shift in meaning but can be a way for the responding actor to find an explanation for the unpredictability. An instance of this was the response 'What's the matter with you? Are you sick?' (Garfinkel 1984: 43). This could be a shift in meaning or a low-conflict strategy to exclude the other as unreasonable. Sickness of some kind is used to explain why the other lapsed temporarily into unreasonableness or to indicate willingness to move beyond phatic communion.

Milgram performed a breaching experiment that violated the norms of behaviour in a subway. One of the practical knowledge rules of subway behaviour is that seats are taken on a first-come, first-served basis. Milgram instructed the student experimenters to request seats from random individuals, without giving justification for the request. In 56% of cases the person got up and gave her seat, and in another 12.3% they slid over, while 31.7% refused (Milgram 2010a: 37). This bore out a generalized propensity towards authority, consistent with his famous electric-shock authority experiments (Milgram 2010b). Upon completion the students were asked for their reaction to taking part in the experiment. Their responses were revealing.

> [They] reported that when standing in front of a subject they felt anxious, tense, and embarrassed. Frequently, they were unable to vocalize the request for a seat and had to withdraw. They sometimes feared they were the centre of attention of the car and were often unable to look directly at the subject. Once having made the request and received the seat, they sometimes felt a need to enact behaviour that would make the request appear justified (e.g., mimicking illness, some even felt faint).
>
> (Milgram 2010a: 38)

This anxiety, distress and embarrassment are typical signs of ontological insecurity. Some were simply unable to carry through with the action, and of those that were successful, some mitigated their unreasonable behaviour by feigning sickness, while others were not feigning but genuinely felt faint.

This suggests that the desire for ontological security forms a significant barrier to the violation of norms. Once an actor has been socialized within a certain taken-for-granted order of things, this creates a fundamental security of self, which is jeopardized by any attempt at structural change. This constitutes a fundamental 4-D ontological predisposition towards the status quo. As structural reproduction is interactive (structuration plus confirm-structuration), the desire for ontological security creates an underlying 4-D predisposition towards collaborative structural reproduction. This means there is an underlying 4-D aversion to 2-D structural conflict.

Two models of the social construction of social subjects

Let us explore how different social ontology emerges in relation with social order. There are two ways of thinking about the development of social subjects. The most obvious proceeds from discursive consciousness. Essentially, the elites of society deliberately mould social subjects by controlling their conduct. This is a top-down view. From a sociological perspective this misses something fundamental: the practical consciousness processes that created the elite social subjects who consider these models felicitous in the first place. It also misses why the less powerful often embrace their 4-D subjectification. Let us begin with a bottom-up perspective, then top-down. These models dovetail neatly as both have push and pull factors and are separate only analytically.

Competition for self-restraint

Elias describes a dual process of sociogenesis and psychogenesis, whereby the psychological social formation of a social subject reflects the process of formation of social order (see Elias 1995: xiii; Mennell 1989: 50). Elias argued that modernity was associated with a massive internalization of self-restraint, which mirrors the development of a social order characterized by centripetal forces of complex interdependence between social actors.

Elias' work focussed upon social transformations that took place in Western Europe, which he describes in terms of the *civilizing process*. The ethnocentric implications of this are so obvious that we do not need to restate them. While making use of some of his ideas, we demote the theoretical centrality of the concept of a *civilizing process* in preference for *internalization of self-restraint in pursuit of status authority*. We will start with a non-European example of what Elias had in mind, as theorized by Erikson, in order to overcome any ethnocentric implications.

In our selective *use of* Elias, we are using his work in a critically reflective manner. As Foucault observed with regard to his use of Nietzsche, the best tribute you can pay to an author is 'to use it, to deform, to make it groan and protest. And if commentators say that I am being unfaithful to Nietzsche, that is absolutely of no interest' (Foucault 1980: 54)

Erikson, the formation of social ontological predispositions

In his account of the formation of ontological security and the self, Erikson emphasizes that no society, whether modern or traditional, can 'afford to be arbitrary or anarchic'. As a consequence, 'they cannot afford to create a community of wild eccentrics, of infantile characters, or of neurotics' (Erikson 1995: 168). Every society is a complex order of interdependence and, consequently, requires specific predispositions of social subjects that constitute that society. The characteristics that these people display will reflect the needs of that society as an interdependent whole.

Erikson compares two Native American tribes, with very different characteristics: the Sioux and Yurok. The Sioux inhabited the plains, roaming widely, and constructed spatial concepts consistent with centrifugal mobility. Their interpretative horizon, especially their sense of time and space, was shaped by following roaming herds of buffalo. Their expansive view of space brought them into contact with shifting enemy bands and, more latterly (1960s), with mainstream US society. The main personality characteristic of the roaming Sioux was generosity, openness to strangers and a comparatively high level of spontaneity. This outward-looking tendency meant that, at the time of Erikson's studies, the traditions of Sioux society were in rapid decline through assimilation.

In contrast, the Yurok lived in a narrow mountainous and densely forested valley, with a river running through it, which provided their only form of animal protein – fish. They restricted themselves to this narrow valley and anyone who wished to go beyond this limited space was considered 'crazy' or of 'ignoble birth' (Erikson 1995: 150). In the terminology used here, any attempt at outward movement, or travelling, was perceived of as infelicitous, and would be interpreted as a sign of profanity. In terms of social dynamics, the main social forces of Yurok society were centripetal, tending inward. As a consequence, at the time of Erikson's research, this society was able to preserve its main traditions.

In Yurok society, a high emphasis was placed upon self-restraint, autonomy and cleanliness. The latter took the form of emphasizing the importance of keeping fluids apart. Consequently, urination in the river was taboo. Training contributing to internalized discipline and self-restraint began *in utero*. The pregnant mother ate little, while she continued doing hard physical labour, which prevented the foetus from being too comfortable. It was a norm for pregnant women to rub their abdomen in order to keep the foetus awake. After birth, the baby was seldom allowed to rest and early weaning was encouraged (Erikson 1995: 159). Once the child could eat solid food, he was socialized into a strict discipline. The Yurok meal was 'a veritable ceremony of self-restraint. The child was admonished never to grab food in haste, never to take it without asking for it, always to eat slowly, and never to ask for second helpings...' (Erikson 1995: 160). When using a spoon the child was told never to heap it too much, and how to hold it *correctly*, according to social norms. Children's stories consisted of fables that emphasized the terrible consequences of lack of self-restraint. For instance, according to a fable, the buzzard's baldness is the effect of the bird being impatient and greedy, therefore putting its whole head into a dish of too-hot soup (Erikson 1995: 160).

The Yurok social subject emerges as highly self-restrained, suited to their social and physical situation. They were confined in space, so the predisposition to wander was dysfunctional. They were highly predictable in a society where mutual dependence was high. For their main mode of food production, they were fishermen who had to sit patiently on the banks of the river. Fishing requires self-discipline, while buffalo hunting requires speed. The emphasis upon cleanliness meant that they did not contaminate their river or food source.

Once a year the Yurok dammed the river to catch a large number of salmon in one go. After that annual event a feast was held, where self-restraint was momentarily relaxed. This served as a safety valve, acknowledging that with repression there is also resistance, which requires an outlet. Echoing the dominant ideology thesis, this was a way for society to release tension in a controlled manner. It is analogous to carnivals in the feudal world where the peasantry and servants were permitted to express their frustration with the hierarchy. In the modern world, sports events serve this same function, with restrained social subjects taking pleasure in physicality and a contained level of violence. Jokes are another aspect of this safety-valve mechanism (Billig 2005).

In summary, in Erikson-Freudian terms, the super-ego ideals of the Yurok are perfectly shaped relative to the social structure of the society in question. In terms of this theory, these self-restrained individuals felt ontologically secure relative to the conditions of possibility that were consonant with the demands of their social order. Their sense of the reasonable and unreasonable amounted to character predispositions that were ideally suited to their circumstances. Yet resistance occurred and there were social institutions where this could be expressed.

In terms of power, these social actors had a 4-D social ontology that was enabling (power-to) of their way of life, and resulted in solidarity (power-with). At first, the child who was, for instance, told to hold his spoon correctly might experience this as a high level of external social control, with parents exercising power-over the minute details of his bodily movements.

However, over time, parental agential exercises of power-over became internalized into the social ontology of the child, rendering their structuration and confirm-structuration felicitous.

A high level of self-control was individually constraining, yet simultaneously enabling, delivering power-with and power-to. Self-restraint constituted a normatively desirable disposition that conferred Y-status authority. The top-down admonition of parents would, in all probability, be replaced by desire, linked to status. Not everyone would have been equally adept at self-control. This would have given those with the greatest level of restraint higher social status relative to those with less restraint. People who heaped their spoon too much would inspire feelings of disgust, while those who got it 'just right' would be felicitous, and therefore have higher authority status. The race for status would, as an unintentional effect, lead to a society with a high number of restrained individuals whose ontological dispositions were functional to the survival of that society. In this way, what starts as an admonition to a child to engage in a purely conventional practice leads to the creation of predispositions that are neither arbitrary nor trivial, once the purpose of the norms of that society are understood. In terms of agency, self-restraint is the road to authority status, thus desirable.

The historical transformation of European social ontology through the pursuit of status

In the work of Foucault, Elias and Weber there is an implicit suggestion that the formation of self-restraint is a uniquely Western modernizing phenomenon. We have begun with Erikson's account of the Yurok to show that this process is by no means unique to either modernity or to Western society.

As we are about to see, Elias' account of the development of European self-restraint is analogous with Erikson's account of the Yurok. Elias argues that pre-modern feudal Europe was centrifugal and highly spontaneous, while modernization was centripetal and tending towards self-restraint. This mirrors fairly closely the contrast between the Sioux and Yurok. Consequently, we resist any implicit suggestion that the process was a uniquely European civilizing process. Similarly, if we look to Japan, the story of the formal use of chopsticks and the development of the tea ceremony are part of analogous stories of self-restraint, thus a civilizing process, in Elias' terminology.

A variation upon this theme is the hypothesis that overall there is not an increase in total levels of self-restraint but, rather, a shift in their nature. Perhaps the Sioux were not more self-restrained than the Yurok, just differently restrained. Similarly, the restraints of modernity are different from those of what went before. This entails a shift in self-restraint, though maybe not an overall increase in density. Feudal society had complex restraints associated with honour that declined with modernity. I do not emphasize the restraints of feudal society because the contemporary condition of 4-D is my focus.

The process that I am about to describe is European in its orientation but, from the above, it should be clear that this does not represent an ethnocentric orientation on my part. I invite readers from other societies to reflect upon analogous processes in their history.

Differences between feudal and modern social ontology

Garfinkel's and Milgram's breaching experiments made visible norms linked to ontological security. Corresponding to the breaching experiments, certain modes of behaviour in the past appear to us, relative to our social ontology, as infelicitous, embarrassing, shameful and of low status.

Elias researched books of etiquette from 1200 up until the 1960s. The early books were directed at the upper classes of society when visiting court. What is surprising is the extent to which some of the advice given suggests the prevalence of social norms that would inspire shame and embarrassment today. Take the following early examples of advice on manners.

> A man who clears his throat when he eats and one who blows his nose in the tablecloth are both ill-bred, I assure you.
>
> (Elias 1995: 69)

> Do not scrape the back of your throat with your bare hand while eating: but if you have to, do it politely with your coat.
>
> (Elias 1995: 70)

> Before you sit down, make sure your seat has not been fouled.
>
> (Elias 1995: 105)

To the modern reader this advice appears extraordinary, especially in light of the information that this was directed at high society – largely young nobility. As a thought experiment, imagine a breaching experiment where these behaviours were recreated. The contemporary observer would feel both inner revulsion and would assume the other has low status. Revulsion and rejection would be coupled with a perceived difference in authority status.

Over historical time there is feedback from the avoidance of low-status behaviour to an actual transformation of the ontological predispositions of social subjects. Elias' description of spitting is particularly informative in this regard. In the Middle Ages advice on spitting included the following injunctions: 'Do not spit over or on the table. Do not spit into the basin when you wash your hands, but beside it' (Elias 1995: 125). Notice that both pieces of advice assume that the person is going to spit. Moving forwards in time, spitting should be done outdoors on the ground and then trodden upon, or into a cloth and so on (Elias 1995: 126–8). In the nineteenth century and the early part of the twentieth century the phenomenon of the spittoon, a bowl for spit, still existed and was found in public places, including trams. After World War II the spittoon gradually disappeared from view in Western Europe, although as late as the 1960s buses still had 'No Spitting' notices (Mennell 1989: 40).

What is absolutely fascinating is that up until the relatively modern period, which saw the demise of the spittoon, spitting was considered a *natural function*, thus unavoidable. It was considered equivalent to urination, or defecation (Mennell 1989: 40). However, unlike the latter bodily functions, spitting is no longer considered a natural function. A person who spits is told *not to spit*. They are not advised how to spit in a more mannerly way. This raises the interesting question of the extent to which what appear to be natural functions turn out to be social in origin (Elias 1995: 131) – the relevance for essentialism and gender construction is obvious.

If we return to 3-D reification, there is always the desire to make your field, in which you excel, more than mere convention. Part of the reason for this is the theoretically mistaken everyday perception that equates conventionality with arbitrariness. The qualities that an elite group so carefully cultivates within a field in order to set themselves apart from the rest are not attributed to hours of hard work devoted to arcane practices, rather to an innate quality of distinction and refinement that the social subject possesses.

The desire to make your cultural status more than a set of learned conventions is beautifully expressed by Pierre Francastel, a great culinary aesthete, quoted by Bourdieu in *Distinction*.

> *Taste* must not be confused with *gastronomy*. Whereas taste is the *natural gift* of recognising and loving perfection, gastronomy is the set of rules which govern the *education* of taste. Gastronomy is to taste as grammar and literature are to the literary sense. ... Not everyone is a gourmet; that is why we need gastronomes. We must look upon gastronomes as we look upon pedagogues in general: they are sometimes intolerable pedants but they have their uses. The belong to the *lower, modest order* ... There is such a thing as bad taste ... and persons of *refinement* know this *instinctively*. For those who do not, rules are needed.
>
> (Bourdieu 1989: 68; italics original)

In this exposition gastronomy signifies the process of learning the rules of the field. However, those who embody the true excellence of the field have *taste*, which is a *natural gift*. Unlike the *lower, modest order*, they have their sense of refinement *instinctively*. Francastel believes that the cultural characteristics that he has acquired are somehow innate. From the perspective of his natural attitude, he feels that these qualities are intrinsic to his being. His social status is not separable from his persona. Even if he is sincere in his experience, this is reification. From the perspective of 4-D social ontology, he accurately describes how he differs from the novice in the field, for whom these qualities are not part of their second-nature being-in-the-world, and for whom the qualities of the field are still an external discursive consciousness effort.

Class status competition and state formation

The process of internalization of restraint was linked to the sociogenic process of transformation of power structures. In the early feudal period centrifugal forces dominated. Political units were small, and constantly breaking apart. Louis VI, who reigned from 1108–39, though nominally king of a much larger territory, effectively controlled only his own family lands, the Duchy of Francia, which centred on Paris and Orléans (Mennell 1989: 62). In this feudal age, kings sought feudal tribute through a complex chain down the feudal aristocracy. Essentially, aristocrats would give tribute in exchange for control of a given territory. As that tribute included soldiers, these aristocrats had their own armies, in addition to powers of taxation, weights and measures and so on. They were mini-states, within states. When the king was short of funds or soldiers, he would grant rights and lands down the feudal structure, which dissipated control from the centre to the peripheries. However, by the twelfth century this process of fragmentation had reached saturation. There was a limit to how many lands and rights could be granted, so there emerged a noble class without fiefdoms of their own, who started to become courtiers.

The gradual emergence of centripetal forces within Western Europe can be reduced to three elements that came together. First, the *monopoly mechanism*, whereby there was a gradual concentration of the means of violence and taxation in the hands of a single ruler, which allowed for the expansion and survival of larger territorial units. Second, there occurred the *royal mechanism*, whereby the internal balance of power within states became centred within courts. Third, a tendency towards *the transformation of private into public monopolies took place*, whereby rights moved from aristocrats to the centre (Mennell 1989: 66).

In competition between units, be they states or companies, there is a tendency for a slight advantage to become magnified through competition, leading to elimination of the less effective units, until finally a monopoly is established (Elias 1995: 347). During the later feudal age, and into the modern period, cities with thriving merchant and manufacturing classes became major repositories of material resources. Commerce requires predictability; merchants and manufacturers were opposed to the complex random system of feudal levies. They preferred centralized royal taxation, which made profit and loss book-keeping possible. As observed not only by Elias but also by Spruyt (1994) and Tilly (1990), centralized taxation from cities gave monarchs an advantage over their feudal competitors. This was accompanied by changes in the technology of warfare, a move away from mounted knights to mass armies backed by gun and cannon. Gradually, courts militarily defeated and subsumed the previously warring aristocracy. This allowed for the emergence of relatively large sovereign territorial states. As Spruyt (1994) argues, as late as 1500 the European political map was still fragmented into lots of multifarious political units, which included city states, the Hanseatic League, the Roman Empire, the Catholic Church and various dukedoms and earldoms, all with different powers. By 1648 the main signatories of the treaty of Westphalia were all sovereign territorial states. These states had the advantage over their competitors by virtue of a dual monopoly: that of taxation and violence.

The monopoly of violence by the state made possible the internal pacification of territorial units. It was no longer possible for private individuals to use violence, as warriors, to acquire lands for themselves. In Europe this started a process, which took hundreds of years, whereby the annual death rate by murder declined from approximately 100 per 100,000 to 1 per 100,000 (Pinker 2013: 75–6). However, what allowed this to happen was not simply the physical monopoly of violence (sociogenesis) but a change in character (psychogenesis). As we shall later see, this decline in everyday murder did not result in a decline in mortality in war.

The establishment of the monopoly mechanism meant transfer of power inward, which is epitomized by Louis XIV's claim that he was the state (Mennell 1989: 74). However, the centring of power around the figure of the king entailed the apparent paradox that the more powerful the king became, the more dependent upon others he was (Elias 1995: 349). The centralization of power meant the emergence of a complex chain of mutual interdependence. In the beginning this meant that a large court became the centre of power.

If we look at the frontispiece of the first edition of Hobbes' *Leviathan* (1914] [1651]) we see the figure of the king as this singular being, whose body is made up of the body politic. This suggests top-down power but, according to Elias, what in fact happened during this period was that the court maintained its pre-eminence as a kind of balancing act. Not only was the French court made up of competing aristocrats; it was full of upwardly mobile bourgeoisie. Similarly, in England, the king became more and more dependent upon parliament (Mennell 1989: 75–7).

Simultaneous is the move from private to public monopolies. This is most obvious with regard to violence. Both armies and policing duties went from private means to public ownership in the hands of the state. In the pre-modern world all bureaucracy was private. The court was an extension of the royal household. However, pretty quickly that became cumbersome, so a publicly owned and paid-for bureaucracy emerged. The private income of the monarchy became distinguished from the state budget. In the nineteenth century, as power shifted away from the aristocracy and towards the bourgeoisie, the process of moving from private to public monopoly accelerated markedly.

The move from private to public happened in lots of small ways, all of which were symptomatic of sociogenesis, with psychogenetic effects. A public postal service emerged, rather than private rights to deliver post. Only the state could set weights and measures. Instead of a multiplicity of privately levied dues, a centralized taxation system developed. In economic life the bourgeoisie started to distinguish their public economic activities from their private economic activities. Companies open to public scrutiny emerged. The bourgeois home became a private space, while the company was a public space, albeit privately owned. A division arose between work, which was public, and the private life of the family.

Although private overall, in the architecture of the bourgeois home we can see the physical representation of the development a public/private distinction. Typically, in the nineteenth century the bourgeois home had a public hallway, a parlour and formal dining-room. The larger and more numerous these front-stage spaces were, the higher the status. Concealed at the back, or in the basement, were the kitchen, utility rooms and a private back entrance. Even more privately, upstairs were the bedrooms and bathroom. In terms of psychogenesis, or social ontology, the bourgeois social subject developed a strong sense of the public/private distinction, which mirrored the way they lived. In the late nineteenth century and the first half of the twentieth century this style of living moved down the social scale, eventually reaching the lower-middle classes, whose houses were miniature bourgeois homes.

The changes in the structures of power had profound effects upon behaviour and subject formation. The feudal knight had a predisposition towards glory and grandiosity. He gloried in battle and was at ease with blood spilled over him. He lived life for status that made him visible both in apparel and in lifestyle. In Elias this appears as spontaneity, while I would theorize this as different set of status restraints. I imagine it was hard work to dress outlandishly, appear fearless, duel anyone who offended your honour and so on.

In court society, knightly-status temperament was inappropriate. The court was a place of intrigue, cliques and manipulation. To be a successful courtier you had to be aware of how others perceived you. Insulting the wrong person or upsetting an alliance could have devastating consequences. This required skill in self-control and understanding of how others perceive you (Mennell 1989: 85).

Courtiers watched for conspiracies and formed alliances, trying not to put a foot wrong. This image of the person is similar to Goffman's account of front-stage self-restraint and impression management (Goffman 1971). In the rivalry of the courts the aristocracy continually tried to set themselves apart from the rising bourgeoisie. In competition with the bourgeoisie, aristocracy tried to excel at what they did best: living an elegant lifestyle, thus showing the bourgeoisie up as having wealth without style. For them, having elaborate carriages and butlers was not a superfluous luxury but a necessity, a restraint, in order to prove their essential reified superiority to the class below them, rising hard on their heels. Many aristocrats sold lands in order to finance their status lifestyle, which led to their economic demise. The attempt to set themselves apart also took the form of having increasingly complex manners. Over historical time, the world of status interaction changed from one in which people ate with their hands, used daggers and drank from tankards (essentially small buckets) to a world with complex silver place settings, fine porcelain and delicate crystal.

The bourgeoisie did not simply acquiesce in accepting this display of distinction by the aristocracy. They rose to the challenge, aped aristocratic manners and excelled in internalized self-restraint. Gradually the bourgeoisie became self-restrained and followed the fashions of complex modes of behaviour.

The upper class developed fields of complex high-status behaviour to differentiate themselves from the class immediately below them. Unfamiliarity with the latest manners became infelicitous and a sign of status inferiority. Complex modes of structural reproduction become known as *civilized*, which had a normative component of superiority; the upper classes are civilized while the lower classes are not. However, the lower classes did not acquiesce in this negative judgement. They imitated the (purportedly) civilized and so made themselves civilized. During the later modern period, the civilizing race extended down the social scale, moving to the working classes and overseas to the European colonies. Alternatively, as resistance, some minorities created their own subcultures.

It is important to understand that this downward movement of self-restraint was not an external imposition by the elites upon the masses. Quite the contrary, it stemmed from classes attempting to empower themselves. The bourgeoisie comprising the merchant class wanted to have the same status authority as the aristocracy, so they voluntarily internalized these restraints. They imposed this power upon themselves, including with regard to sexuality (see Foucault 1981). Self-subjectification (Foucault 1982) gave them high status authority distinction. However, the next segments of the bourgeoisie – first the manufacturers, then the professionals – did not simply accept status inferiority, but imitated whatever manners conferred status. This competitive process for distinction-cum-restraint continued right down the scale and, eventually, culminated in working-class children perceiving the cultural capital of their teachers and internalizing that in order to get ahead. This is a dynamic process where everybody exercises agency. As observed by Bourdieu:

> It follows that all the groups involved in the race, whatever rank they occupy, cannot conserve their position, their rarity, their rank except by running to keep their distance from those immediately behind them, thus jeopardising the difference which distinguishes the group immediately in front; or, to put it another way, by aspiring to possess that which the group ahead already have, and which they themselves will have, but later.
>
> (Bourdieu 1989: 161)

Self-restraint and interdependence

In both Elias' account of the internalization of restraint of the Western middle classes and Erikson's characterization of the self-restraint of the Yurok, these processes are functional to the social order in question. The self-restraint of the Yurok made for good fishermen, while the restraint of the modern social subject creates a subject predisposition suitable for living in a modern complex interdependent society.

Elias provides a graphic depiction of the contrast of functionality of subjective predispositions and social orders by comparing a country road in a simple warrior society of the eleventh century with a modern highway (Elias 1995: 446). The former is a lonely place with few vehicles and no public lighting. The demarcation between the verge and surrounding woods is indistinct. As a thought experiment, imagine that you are travelling on horseback, the light is fading and sleet is falling, obscuring your vision. Peering into the distance, you perceive another figure on horseback. What do you do? You either make sure your weapon is ready and/or you prepare to gallop off the road at a moment's notice. In other words, the appropriate social ontology is one with a predisposition for fight or flight: a capacity for rapid reaction in response to contingent, unforeseen situations.

In contrast, imagine you are travelling on a six-lane highway, around a major metropolis, approaching an intersection that splits into three, with a multitude of roundabouts and spaghetti junctions. You are travelling at 100 km per hour, articulated trucks on both the inner and outer lanes, and you need to change lane in preparation for the next intersection. Is a fight-or-flight temperament appropriate to this situation? Certainly not; self-restraint linked to foresight is the order of the day. You moderate your speed sufficiently to slip behind a truck in order to change lane, as required. If you find yourself unable to enter the correct lane, you plan to take the next roundabout to bring you back to where you were. Massive foresight and restraint is required of the modern driver. Of course, every once in while a driver cannot tolerate the self-control required and gives vent to so-called 'road rage'.

Education and the Panopticon as 4-D

In addition to competition for status through self-restraint, from the nineteenth century onwards the state took upon itself responsibility for the mass socialization of citizens through public education and, in the case of recalcitrance, the use of correctional facilities. This was a top-down pressure, or overt control, which then spawned its own self-subjectifying upward pull through competition for educational qualifications.

Part of the impetus for this was the emergence of modern nation-states. Gellner (1983) argued that nationalism arose out of conditions specific to the modern world. Nationalism is the belief 'that the political and the national unit should be congruent' (Gellner 1983: 1). A nation is defined by a shared culture, combined with recognition of others as belonging to the same nation (Gellner 1983: 7). Nationalists believe that the political unit and shared culture should be isomorphic.

In terms of world history, nationalism is actually a fairly odd belief: a social construction of recent date. In a traditional society, the culture of the ruling class and that of a lower class were usually not the same. In a traditional social order a small literate class shared a broad high culture. In such a society the idea that all of society should become literate and share the same culture would have been an idle dream (Gellner 1983: 17). The needs of industrial society changed all that. All of a sudden there was a requirement for a large mobile workforce who were literate and numerate. In the pre-industrial society different languages and dialects were spoken everywhere. In contrast, large territorial states, with industrial economies, required a workforce who spoke the same language. For instance, in the

UK of the nineteenth century mass education required the homogenization of peoples who spoke Cornish, Welsh, Scots Gaelic and Irish into a single English-speaking workforce. Mass education meant socialization and homogenization of a diverse population. As a consequence, society moved from socialization of the farmstead, apprenticeship and all the motley places of socialization of the pre-modern world to state-sponsored education. This process was far wider than simply language. It involved the ordering of everyday socialization. As comprehensively explored by Dean (2010), this involved a new mentality of government, or governmentality, whereby the state took upon itself to manage the 'conduct of conduct' (Foucault 1982). As argued by Dean, conduct has a double meaning: it refers to the conduct, as in behaviour, of social subjects, and conduct, as in conducting or directing the state (Dean 2010: 17–18).

The modern state is not simply characterized by the monopoly of violence and taxation; it is also characterized by the monopoly of education (Gellner 1983: 34). For the first time in history, the state attempted to impose a common culture upon all of society. Enthusiasm for, and resistance to, particular manifestations of that project lie at the core of nationalism.

The image of the Panopticon is in some respects a metaphor for modern internalization of educational discipline and governmentality. The Panopticon is an all-seeing machine. As envisaged by Jeremy Bentham, it is an observation post from where everyone can be seen, while those observed are never sure when they are observed, so assume they are always observed (Bentham 2017; Foucault 1979). The subjects of the Panopticon learn that they are observed and so observe themselves. Becoming a social subject is not simply about being subjected to control. It is about being able to understand how the self appears from the perspective of the other. To use Mead's image, it concerns the *I* and the *me* (Mead 2015: 173–8). The *I* constitutes the interpretative ego, who requires ontological security. The *me* concerns the 'attitudes of others which one assumes as affecting his own conduct...' (Mead 2015: 176).

The Panopticon constitutes a metaphor for subject formation in an age of high levels of interdependence. Elias' account of court society and the Panopticon are analogous. The person at court constantly monitors what others think of them. Complex interdependence presupposes social beings who are constantly moving back and forth between the *I* and the *me*. If the courtier misreads how others interpret him that constitutes an infelicitous moment in which the *I* feels ontological insecurity. The student sitting at her desk or taking an exam learns that she is constantly visible. She develops a sense for how the teacher sees her *me* as a subject persona. The classroom is analogous to a court society for the mass of the population.

Having a strong sense of *me* is a resource for negotiating complex social situations. Complex societies are places where the individual spends most of their day front-stage (Goffman 1971), constantly monitoring the *me* perceptions of self. If that individual, the *I*, has certain goals that can be realized only in collaboration with others, the sense of *me* is an essential resource in the context of a complex modern society.

Exclusion takes place as a consequence of failure to participate in this race for self-discipline. Correctional facilities became a tool for dealing with these problem social subjects. As Ryan (2007) has explored in fascinating detail, policing the poor was a major nineteenth-century state project, where the objective was to bring those who were excluded back into productive society. Crucial was the distinction between the so-called *deserving* and *undeserving* poor. The former were social subjects who had internalized discipline but, through bad luck, were poor. They deserved charity without correction. The second category referred to social subjects who were (supposedly) undisciplined, feckless and required training in workhouse and other correctional facilities. These institutions were additional to the educational mass socialization of a population into discipline and self-restraint.

Educational qualifications as deferred gratification

Together with mass socialization goes a plethora of educational qualifications, which create a pull towards self-subjectification. These educational qualifications must be perceived to be objective in order to count. Their perceived external objectivity is every bit as important as that of fiat currency. Just as a person cannot become wealthier by minting currency in a private space, so they cannot gain meritocratic advancement by printing their own educational certificates. Nowhere is the move from private to public more pronounced than in the state certification of educational qualifications.

As modern society advances, the legitimacy of authority shifts towards meritocratic principles. Those with the highest educational qualifications, coupled with experience, achieve social advancement. The training to become a medical doctor or other specialist entails massive accumulation of certificates that presuppose self-subjectifying deferral of gratification. What we term meritocracy is essentially a society where social mobility is increasingly based around a currency of state-backed educational qualifications, which require deferred gratification.

Consider the contrast between the lads and the ear'oles described by Willis (2016), in his account of a working-class school. The lads revelled in the capacity to have a good time, to have a laugh, as they put it, while the ear'oles sat still and just listened. The capacity to enjoy themselves did confer status authority to the lads among themselves, and ontological security among their group. So, this should not be perceived as a pure negative. However, the ear'oles' *inability* to enjoy themselves (as interpreted by the lads) was a manifestation of a disciplinary *ability* to defer pleasure, as viewed from the perspective of the educational-cum-meritocratic system of social mobility, thus to self-subjectify. While a defect from the viewpoint of the lads, this constitutes a resource for social mobility – a point the lads acknowledged. This capacity for deferral of gratification is an ontological status authority useful in complex modern societies. In this regard it is no different from the way the Yurok capacity for self-restraint was useful to their ability to become good fishermen.

Killing and self-discipline

While the decline of the temperament appropriate to feudal society meant a decline in blood and gore in the streets of Europe, it did not translate into a decline in numerical killing; quite the contrary. As has been pointed out by many critics of Elias, including Malesevic and Ryan (2012), the twentieth century was one of the bloodiest in history. However, the point is that the dominant *mode* of killing has changed, reflecting a changing social ontology of self-restraint. The overall effect is not a decline in the effectiveness of killing but its visibility.

The feudal warrior killed in close combat and considered it glorious to get close to the blood and gore of battle. The pursuit of glory was a form of feudal restraint and status. In the mid-sixteenth century a confrontation took place between the armies of the Duke of Montmorency and King Henry IV, which is archetypal of the confrontation between a feudal and modern social ontology. The duke's army was at the top of a hill, while the king's was at the bottom, which conferred strategic advantage to the duke. The duke had a well-disciplined army approaching from the rear. In terms of modern instrumental strategy, the duke should have prepared his well-disciplined forces on the high ground, exploiting geographical advantage. However, the duke 'was a knightly, princely man, generous and brilliant' (Elias 1995: 482). In other words, unlike his troops, he was not disciplined in a modern way. When he saw the king's forces positioned below, his officers advised him to wait. However, the duke was 'already gripped in a belligerent frenzy'. Unable to restrain himself, without giving his forces sufficient time to follow, the duke galloped his 'magnificent stallion' 'splendidly adorned with red blue and dun feathers' (Elias 1995: 482) down the hill towards a shower of bullets, to inevitable, but glorious, death.

The duke was a person of feudal social ontology confronting an army of early-modern disciplined social subjects. As described by Foucault, while the feudal soldier was someone who could be seen from afar, with status derived from visibility in individual combat, in early modernity the 'soldier became something that can be made'.

> Recruits become accustomed to holding their heads high and erect; to standing upright, without bending the back ... remain motionless until the order is given, without moving, the hands or the feet ... lastly to march with a bold step.
>
> (Foucault 1979: 136)

In contemporary society, the most militarily effective armies typically wage war using self-disciplined social subjects that rarely come into direct contact with their opponents. Typically, at the start of contemporary war, preparatory killing is carried out using bombs dropped from 20,000 feet, combined with unmanned drones and laser-guided missiles. When the modern army enters enemy territory, this is usually done using tanks. These technically advanced tanks are managed by soldiers without a direct sense of the actual space where they are in combat. The contemporary tank does not involve direct eyeball contact between combatants. Rather, it is equipped with computer screens, where targets are lined up, and the successful hit appears as a visual representation, a mere puff, on the screen. In many ways, this experience is indistinguishable from virtual-reality war games. The next stage of tank warfare will be robotic – literally, a virtual war game.

Modern soldiers kill without getting blood spattered on their uniforms. But this does not mean that they kill less. Armies require the same self-restraint as any other high-technology sector and are all the more efficient for it. Ironically, the self-restraint that takes violence off the streets, out of everyday sight, actually makes contemporary social subjects more efficient killers in situations of war – constraint confers power-to kill.

Felicitous performance and status authority

The processes we have described are far from unique or culturally specific. Mirroring Erikson's observation that societies do not reward social eccentrics, society does not confer status upon those who fail to internalize what is considered felicitous discipline for that society. This entails a social process whereby social status authority is created that is particular to a specific self-subjectifying disciplinary context. For instance, in a traditional society of pearl divers, those who can discipline their breathing and, consequently, hold their breath longer than the rest will have high authority status. The social actors who have the highest level of disciplinary restraint will (other factors being equal) gain higher authority status than social actors who fail to internalize that restraint and are constantly infelicitous.

The connection between restraint and status authority also has an element of ontological revulsion as a push factor. Not only does the person with low restraint tend to be someone of low status; they often inspire a feeling of active embarrassment in the eyes of others. To the extent to which these subjects perceive that reaction, they understand that they are infelicitous, giving rise to anxiety tinged with shame and self-contempt. Conversely, those who learn to structure the field well gain authority status. This creates continual social pressure to conform, to internalize these restraints from above and below. Most social actors do not wish to appear unreasonable or be ontologically insecure. Simultaneously, they desire the status authority conferred by a performance that is well executed. The latter forms the source of *agency* for the individual, making them other than cultural dupes (see Mik-Meyer and Haugaard 2019).

Even if, to the outsider, the performance of certain roles appears an act of self-subjectifying subordination, for those actors involved they are activating agency within the structured conditions of possibility available to them. If, for instance, the local field is one of gender norms, the woman who performs well is not simply passively internalizing subordination; she is realizing agency within her field. To an outsider, a Western feminist, this woman's social practices may appear as a subservient activity but to her this constitutes the realization of agency within the conditions of possibility that she is familiar with. The better she performs, the more ontologically secure she feels and, simultaneously, the more authority power she has within that field. From the perspective of another field, that of Western feminism, this may appear as loving your own subordination, with the psyche turning against itself (Butler 1997). While this may be partly what is going on in extreme cases of 4-D (which will be discussed in the next chapter), there is also agency and empowerment that transcend subordination.

Clarissa Rile Hayward gives a superb instance of this process in the opening of her book *How Americans Make Race* (Hayward 2013). Following a thought experiment suggested by Richard Ford (2005), Hayward invites the reader to imagine the reaction to a female tango dancer who refused her gendered role in the dance; she would be sanctioned by her dance instructor, who would correct her mistakes; she would be sanctioned by the other female dancers, who would let her know that she should behave appropriately; and she would be sanctioned by the male leads, who would refuse to dance with her (Hayward 2013: 1). These would be the negative sanctions of infelicity and unreasonableness. Against that, on the positive pull side, changing her behaviour to local conditions of felicity would mean acceptance, approval and status rewards within that field.

Near the time of writing Hayward had bought a pair of *Comme Il Faut* dance shoes, which means *proper* or *according to accepted standards or conventions*. Aside from the translated meaning, this refers to the brand name of

> top-of-the-line Argentine tango shoes, which are handmade exclusively in Buenos Aires. Online the retailer describes Comme Il Fauts as 'ultra chic, outrageously sexy, and superbly crafted with ... a very distinctive stiletto heel.'
>
> But that is not all they did. The ad continues: 'Don't let the heel scare you – it is specifically designed for walking backwards and is perfectly positioned for incredible stability.'
>
> (Hayward 2013: 2)

When Hayward tried the shoes they did indeed enable her to walk backwards and pivot on the ball of her foot, and tilt her body forward, 'heightening both my capacity and my disposition to read and to respond to the moves that he led' (Hayward 2013: 2). In that sense, the tango shoes 'prompted me to perform my gendered role well' (Hayward 2013: 2). Now, of course, the idea of her responding to the male lead entails confirm-structuration to the gendered norms of patriarchal society. This suggests subordination. However, the words *ultra chic, outrageously sexy, and superbly crafted with ... a very distinctive stiletto heel* suggest the capacity for high status authority within that field. The tango dancer who is *ultra chic* and *outrageously sexy* realizes agency by engaging in a gendered performance that commands high Y-status authority within her field.

While there is a larger story of gendered inequality, for the female social actor who plays that field well significant rewards are at stake, which points beyond the desire for subjection, towards agency. With regard to gendered norms, there is the push factor of knowing that a gender-inappropriate response will be infelicitous, and thus inspire ontological insecurity, and the pull factor that a felicitous performance will be well received and, if well executed, confer high-status female-gendered authority. Of course, the latter may have less, or more circumscribed, authority than that of high-status male-gender constructions. But changing that structured bias entails changing the social system, which is beyond the 2-D conditions of possibility for an individual social actor.

Resistance to self-restraint

Social actors are active. Many compete for status but some resist. There are several forms of resistance. The first entails creating private spaces where suppressed desires are expressed, as in the dominant ideology thesis. This does not lead to change but constitutes symbolic resistance that serves as a safety valve for pent-up frustration. Second are those who refuse to join the main race for status, while creating their own lifestyle that provides ontological security. Third is the rejection of status authority through informalization, which contains its own self-subjectification. We will explore each briefly.

Spaces of symbolic resistance

To return to the image of the highway, while most drivers are remarkably restrained, there is constant venting of resistance to this self-restraint. In most Western societies, night is when the joy rider appears. Under the cover of darkness, young drivers spin cars at speed in such a way as to leave black tyre tracks across the lanes. Next morning, the white lines stand violated, with great black tracks of rubber crossing them out: a testament to defiance.

When the disciplined driver arrives home, frustrated at endless tailbacks, they seek relief in the latest Hollywood movie, populated by spontaneous heroes of the highway, whose character is reminiscent of the feudal knight. Imagine a good cop (whom the viewer identifies with but who is constantly in trouble with his boss for breaking the rules) who finds himself on the wrong highway chasing a terrible villain who has just exited onto a highway below. Instead of waiting for the next exit, a determined look crosses the good cop's face. He grits his teeth and presses the accelerator, drives off a bridge, spins the car on the roof of an articulated truck, drives off the truck on to the bonnet of the villain's car, and shoots him dead (loosely based on Elias 1995: 452–3).

The feudal knight gloried in contact with blood and the dismembered bits of his victims. The contemporary soldier is trained to kill in a controlled manner, preferably at a physical distance from the actual blood and gore. This abhorrence of visible violence extends across society, all the way down to the family unit, where physical violence is prohibited. However, within the 'peaceful' home there is an insatiable demand for violent films and video games. In contrast to the self-disciplined soldier, the imaginary hero is someone who does not obey orders and kills in close combat (see Smith 2008). In essence, Rambo is a modern reimagining of the Duke of Montmorency. The main difference is that, somehow, Rambo has a unique ability to run into a hailstorm of bullets and not get killed, which is the difference between fact and fiction.

When states can no longer go to war with one another because of mutual interdependence, they stage sporting events, which are a form of ritualized war. When spectators attend these events they revert to forms of spontaneous behaviour. A self-restrained individual is suddenly transformed into someone jumping up and down while cheering or jeering.

As we saw, the normally highly self-restrained Yurok have one day a year when their self-restraint gives way to hedonistic pleasure. Western modernity has many more such days, and the public/private distinction creates back-stage spaces of release that are constantly available.

Resistance as sub-group status

While the race between competing classes goes on, there will be subgroups that are not at the 'status races', so to speak. They resist exclusion by creating their own competition, which preserves their sense of self-worth and ontological security. That field of status will have its own norms, which typically constitute an inversion of the main, systemically higher-status, dominant race.

As Willis (2016) argues, in working-class schools *the lads* reject the dominant culture of their school and form a sub-group that resists. To *the lads* the hardworking students were *ear'oles*, which suggests passivity and low status. Being an *ear'ole* entailed the capacity to sit still and just listen while the teacher spoke, which suggests abjection. The *lads* fidgeted, learned nothing, but they had pride in their 'masculine' resistance. In their field, status is associated with never being abject and enjoying yourself publicly in a way that violates the rules of the establishment.

If a member of the self-retrained high-status group observes someone spitting, this inspires revulsion. Against that, there will be resistant reactions by groups who deliberately violate these norms. In their social field the act of spitting constitutes an expression of manliness, defiance and local status authority. In inner-city neighbourhoods in Limerick (which middle-class Irish society would define as low-status), spitting is a local source of cultural capital. The *hard man* holds his head high as he spits, while walking down the street, taking pleasure in the discomfort of those in whom his behaviour invokes displeasure (Lappin 2017). *Hard man* is a Y-status authority function particular to a local field of resistance. It constitutes a local authority currency that is valueless outside that field. However, for those social actors inside the field, it provides ontological security, positive feelings of self-esteem and status authority. This field will entail specific constraints, which confer local distinction. Their protest is not simply the absence of rules. Strict codes govern how to resist, which confers status authority within the subculture.

Informalization

Since the 1960s a process of informalization has been taking place, which suggests a decline of self-restraint. Informalization is a sign of resistance to 4-D self-subjectification, as restraining social norms are deconstructed. However, we have to be careful of this reading. First, what appears as informal may have its own pursuit of status built in, and not be as deconstructive of norms as it may appear. Second, a bid for freedom may actually presuppose high levels of self-restraint and self-surveillance. The latter does not mean that this is not resistance, but that some forms of freedom are premised upon a 4-D social ontology of restraint.

The pursuit of the casual entails a form of critique based upon a disregard for status-based conventions of distinction. Social conventions of self-restraint are exposed as made and therefore to be un-made. From an egalitarian perspective, the deconstruction of the norms of formality can be liberating from restraints, whose only purpose was status snobbery.

While informalization can be genuine social critique, this mode of deconstruction of 4-D has the potential to reproduce its own status conventions. Take the architecture of the home as an instance. The front regions have lost their status and everyone is now invited into the back region of the contemporary middle-class home. The dining room has largely disappeared, while the kitchen has become public, which appears informal. However, in becoming public, these kitchens have become designer items rather than functional utilitarian spaces. The status of mahogany is replaced by surgical kitchen counters crafted from exotic polished stone and the status of silver and porcelain are replaced by complex cookers and electronic gadgets controlled from smartphones. The extent to which social actors now feel compelled to replace their kitchens every few years, to follow the latest trend, means they have simply exchanged one set of status constraints for another.

While more spaces of the home are now front-stage, there is also a corresponding increase in anonymous taste that mirrors public spaces, as homes come to resemble hotels. This reflects how times of relaxation, which used to be private, are increasingly displayed on public media, such as Facebook, Instagram, WhatsApp and Snapchat. While it may appear informal to invite others to observe the inside of your home there is a danger that the more expansive the public areas, the greater the requirement for 4-D self-surveillance. What used to be back-stage actual relaxation now becomes front-stage posed, therefore restrained, relaxation. There is a creeping Panoptical self-surveillance at work here.

A second aspect of informalization concerns the complex relationship between self-restraint and freedom. In everyday discourse they appear inverse; the greater the freedom, the less the restraint. In fact, many forms of freedom presuppose self-restraint as a condition of possibility. Typical is greater bodily freedom. In the Victorian age bodies were clothed and covered; now they are increasingly uncovered. In the past, swimming was done semi-clothed; now there is a proliferation of nudist beaches across Europe. To the dedicated naturist, this appears as freedom from the constraints of society. However, in reality, the capacity for adults to stand around together while naked, without this becoming an overtly erotic situation, presupposes massive self-restraint. This is linked to a wider perception that revealing the body in public does not equate to an erotic invitation. The conditions of possibility that make this possible presuppose a uniquely self-controlled social ontology. In traditional monotheistic societies, where bodies tend to be covered up in public, that social ontology is less developed, so naturism and similar bodily freedoms lie outside the ontological conditions of possibility. This points to the complex relationship between freedom and restraint. The freedom of naturism is a real freedom but it presupposes a complex social ontology of 4-D self-restraint.

8

The fourth dimension continued:
Social death through slavery,
death-camps and solitary confinement

In the previous chapter we looked at the 4-D social transformation of social ontology in terms of a race for self-restraint, which delivers status authority but also inequality. This was cast within a frame that emphasizes the agency of both the more and the less powerful. Self-restraint is not simply imposed from the top down. A dynamic process is at work whereby social actors seek restraint in order to acquire status and empower themselves.

It should be clear that power is not zero-sum. While domination occurs, we should be cautious of characterizing the less powerful as passive victims of it. Typically, the less powerful have some agency. Contrary to everyday perception, power and freedom are not opposed. There is also a normative issue here. All too often well-meaning binary discourses of victims-versus-oppressors are condescending towards the less powerful. However, against all this, it is important to acknowledge that power can be top-down, opposed to freedom and deeply destructive to victims of domination.

In the previous chapter, in the discussion of the Panopticon and the mention of workhouses we touched upon top-down imposition of constraint. In this chapter we will focus upon the most extreme forms of 4-D domination associated with slavery, concentration camps and solitary confinement. This exposes the most disturbing aspects of domination, while it gives us an insight into the core of human social ontology. Here the binary discourse of victims and perpetrators is more pertinent. Although, as we shall see, even these victims attempt some resistance in order to obtain the minimal agency necessary in order to avoid social death.

Slavery and social death

In Chapter 1 we examined Primo Levi's account (Levi 1991) of being denied the status authority of a person. Orlando Patterson (1982) theorizes this phenomenon as *social death*. He develops the concept of social death with regard to slavery.

In his study of slavery, Patterson rejects economic definitions of slavery, which define slaves as property, in favour of a conceptualization in terms of power and authority. His definition is as follows: '*slavery is the permanent, violent domination of natally alienated and generally dishonoured persons*' (Patterson 1982: 13; italics original). In Patterson's theory, the word *honour* covers similar conceptual space to *status authority* in the language game of this theory. Someone is dishonoured when they have no authority agency of their own (Patterson 1982: 10). Natality refers to their birth into slavery, which is interpreted metaphorically. It is not that a slave is literally born into slavery, but that their membership of society is defined by the state of subservience.

Free persons are social subjects who have agency, while slaves have no agency. Even their very constitution as social subjects belongs to another. As an ideal, this state of abjection is created partly by removing all social ties that do not come through the master. In this respect Patterson quotes the view of the Ahaggar Tuareg of the Sahara that 'without the master the slave does not exist, and he is socialized only through his master' (Patterson 1982: 4). The slave is cut off from God, and the sacred. This creates a unique relationship whereby, according to the Tuareg saying, 'All persons are created by God, the slave is created by the Tuareg' (Patterson 1982: 4). In this regard, the discourse of slavery often entailed a view of the slave as infidel. The European colonial idea of the slave as a *savage* mirrors the idea of slaves as without society.

This image of the slave is consistent with Hegel's theorization of the master–slave dialectic, as follows: 'The one is independent whose essential nature is to be for itself, the other dependent whose essence is life or existence for another. The former is Master, or Lord, the latter is Bondsman [Slave]' (Hegel 1961: 234).

Archetypically, slavery was often a substitute for death in war (Patterson 1982: 5). The captured slave was a defeated person who could either be killed or enslaved. When enslaved, their social self was essentially given over to their captors, who refashioned the subjectivity to their pleasing. Based upon his experiences as a black freeman who was captured and enslaved in the South of the USA, Solomon Northup observes that the whippings that slaves receive have a specific purpose, which is to break their spirit, and in so doing mould them into a state of slavery (Northup 2012: 170–3). This use of violence is not so much coercive, in the sense of goal-directed (do X or you will be punished). It is ontological, for the 4-D purposes of moulding the social subject. Through fear, they become a body, devoid of the social, to be reprogrammed with a practical consciousness that hinges around deference. This practical consciousness is not that of an autonomous agent. Rather, all action is directed through the master because 'the slave had no socially recognized existence outside of his master, he becomes a social nonperson' (Patterson 1982: 5). As an ideal type, fear and anxiety are intended to make the slave constantly willing to please.

To return to the ancient origins of slavery, when captured in battle, the slave left a social order that was theirs and entered into that of another. As they could be killed, their survival was at the whim of another. So, they exchanged bodily survival for social death from their previous society. Therefore, it was considered justifiable that their new master could natally reconstruct them as desired. Obviously, many slaves were not captured in battle, so in that case, initiation into violence was a symbolic conquest that severed all previous social ties. In that sense we see intrusive slavery, where the slave genuinely did not belong, and extrusive slavery, where this condition of social death was created artificially (Patterson 1982: 44).

Under normal circumstances, especially in traditional societies, the birth of a social subject entitles them to social ties. In slavery, these ties are severed. The person captured in battle has lost all social ties. The person enslaved artificially, the extrusive slave, has those ties symbolically severed. Social death entails a severing of normal natal social ties (Patterson 1982: 5–6).

The term *natality* also has a second reference. For Arendt the act of birth is the origin of action. She writes: 'To act, in its most general sense, means to begin ... to set something in motion ...' (Arendt 1998: 177). So, deprived of natality, the slave is deprived of all action. The natally enslaved is someone without agency. Any action she engages in only contributes to the agency of another. When Levi started to find agency within the camp, it was a way of not giving in to the condition of social death. Famously, Northup (2012) also refused to acquiesce his spirit to repeated whippings, in order to hold on to his sense of self.

In theory, in its extreme form, slavery entailed that family ties were not sacred to the master. The ultimate control of slavers was the capacity to break apart the slave's family. To sell a wife from a husband was considered the ultimate power, and worse than any whipping.

> Peter Clifton, an eighty-nine-year-old ex-slave from South Carolina, was typical when he said: 'Master Biggers [his master] believed in whippin' and workin' his slaves long and hard; then a man was scared all the time of being sold away from his wife and chillun. His bark was worse than his bite tho', for I never knowed him to do a wicked think lak dat.'
>
> (Patterson 1982: 6)

In this context, the fact that the master never did sell the wife or children of the slave allowed the slaves some level of autonomy, which would have been crucial for their ontological survival. A person devoid of control of their most intimate ties breaks down. However, even if slave masters rarely exercised the power to break apart families, the fact that they had the power to do so would have been a significant source of anxiety.

As Pettit argues (1996 and 2014; Haugaard and Pettit 2017), domination takes place when the powerful has the arbitrary dispositional power to make another do something unstructured, even if he never actually exercises that power. As long as the less powerful individual is aware that the powerful has this dispositional power, she will fawn and please the powerful other to make sure he doesn't exercise it. In the case of slavery, even if it was relatively uncommon for husbands and wives to be sold from each other, the fact that it could be done was a continual source of ontological insecurity that would make the slave prone to an abject predisposition. The sale of slave children was relatively common, and deeply traumatic.

Another source of humiliation and insecurity was the potentiality that the master might use the wife or daughter of a slave as a sexual object. In that case, the slaves would just have to accept the situation. A variant on the slave's impotence was to force them to witness a family member being whipped, while unable to come to their aid. As we saw, in the account of dominant ideology (Chapter 2), a slave may outwardly acquiesce to this humiliation, but inwardly may have their own back-stage counter-hegemonic discourse in which they realize revenge (Scott 1990: 5). The latter agency enables them to resist this extreme form of 4-D power.

The family structure was a possible source of agency for the slave, which would lift her out of slavery momentarily: 'the slave's natural love for and attachment to kinsmen worked against the master's attempt to deny him all formal claims of natality ...' (Patterson 1982: 13). Among slaves, having your own living space, however basic, was desirable. In the American South, slaves who did household work often lived better materially, with accommodation in the main house and access to food coming from the kitchen. This was significantly different to those who worked in the fields, who had only basic sustenance and usually only rudimentary shelter. Yet, being an agricultural slave, with some space for personal agency, was generally considered preferable to the all-embracing nature of domestic slavery. Having a shack away from the main house provided that tiny private space, where the slave could form their social ties to family and have a space of autonomy, and thus honour, in Patterson's sense.

The fact that the slave is severed from sociality obviously provides the master with the rationalization that slaves are incapable of sociality. In the *Social and Mental Traits of the Negro*, it was claimed that 'The Negro has little home conscience or love of home, no local attachments of the better sort ... He has no pride of ancestry ...' (quoted in Alexander 2006: 272). Notice the last words, alleging no pride in ancestry. They make the fact of natality, inflicted by violence, an essential reified characteristic.

Essentialist rationalization is part and parcel of the justification of slavery. In Viking discourse, slaves are said to be ugly, with 'swarthy skin' and 'hideous countenance' (Patterson 1982: 177). The reference to trolls seems obvious. Slaves are made equivalent to trolls, and therefore intrinsically not fully human. In the American South the wider society was patriarchal. Consequently, autonomy status was associated with male gender. Male slaves were essentialized as visibly lacking 'manliness' in demeanour (Patterson 1982: 177). As the quality of (so-called) manliness is tied to honour of full agency, a slave disposition entails the absence of these qualities.

Social death and resistance in the Nazi camps

In our discussion of the breaching experiments performed by Garfinkel and Milgram, we saw how social subjects experience ontological insecurity because singular acts of structuration are met with an inappropriate response. Imagine the level of ontological insecurity that could be created by deliberately recreating such conditions in every aspect of interaction. Over a short period of time, the person's sense of inner certainty about the world would be undermined, and slowly the sense of self could be stripped away.

The psychologist Bruno Bettelheim gives an account of this process, based upon his own experiences in concentration camps (Bettelheim 1986). The first experience of radical ontological insecurity started in the transport in the cattle cars to the camps. Jews were locked into the cars for days, with no place to defecate and with little, if any, food or water.

As described by Goffman (1971), modernity entails a sense of social agency that includes the capacity to maintain the distinction between *front-stage* and *back-stage* behaviour. As part of the process described by Elias, from the sixteenth century onwards defecation moved to back-stage behaviour. In twentieth-century modernity, defecating in public view, or front-stage, is a fundamental breach of social norms, which causes ontological security. Part of the same process of internalization of restraint means that food is never grabbed roughly and, if at all possible, utensils are used (although, since the 1940s there has been significant informalization with regard to the latter). In the cattle cars, the Jews were enclosed without food and water for long periods of time. In many cases the inmates received food and water from bystanders who passed sustenance to them through gaps in the cattle cars (Lanzmann 1985: 1(26)). The prisoners would fight and struggle for food, especially for water. Thirst was a more powerful bodily force to control than hunger. Quickly, they became incapable of the usual restraints associated with eating at a table with others. Self-restrained social subjects grabbed/fought over sustenance, and faced the regular humiliation of public defecation. This was a fundamental attack upon ontological security. In many instances, those of higher status, who had internalized these norms more deeply, found this particularly disturbing.

From the perspective of their oppressors, a 3-D process of reification was taking place. Because of the material restraints of the cattle cars, these victims were forced to behave in an unrestrained manner associated with animal behaviour, as characterized in everyday discourse. Consequently, legitimacy was given to an essentialist discourse of negative Y-status authority. In the eyes of the oppressors, the behaviour of the Jews in the cattle cars revealed their true essence as animals and therefore it was reasonable to treat them as such.

For many prisoners the cattle car transport was sufficient to tip them into suicide or withdrawal into ontological breakdown (Giddens 1984: 62). In the Zimbardo prison experiments, in which students were randomly divided into prison guards and prisoners, a similar process took place. Zimbardo describes the prisoners as becoming 'zombie-like' (Zimbardo 2009: 196). The title of Levi's book, *If This is a Man*, suggests that the definition of being a man is more than bare animal existence. Expressed in ungendered language, where *person* is substituted for *man*, the essence of personhood goes beyond mere animal existence, or what Agamben refers to as *bare existence* (Agamben 1998). Social death is bare existence.

When the prisoners arrived at the camps, disembarking from the misery of the cattle cars, they were greeted by chaos: shouting, dogs and random insults from the SS (Lanzmann 1985: 1(21)). The point of this ritual of physical and symbolic violence was to break down the new arrivals psychologically (Levi 1991: 34–5).

In Chapter 1 we theorized violence as a resource for coercion, while signalling that violence also has a 4-D dimension. The former, coercive threats of violence, are usually structured, with an objective goal. Coercion is an added incentive to confirm-structure systemic bias against the confirm-structurer. In contrast, the use of this form of violence is different. The objective here is to instil fear in another, and so render them docile. When confronted with randomized acts of violence, the person shifts into bodily survival mode. Justifications for social structures are no longer part of the equation. The physical self is set against the social self, and the social self does everything it can to ensure that the physical self survives. When violence is random, and fear is predominant, the victim simply focusses upon pleasing the oppressor. Social death constitutes a change in personality structure, whereby the relatively powerless becomes docile and fatalistic.

The latter stems from a sense of arbitrariness, as there is no longer any justification at the core of the order-of-things, except the de facto arbitrary desires of the powerful.

On the arrival platforms in the Nazi camps, Jewish families were separated from one another into groups, the minority for temporary survival as slave labour (largely physically fit males and some females) and a few children (especially twins) for the purposes of experimentation. The majority, consisting of children, older people and most of the women, were placed in a line for immediate death. The separation was an inversion of moral order. The vulnerable were designated for immediate extermination, while the remainder were to be worked to death. The normal practical consciousness would have followed the logic epitomized in lifeboats, where the vulnerable are the first to be rescued. Some of those in the lines for slave labour mistakenly assumed that women, children and older people would be treated better. Consequently, they urged relations in borderline situations (such as teenagers and the middle-aged) to go into the files that turned out to be the lines to death. The realization that this advice, typically given by parents to teenage children, had sent the persons closest to them to immediate death proved exceptionally traumatic (Haugaard 1966).

One cattle car contained someone who had been through the process before, had escaped and had been recaptured. He knew that at the next station the Jews would be moved from one train to another, as the tracks did not connect. This was an opportunity for break-out, as there were only a few guards, who might shoot, but would be unable to shoot everybody (which was better than the odds of survival at Auschwitz). However, the experienced prisoner was only able to convince a single other person to attempt to escape with him. As it turned out, both were successful as the guards refrained from shooting them, and one even facilitated their escape. However, the majority in the car clung to what they knew, rather than their new bizarre reality; they changed trains in an orderly manner, acquiescent with the master plan of death (Haugaard 1966).

Once inside the camps the personhood of the new arrivals was symbolically erased through the removal of their names. A number was tattooed upon their forearm, which symbolically represented their loss of Y-status as a citizen person. Their heads were shaved, which, in the case of women, made them appear androgynous. Clothing was removed and replaced by striped pyjamas, shoes were replaced by clogs and any personal possessions were removed. Everything that was theirs, including their hair and everybody they loved, was removed from them. When fleas, parasites, starvation and cold were added to this mix, the person was gradually reduced to a bare life of animal existence – social death was complete.

The jobs allocated were usually pointless, so excelling at your work, by striving hard, was a disadvantage as it sapped vital energy. The taken-for-granted everyday view that a job well done would be rewarded was turned upside-down. Many jobs entailed instructions that, once understood, were appalling in their implication. Filip Muller relates how he was instructed to stir well and hard, without understanding what this meant, only to learn that he was stirring the bodies, bones and finally ash in the crematorium oven, next to the gas chambers (Filip Muller in Lanzmann 1985). All the inner certainties of normal society were disconnected from the outer reality of survival. Consequently, the new entrant was reduced to a hollow resemblance of self, as the dividing line between life and death became indistinct (Levi 2013: 29).

For the majority, the combination of senseless tasks, the lack of any time to oneself and the inability to plan ahead was so deeply destructive that they became like walking corpses (Bettelheim 1986: 148). As argued by Giddens, this resulted in a gradual stripping away of the person.

> The disruption and deliberately sustained attack upon the ordinary routines of life produced a high degree of anxiety, a 'stripping away' of the socialized responses associated with security management of the body and a predictable framework of social life. Such an upsurge of anxiety is expressed in regressive modes of behaviour, attacking the basic security system grounded in trust manifested toward others.
>
> (Giddens 1984: 63)

The majority of victims were unable to overcome this attack upon their self and became incapable of interaction. As has been frequently recounted, such individuals would develop a characteristic empty stare, a dragging of the feet and a shutdown of their capacity to interact. This breakdown of the person would characteristically be made manifest by the inability to look the other in the eye. Indeed the eyes would become so vacant that it appeared as though there were no thoughts at all in the mind behind them (Levi 2013: 100–101).

In contrast, those who resisted social death became new persons with a practical consciousness relevant to their situation. They fell into two classes. Many, including Levi and Muller, managed to survive by creating tiny spaces of agency, autonomy and even resistance within the camp. Others internalized the knowledge structure of the Nazi worldview, often identifying with the SS (Giddens 1984: 63).

Central to psychological survival was the capacity to create a new sense of autonomy and agency within a situation that was entirely abnormal. Levi experienced his first lesson in this strategy when he went to wash.

Very little water was available and most of it was dirty. Nor was there any-thing like soap or washcloths and so on. Given that they were living in conditions of total squalor with no future, and as they were almost cer-tain to die, washing seemed an utterly pointless ritual. So, Levi was about not to do so, when one of the inmates, an old hand in camp, instructed him to wash meticulously, as if his life depended upon it (Levi 2013: 43–5). While at the time this appeared absurd, Levi learned that performing small everyday tasks with a sense of purpose was part of the key to sur-vival. The act of washing was a moment, however fleeting, of agency and limited autonomy. Levi also learned that having lost all his belongings, the few new possessions of camp life, including a spoon and bowl, had dispro-portionate significance.

When Levi was assigned to work in the chemical plant, he gained entry into a world that increased his agency further. Through minor pilfering, he gained access to possessions of value within the camp (Levi 2013: 163). Equally importantly, he created a space of some autonomy and agency. Levi was active within a black market, which was not regulated by those in official authority. Therefore, it constituted a space of agency and symbolic resistance.

Social bonding between victims was significant. At one point, when extremely thirsty, Levi found a small amount of stagnant water in a pipe. He was alone, so could have drunk it all. However, he chose to share it with a friend. Thus, altruistic behaviour enabled social bonds to be reproduced (Levi 1991: 84–5).

As Levi acquired survival skills, he also gained status authority among the other inmates. A significant source of Y-status authority among the prisoners was having a low number (Levi 2013: 30). The longer you survived the more your number became a testament to your survival skills. In a sense, the prisoners created a field of social status for themselves that was beyond the control of the guards.

Muller, on the other hand, was given agency as a consequence of a chance event. He witnessed a group of Jews being forced to undress and herded into the gas chamber. They were not willing subjects and had to be beaten with clubs by the SS. As an act of symbolic defiance, inside the undressing room, they broke out into a chorus singing the Czech national anthem and the Hatikvah. Muller found himself overcome with the mean-inglessness of trying to survive under these circumstances. So, resolved to die, he decided to join them in the gas chamber. However, once inside, before the chamber door closed, some women begged him to save himself with the following words: 'So you want to die. But that's senseless. Your death won't give us back our lives. ... You must get out of here alive, you must bear witness to our suffering and to the injustices done to us' (Muller in Lanzmann 1985: 4(4)). These words gave Muller a purpose for survival, in the inner circle of hell, where he worked around the ovens and gas chambers. He dedicated his life to bearing witness, including writing his own grueling account of these experiences (Muller 1999).

The ability to create private space ties into Goffman's (1971) account of front- and back-stage regions. Part of breaking down the person's onto-logical security is to convert their existence entirely into a front-stage world, which is Panoptical. If there is no back stage, you eliminate any pri-vate space of reflexivity, which could allow for an alternative interpretative horizon. However, once the prisoners develop a back stage and social ties among one another, there arises the possibility of a counter-discourse. If this occurs, the person can develop the kind of split self that Scott (1987 and 1990) describes. This consists of a front stage of compliance and a back stage of agency or resistance, as in the dominant ideology thesis. Their sense of self is not synonymous with the dominant discourse. In the private space they can realize agency simply by thinking for themselves (even if just fantasy) or, as resistance, articulating counter-hegemonic social knowledge.

Aside from agency back-stage, there is also the possibility of survival by internalizing the discourse of the camp. Levi describes a young Jewish inmate who, when freed from Auschwitz, still fully identified with the Nazi morality of the camp (Levi 2013: 217). The Kapos were Jewish inmates who kept order on behalf of the Nazis. This individual had been admitted to the camp as a 12-year-old child and served as under-servant to the chief Kapo. Obviously, his young age would have made him particularly vulner-able to 4-D power colonization of his subjectivity.

While morally very different, the two diverse modes of survival tell us the same thing about social ontology. The camp was a process of social death, which entails de-socialization and deep ontological insecurity. Most never survived that breakdown and lost the will to live. Social and ontological death became physical death. However, there were two possible modes of survival in these critical circumstances. The social subject can preserve part of the self by creating private spaces where they have a local inter-pretative horizon that is theirs. In a context of *near*-complete control this constitutes agency and/or resistance. The other alternative is to reform the self through internalizing the interpretative horizon of the camp, including the demeaning view of self, which is a strategy that has an affinity with Stockholm syndrome.

Social death and solitary confinement

As an ideal type, social death is probably most effectively realized in the phenomenon of solitary confinement. As observed by Jack Henry Abbott,

who spent years in this condition, 'Solitary confinement can alter the ontological makeup of a stone' (Abbott 1991: 45; Guenther 2013: xi). The
point of isolating the person physically from all social interaction is to turn
them into an asocial being, to then be reconstructed as a social agent with
the desired social ontology. Failing the latter, the objective is to break the
will, for the purposes of control. As argued by Guenther (2013), in the USA
the origins of solitary confinement lay in the desire to reform. However,
in contemporary supermax prisons the objective is merely control because
the reform model has failed.

The preeminent early-modern theorist of solitary confinement was
Benjamin Rush. He was a prominent physician, psychiatrist, educator,
abolitionist and a signatory of the Declaration of Independence (Guenther
2013: 5). For him, punishment was of supreme importance for the
purposes of creating a new American republic, bound together by citizens
of good character.

> Sympathy and sensibility would have to do the work of forming citizens or, in
> Rush's own words, converting them into 'republican machines' governed by
> reliable mechanisms of self discipline, emotional restraint, and industrious
> habits of work, study, and prayer (Rush 1806). This production of republican
> machines was necessary in order for citizens 'to perform their parts properly,
> in the great machine of the government of the state' (Rush 1806: 14–5).
> (Guenther 2013: 6–7)

In a manner analogous to Foucault's description of the shift from punishment of the body to the control of the soul (Foucault 1979: 16), Rush was
impressed by a scene he witnessed where a culprit was admonished for half-
an-hour, then expected to be whipped, but was surprised to be dismissed
with the words: 'There go about your business. I mean shame and not pain
in the present instance' (quoted in Guenther 2013: 5). Rush thought that
'the beauty of shame was that it inflicted a psychic wound that was invisible
and yet visceral, affecting transgressors right at the level of their personhood' (Guenther 2013: 5). Shame is more effective than the whip because
'physical pain tends to produce resistance in the offenders by providing
them with a concrete object of aversion, shame undermines resistance
from within' (Guenther 2013: 5). When resistance occurs, this creates a
space for autonomy, which undermines 4-D domination. However, shame
works directly upon the self, not allowing a gap between the powerful and
the object of domination.

Rush thought the glue of society was *sense and sensibility* (Guenther
2013: 7). He believed that sensibility was undermined by irregularity, over-
excitement and over-stimulation. When the person was over-stimulated

or improperly stimulated the result was both disease and criminality (Guenther 2013: 7). Thus the cure for vice was the removal of all stimulation through solitary confinement. Rush took this idea so seriously that he applied it to the treatment of his own children, both as infants and adults. One of his sons, who showed signs of depression, was admitted to Rush's institution of solitary confinement, the Pennsylvania Hospital. He died there after 27 years of confinement (Guenther 2013: 9).

Rush's purpose was to create 'a machine for isolating, breaking down, and resetting the habits of diseased criminal subjects, and of (re)producing healthy citizen subjects' (Guenther 2013: 13). The theory had logic to it: the person was mal-socialized, so in solitary confinement all social interaction would be removed. Even more radically, all stimulation of the visual and auditory senses could also be suppressed in a dark cell with neither light nor sound. Once confined for a period, without any stimulation, the person would become a *tabula rasa*, which could then be re-socialized into a model citizen. In other words, social death could be followed by resurrection (Guenther 2013: 15).

The utopian 4-D social experiment failed miserably. Instead, '[p]risoners emerged from this machine with eyes like blanks, a deranged nervous system, and diminished capacity for coherent thought or conversation' (Guenther 2013: 15). Imprisonment in solitary confinement was, in the words of Hans Christian Andersen, 'a nightmare for the spirit' (quoted in Guenther 2013: 16). Charles Dickens described solitary confinement in terms of demolishing the person both 'body' and 'soul', with the prisoner emerging as a 'living ghost' (Guenther 2013: 19–20).

Dickens describes prisoners who developed strategies for survival. One managed to pilfer fluff to make a hat. Although totally deprived of human interaction, another was allowed to keep rabbits. However, neither the hat nor the rabbits were sufficient to preserve some semblance of personhood. Dickens describes the rabbit-keeping victim as ' "unearthly as if he had been summoned from the grave", and when he darts in pursuit of a rabbit ... it is "very hard to say in what respect the man was the nobler animal of the two" ' (Guenther 2013: 22). These prisoners attempted agency but the space for autonomy was obviously not sufficient for their being-in-the-world to be preserved.

Abbott describes in detail the process whereby the deprivation of the senses and interaction with other humans slowly breaks down the capacity for coherent thought. In the darkness his eyes hungered for light and his ears for sound in a manner that was analogous to a thirsty or hungry person hungering for water or food (Guenther 2013: 36). This deep desire of the senses to be stimulated resulted in synaesthesia for the eyes. Deprived of light, the eyes could be stimulated by touch. Abbott put his fingers to his eyes, with the result that he could stimulate the sensation of flashes of light (Guenther 2013: 36). Devoid of sound he would scream, and his ears would hear his own screams as voices of others from far away. Slowly, as Guenther emphasizes, Abbott became *unhinged* from reality.

Guenther uses the word *unhinged* both in the colloquial sense of insane, and as a precise description of the phenomenological deconstruction of the person. The person is a being-in-the-world who interacts with it. Based upon Husserl and Levinas, she theorizes the transcendental ego as analogous to a hinge that joins together inter-relational subjectivity. We are not simply atomistic individuals in a world-out-there. We are subjects that constitute ourselves like a hinge between self, embodied others and the world. If all external reality is denied, that hinge is broken, and the person falls apart (Guenther 2013: xii, 31 and 35).

Guenther argues that the transcendental ego has the power of constituting the self by drawing inner and outer reality together (Guenther 2013: 28). She quotes Husserl, as follows.

> The apprehension of a man as a real personality is determined throughout by such dependencies [upon social others]. A man is what he is as *a being who maintains himself* in his commerce with the things of his thingly [sic], and with the persons of his personal, surrounding world, and who, in doing so, *maintains his individuality throughout*.
>
> (Husserl quoted in Guenther 2013: 29; insertions in square brackets by Haugaard)

As theorized above, the transcendental ego constitutes the bringing together of external and internal, which includes persons and things. The human mind is exposed to external stimulus, imposing concepts upon it, and in the process is re-constituted as a social subject. The transcendental ego is the interactive hinge, which draws these elements together. Deprived of external reality, the mind hungers for stimulation and, consequently, fakes it. In the early stage of solitary confinement people imagine things that are not there. The eyes deprived of light try to reconstitute themselves as organs of touch. However, deprived over time, the transcendental ego simply collapses. In this state of deprivation the person feels deep anxiety, paranoia and finally a total breakdown of the personality.

In the concentration camp or in situations of slavery the social actor experiences prolonged destructuration and many break down. However, in slavery and in the camp some manage to create spaces of resistance and solidarity with fellow victims. Solitary confinement is a step further in the 4-D deconstruction of the person. Deprived of the possibility of interaction, acts of structuration are never confirm-structured. The social actor has no idea if they are speaking the private language of the unreasonable or whether they are constructing felicitous concepts.

Contemporary prisoners relate that the only stimulus from others is someone reaching into the cell to put handcuffs on their wrists and a hood over their head, to transport them from nowhere to nowhere. The existence of the other and the external world disappears from the eyes and ears. The only channel of communication to sustain the transcendental ego is the tactile sense. The self, who is an immensely complex processing machine, comprised of multiple interpretative horizons particular to the social fields, is stripped of all stimulation. This is the end point of 4-D power as an ideal type of pure domination. Unlike most ideal types, in the silent, window-less cells of solitary confinement, it actually exists and is made real, as a dystopian ideal.

9

Normative analysis of the four dimensions of power: A pragmatist approach: what is power for?

This is an overview of some of the normative implications of the theory of power as developed so far. Constructing normative foundations entails shifting language game. The issue is not how *power is* but how *power should be*. As this entails a switch in language game, some readers may agree with the sociological theory, but disagree with what I argue constitute the normative implications. The normative theory is premised upon the sociological theory, not the other way around. So, the sociological theory is free-standing, while the normative arguments are not. These normative arguments deserve a book of their own, so are not as developed as the sociological account in the previous chapters.

Our normative starting point is philosophically pragmatist: what is social and political power for? The simple answer is that political structures are there to empower social actors: to give them power-to. So, political structures are normatively desirable to the extent to which they empower. We have already seen that power-to presupposes power-over. In plural societies conflict between social actors is inevitable. Democracy is a set of political structures the purpose of which is to structure such conflict in a manner that the outcome of conflict is positive-sum, guaranteeing the losers sufficient dispositional power that they can fight another day.

In terms of structure, I will take a two-part strategy here. First, I will briefly sketch a moral compass concerning these social subjects for whom power is created, which is rooted in some widely held intuitions that lie at the core of the modern democratic order. Second, the main part of the chapter will take the reader through normative aspects of the four dimensions of power. In many respects this account will be analogous to a process Rawls terms *reflective equilibrium* (Rawls 1993: 28 and 94–7). Rawls moved between moral intuitions and principles. In contrast, our reflective equilibrium moves between normative and sociological theory.

A normative compass concerning social subjects

All statements occur within a field, which constitutes a local language game. So, we will not claim to construct a view from nowhere. Such a strategy would be at variance with our sociological theory. Rather, we look to what is the essence of a particular normative language game.

Based upon Kuhn, specific language games have paradigmatic instances that seem to embody the essence of that language game. In our discussion of political authority we began with the case of Primo Levi who moved from the Y-status of *Italian citizen* to prisoner in a concentration camp where he had virtually no authority to speak, thus negative Y-status, because of his race. The image of Levi's feet being swept as if they were part of the furniture was symptomatic of his lack of authority to speak, which is paradigmatic of how a citizen *should not* be treated.

The perception that Levi should not be treated this way comes from an understanding that this is an inversion of a liberal and republican democratic ideal that the *ordinary life* is of intrinsic value (see Taylor 1989). Ordinary people should have the authority to speak for themselves. This is why paternalism applied to adults, even when well intentioned, is normatively undesirable (Fives 2018).

In Pettit's characterization of republican citizenship (1997, 2012 and 2014), he places citizenship and slavery in conceptual opposition. A citizen is a person who has a *telos* of their own, while a slave has a *telos* that is subservient to the desires of another. This means that the citizen is not subject to the arbitrary power of another (Pettit 1996 and 1997). Arbitrary power in this case does not simply mean unpredictable power; it means power whereby the less powerful become as if they were slaves, or without the right to speak for themselves. Pettit (2014: xiii–xvii) uses the example of Ibsen's play *A Doll's House* to interrogate freedom. In the play Torvald is a wealthy and considerate husband, married to Nora, who desires freedom. Torvald is generous to Nora, and facilitates her in many ways. Yet, the background structural conditions of nineteenth-century society entail that Nora's freedom is conditional upon Torvald's benevolence. In short, Torvald and Nora's relationship is close to the ideal type of benign paternalistic patriarchy. It is comparatively benign because, in practice, Torvald's power-over tracks Nora's interests. Yet, it is normatively objectionable that, in the final instance, Nora's freedom is conditional upon Torvald's benevolence. Torvald has arbitrary power-over Nora, even if he never exercises it to curb her autonomy. We would say Torvald has dispositional power-over Nora, which he never exercises as episodic power. Yet, the very fact that Nora knows that Torvald could limit her freedom deprives her of full autonomy because her 3-D knowledge of the social structures influences her behaviour. This knowledge has the effect that she will be disposed to a strategy of 4-D social ontology of deference, which typically manifests itself in self-deprecating behaviour. In this respect the excessive politeness and modesty of eighteenth- and nineteenth-century middle-class European women was paradigmatic of this kind of 4-D domination.

Torvald is a full citizen, while Nora's authority status still contains traces of slavery because her freedom is exercised through the goodwill of another, which manifests itself in 3-D and 4-D dispositions of deference. Her freedom is dependent upon 1-D benevolence, not 2-D structured rights and constraints.

In essence, Nora's refusal to confirm-structure is symptomatic of her desire for *citizen's authority*. Citizen's authority is the authority to author your own life. It is the authority to speak for yourself. Citizen's authority lies on a scale; Levi lacked it in extreme form, while Nora lacked it to some extent. Arguably, the social movements of the twentieth century represent a slow process whereby the normative implications of citizen's authority have been understood and extended.

Those with the fewest resources, including the homeless, are the most likely not to have full citizen's authority, or only to have it in an attenuated form. In collaborative research with Mik-Meyer, we investigated the extent of citizen's authority of the homeless when interacting with service providers in Denmark. We found citizen's authority present in all interactions, although in some it took largely symbolic form (see Mik-Meyer and Haugaard 2019).

In the feudal order, a life spent in pursuit of glory had higher value than one dedicated to everyday tasks. In contrast, in contemporary liberal democratic theory there is a common baseline whereby all persons are of equal moral worth as citizens. The fact that we grant every adult an equal vote, irrespective of their knowledge of the policy issues, has an irrational element, when viewed functionally, relative to best policy. In the nineteenth century, John Stuart Mill (1972: 286) thought that votes should be weighted in order to create a balance in favour of the most considered decisions, which is a procedure that would have a positive policy function. However, in contemporary parliamentary democracy the normative objective of one person, one vote is not measured relative to best policy. Rather, the vote constitutes an expression of a liberal democratic normative sensibility. We grant the vote to every citizen as a way of reflecting that every person has to have the authority to speak for themselves, so therefore should have the authority to choose who exercises power-over them.

Throughout the nineteenth and twentieth centuries a repeated theme of fiction emerging from the European liberal democratic tradition concerns the right of young adults to author their own lives. Arranged marriages, however well-intentioned (as we saw with the example of Zexer (2016)) are normatively undesirable because they do not respect this right of social actors to author their own lives. Those who fight for their right to marry for love are, in essence, fighting for citizen's authority as a moral foundation.

In contrast, most traditional societies saw their moral foundation in the collective order, hence the importance of arranging marriage that respected traditions and norms. In those social orders the sacrifice of the individual social subject for the collective was considered the height of altruism. Hence, the sacred was associated with sacrifice of the individual for the whole. This moral foundation is graphically represented by the image of Christ on the cross. Christ gave his life to redeem the sins of others. The normative sensibility of modernity, both liberal and republican, turns this kind of traditional moral order upside-down. However, in contrast to natural science, in social life there is never outright victory of one paradigm over the other. The older collective moral foundation lives on in contemporary society as an alternative morality. It is still strong in nationalism and other forms of collectivist political theory, including current populism.

If all citizens should be authors of their own lives, this means that their lives have equal moral worth. Hence, all moral principles have to relate to everyone equally. All moral precepts are universalizable, as in Kant (2012: 17). The moral *ought* applies equally to all and to the benefit of each subject, not just to an exceptional few. There is not one *ought* for the more powerful and another *ought* for the less powerful. This does not mean that everyone becomes equally powerful or wealthy. Rather, that even when unequal in wealth and power, all citizens are expected to be constrained by the same moral principles.

This universal principle is not true for all normative language games. In antiquity, Plato (2007) thought treating unalike persons as if they were equal was unreasonable. If everyone is of equal moral worth, then they should be regarded as such relative to each other. In contrast, if persons are of unequal moral worth, those of lesser moral worth should be sacrificed for those of greater worth. Similarly, in the feudal great-chain-of-being, those at the bottom should be sacrificed for those on top. Hence, it appeared reasonable that slaves and serfs should enable their master or community collective to accomplish glorious or magnificent acts. However, because contemporary social subjects are deemed of equal moral worth it follows that no social subject exists for the sake of another subject, or for the sake of the political system. In short, everyone is an end in themselves – not a means to an end (Kant 2012: 40–1). Every person is part of the kingdom of ends (see Korsgaard 1996). The reason that slavery is so deeply offensive to the modern sensibility is that it is the paradigmatic instance of someone being a means to someone else's end, rather than an end in themselves.

If the social subject is an end in themselves, this means that they do not exist for the purposes of political structures or as an object of power. As argued by Dewey (1998: 4), pragmatism is a theory of action. From the perspective of these social subjects, who are ends in themselves, they are enabled to act because they have power-to. Power structures are normatively justified by the extent to which they enable social actors to act. These power structures are normatively desirable to the extent to which they enable social action. As theorized here, the pragmatic perspective is a purpose-related perspective. The question is: what is politics for? The answer: to enable social subjects, who have the status of citizen's authority, to have power-to and to manage power-over.

In the analysis of social construction I was careful to demonstrate that, contrary to everyday perception, conventionality does not equate to arbitrariness. In this analysis we saw that what made some social conventions better than others is their capacity to realize the purpose for which they have been created. So, from the perspective of complex mathematics, the conventions of Arabic numbers are superior to the conventions of Roman numbers because they enable complex multiplication. Similarly, certain structured power relations are better because they enable actors to act more effectively than others. Similarly, certain political arrangements are better tools for realizing power-to than others.

As we go through the dimensions of power we will see that certain structures facilitate positive-sum power, which, in turn, results in political stability. This arises from the fact that social actors voluntarily collaborate in structural reproduction in positive-sum situations, while in zero-sum power relations they have to be coerced. Stability is symptomatic of the fact that the political structures are fulfilling their function effectively, judged relative to the goals of social actors. From a pragmatic perspective, this has normative force, as these social structures are fulfilling what they are intended for.

In terms of structure I will explore how this normative orientation applies to the four dimensions of power, taking two at a time.

The first and second dimensions of power

In complex political systems and organizations those endowed with authority claim confirm-structuration as an obligation (as a *should*) to their acts of structuration. To return to Dahl's example, if the police officer directs a driver left where she would normally turn right, the driver *should* confirm-structure the police officer's act of structuration. This confirm-structuration is something that the driver should do, relative to the function of the Y-status authority of the traffic police. To be normatively desirable that *should* constitutes both a sociological *should* and a normative one. If all the members of the organization are of equal moral worth, the social structures exist for the purposes of both structurer and the confirm-structurer. *Normatively*, it *should* be the case that the act of confirm-structuration contributes to the reproduction of an authority structure that benefits the driver. To be normatively desirable, the driver should obey the police officer because it is in her interests to do so. Obviously, if compliance entails a long detour, that is a momentary episodic loss. However, if the longer-term effect is to make the traffic flow more efficiently then it is simultaneously a dispositional gain. The core of legitimate power-over hinges upon the distinction between episodic and dispositional power. It is normatively defensible for citizens to be momentarily made to do something that they would not otherwise do (1-D episodic power-over) if this results in longer-term dispositional gain in power-to.

All organizations entail some level of power-over. As observed by Clegg, Courpasson and Philips, 'Power is to organization as oxygen is to breathing' (2006: 3). All organizations entail positions of authority, which command power-over others. To be normatively desirable there must be a feedback process from episodic power-over to dispositional power-to gain, which is only possible because power is variable-sum. If power were inherently zero-sum any exercise of power-over would take the form of straight gain versus loss. Thus the less powerful would be a means to an end for the powerful. Hence all power-over, thus all organization, would be normatively undesirable. This is the normative foundation of anarchism. However, in contrast to anarchism, because power has the potential to be positive-sum, there exists the possibility that episodic loss contributes overall dispositional gain for the less powerful. This is the key to the condition of possibility for normatively desirable power-over, and liberal democracy.

Normatively desirable authority

To be normatively justified any authority exercised should be framed for the power purposes that the creators of the organization desire. If a political organization is set up by X persons, and those persons elect one of their members to Y-status position, the authority that Y has bestowed upon her derives from the purposes of empowering the X persons (see Raz 1990 and Haugaard 2018). When an X confirm-structures Y's authority, by obeying Y's structuring commands, the outcome should entail dispositional empowerment of that X social subject.

The Y-status position has a specific scope of power that defines the position. It is in the interests of the less powerful to have that scope of power specifically tailored to the position that this person occupies in the organization. In other words, they will create 2-D structural constraint upon the Y-status position that confines Y's scope of power.

To be normatively justified, any increase in scope or intensity of power must have benefit for the members of the organization. In terms of normative justification their ends remain paramount. For instance, Y-status may be increased to make the organization more efficient by allowing those with Y-status wider scope of power. However, it is normatively unjustified for the person occupying status position Y to attempt to expand that authority solely for reasons of personal gain, without increase in dispositional power for the less powerful. Furthermore, there are specific limits upon the expansion of Y-status authority.

Limits upon legitimate authority

There are two limits upon political power-over authority. The first is that authority cannot be so excessive that citizen's authority is lost. This condition overrides gains in efficiency or other justifications. Possibly the best way of understanding this is through the metaphor of the *eyeball test*, developed by Pettit (see 2012: 84–5 and 2014: 98–101; Haugaard and Pettit 2017: 27; Savery 2015). Imagine an interaction where A exercises power over B. To be legitimate, rather than domination B must retain the capacity to look A in the eye during and after compliance with A's power-over.

The eyeball test can only be passed when the less powerful actor knows that the more powerful actor does not have *arbitrary* power-over her. Within this context, the absence of arbitrary power means that the person granted Y-status authority never has power-over others in a manner that negates their citizen's authority. The minimal threshold for citizen's authority is that the less powerful should retain sufficient power-to resources to prevent the more powerful from using them as a means to an end. This pertains not only to authority resources but also includes economic resources, as material poverty renders the social subject vulnerable to arbitrary power, conferring all the 4-D dispositions that go with precariousness (see Savery 2015).

To prevent arbitrary power, Y-status authority should be structured to be scope-specific. If the scope of Y's power is known to actors, and adhered to, the power of the more powerful is not arbitrary; it is 2-D structurally constrained. Once the less powerful knows with confidence that the authority of the more powerful has very specific parameters, there should be no reason for the less powerful to show fear or deference to those with Y-status.

Once the responding, less powerful, social subject feels confident that power is not arbitrary, the less powerful will not feel compelled to adopt a

4-D social ontology of deference. They know that the person occupying the Y-status position cannot exact random revenge or extortion.

The second limit that renders Y-status authority normatively legitimate is that the increase in Y-status must be justified relative to the power-to of the *least powerful* actor. As in Rawls' account of the second principle of justice (1971: 60–75), the measure of legitimacy should be measured from the perspective of the least powerful confirm-structurer. To the extent to which the least powerful is deprived of power episodically, they should receive dispositional power in return.

In practice, the extent to which the less powerful confirm-structurer gains dispositional power-to is scalar (on a scale). From the perspective of the less powerful, the greater the dispositional gain, relative to episodic loss, the greater the normative rightness. Again we have to move away from the idea of binary logic here. Political and organizational systems are more or less legitimate. The cut-off point where any normative desirability gives way to normative illegitimacy (at the extreme end of the spectrum) is where the less powerful gains zero dispositional advantage from compliance (for instance, slavery). In that case, the reason for compliance will always be the consequence of the threat of coercion, or justification based upon 3-D reification, or a 4-D disposition of subservience. At the other end of the scale is authority where we can say that the interests of the least powerful are maximized. However, these two are extremes of normative right and wrong. In between these polar opposites are a host of positions that are more or less normatively justifiable.

Power-over: democratic conflict

Citizen's authority makes it entirely reasonable that different citizens, with different views of what constitutes the good life, should have conflicting goals. Democracy is a set of tools that structure social conflict in such a way that power is not zero-sum and, consequently, even the losers gain some power-to. The right of citizens to author their own lives invariably delivers a plurality of visions of the good life. As argued by Mouffe (2000), conflict is inevitable. The idea that we should come to a level of consensus whereby conflict is eliminated suggests totalitarianism, through 3-D and 4-D domination. Democracy constitutes a structured mode of turn-taking that allows social conflict to be managed (but not eliminated) in a manner that respects the right of each to author their own life.

As we saw, power has both an episodic and dispositional element. The former is the momentary exercise of power, while the latter refers to the power dispositions that actors have. The moment the outcome of an election is declared, there are winners and losers. However, that is an episodic event and the losers are not perpetual losers. An election is won when the losers confirm-structure the victory of the winners. In that moment, the winners gain episodically, while everyone gains dispositionally. *Both* structures and confirm-structurers gain because the social structures of the democratic process are reproduced. Essentially, democracy constitutes a positive-sum iterative game in which all the players, including those episodically defeated, have dispositional gain.

The democratic process is a way of distancing politics from the friend/enemy opposition (see Schmitt 2006; also Mouffe 2018 and for a critique Muller 2003), which presupposes a zero-sum concept of power. In the feudal system, social life was largely a friend/enemy relationship. In early capitalism this was still the case. Through a combination of democratization and unionization concessions were made. During the nineteenth century it would have been obvious that the alternative to concession was revolt and coercion, as there was a constant threat of 2-D overt conflict. Slowly, revolt was bought off by concessions. At a certain point, the level of concessions reaches an equilibrium point where the binary logic of friend/enemy is transcended. The majority of people regard themselves as friends with reasonable disagreements. The majority of the population gained some stake in the system, thus became reasonable players who accepted episodic defeat in exchange for overall dispositional gain.

There will always be some who are excluded from the reasonable, who remain (so-called) unreasonable enemies. Actually, their 'unreason' is a matter of perspective; maybe they do not receive sufficient dispositional power-to gain to consider participation worthwhile. Or, it could be that they are actually unreasonable, which means that they do not accept episodic defeat even though they gain significant dispositional power.

Political systems become stable when the majority of actors gain significant dispositional power. A zero-sum friend/enemy-type conflict is binary and coercion is overt. Consequently, the winners have to coerce the enemies into compliance. As confirm-structuration is always coerced, the system is suboptimal in terms of the production of power. It is unstable, as the potential for revolution, or overt 2-D conflict, is always lurking in the background. In comparison, a democratic regime constitutes a stable, structured system because it manages, without eliminating, power conflicts. In competition between systems there will be a natural selection in favour of the more stable, positive-sum, systems.

In a democratic process, even when citizens lose they should not be a means to an end. After their defeat they should retain sufficient agency to fight another day. Normatively, that retention of agency means that the defeated party retains the position of someone who can look the other (the victor) in the eye. In terms of the phatic communion ritual of politics, this is symbolically represented by the custom of party leaders shaking hands. According to the symbolism of this ritual, it is the episodically *defeated* who structures by offering their hand to the victor, while the victor confirm-structures. Even in defeat, the social subject has power-to initiate agency. It is her agency that confers power upon the victor. Hence, the defeated is still a player in an iterative contest. Episodic defeat does not equate to abjection, or zero-sum deprivation of agency; thus citizen's authority is retained. In US presidential elections the handshake has been replaced by a phone call from the defeated party to the victor, conceding defeat. The defeated party then makes this call public knowledge and the election is deemed to be over.

The dispositional power of the loser should be real, not hypothetical

It is important to understand that for the democratic process to have normative purchase, as well as to gain stability, the dispositional powers of the loser must be real, not hypothetical or symbolic. This has a number of aspects, which I will deal with in turn.

With regard to the democratic process, the level of pluralism and type of electoral system can influence the extent to which the worst-off, or the losers, have dispositional power. In permanently divided societies, with simple majority electoral systems, where the winner takes all, the minority may experience zero-sum loss of dispositional power. If they never win, the minority learns that they do not have the dispositional power to fight another day. So, democracy becomes simulacrum democracy, where elections constitute the symbolic trappings of democracy, while the reality is that there are minorities who have little dispositional stake in the system.

When permanent losers have no consequential reasons to confirm-structure, this system is unstable. In such a situation it is unreasonable to confirm-structure. As a consequence, the defeated will be proto-revolutionaries, desiring 2-D conflict in order to create a new system that gives them greater power-to. Instability is symptomatic of the normative fact that the defeated do not consent to defeat because of positive-sum advantage. The losing party does not have true citizen's authority, as they know that they will invariably lose again. Furthermore, as the majority learn that they are permanent winners, and consequently will never be governed by the minority group, the most obvious external constraint to despoiling the minority is removed. The fact that today's loser could be tomorrow's winner is a significant constraint upon arbitrary power, preventing the slide from positive-sum into zero-sum power.

Proportional systems are, in general, more democratic than winner-takes-all systems. The reason usually given in favour of majoritarian systems is that it provides stable government. However, the flipside of this is that the defeated party has less dispositional power. This leads to a two-party system in which minority parties stand very little chance of becoming part of government.

The nature of the social divisions of a society affects the level of democraticness. Plural electorates, with large numbers of swing voters, can mitigate the undemocratic nature of majoritarian electoral systems. In contrast, societies with binary divisions (be they ethnic, or based upon other identity issues) render simple-majority, first-past-the-post electoral systems unsuitable. Where these divisions are longstanding and strong, even a proportional electoral system may fail to deliver turn taking. For instance, parties representing Israeli Palestinians or Arabs have not, as yet, been part of government in Israel, although a recent survey has shown that 68% would like their party to join a Centre-Left government (Maltz 2019).

In systems where permanent divisions occur, consociational democracy (see Lijphart 1977 and 2008) divides political power in such a way that governments either include the minorities and/or give them a veto. In Northern Ireland prior to 1972, nationalists found themselves in a minority vis-à-vis Unionists because voters did not switch sides, and the Nationalists drew their support from a minority of about 40% of the population. Consequently, majoritarian democracy meant continual and certain defeat. The objective of the 1998 Good Friday Agreement was to establish a form of consociational democracy for Northern Ireland, whereby government included the minority. This solution moved the province beyond a state of constant civil war. The willingness of Sinn Féin/the IRA to relinquish the armed struggle was linked to their perception that the new Stormont democracy would mean real political power for them. The agreement entailed moving from zero-sum to a positive-sum situation. The willingness to suspend violence was symptomatic of a move from a friend/enemy dynamic of politics to a position of mutual cooperation. The symbolic representation of this was the frequently reproduced image of Ian Paisley (first minister) and Martin McGuinness (deputy first minister) smiling and laughing together – they became known as the 'Chuckle Brothers' (*Irish Independent* 2017). In this case, sharing a joke together is symbolic of both being able look the other in the eye. Once parity of esteem was established, the zero-sum friend/enemy dynamic was broken.

Political stability

In his theory of political liberalism, Rawls notes an empirical correlation between justice and political stability (Rawls 1993: 140–4). In that discussion it is not entirely clear if Rawls thinks this is a mere correlation, or constitutes a normative foundation. Relative to the pragmatist theory developed here, stability has normative implications because it is symptomatic of the fact that, in the eyes of the actors involved, the democratic process is positive-sum, delivering power to the less powerful in sufficient quantity that they have a stake in the system. Once they gain dispositional power from the system, they are not a means to an end but an end in themselves. So, political stability and justice are not a mere accidental correlation. There is a direct relationship between the positive-sum dispositional power gain of the less powerful actor, political stability and normative desirability.

As a qualification on the above, stability only equates to normative desirability when acquiescence does not entail 3-D and 4-D domination, which we will explore later.

Modus vivendi

In many instances resigned acquiescence constitutes *modus vivendi*. This is an arrangement that occurs without a deep sense of normative commitment towards the other. However, as there is no outright victor, both parties compromise. In international politics the 1978 Camp David Accords, followed by the 1979 Egypt–Israel Peace Treaty, would be an instance of *modus vivendi*. This agreement was not symptomatic of the fact that these two countries had become committed friends. Rather, the Egyptians decided to recognize the Israelis because they were unable to defeat them, having tried to do so several times.

Typically *modus vivendi* is not considered highly normatively desirable. Rawls, for instance, is at pains to distinguish *modus vivendi* from overlapping consensus, characterizing the former as 'altogether inferior' to the latter (1993: 147). In contrast, I would point out that *modus vivendi* can be the starting point to a positive cycle towards a more equal distribution of power, which results in normative desirability. Essentially, over time, if social actors buy into a state of *modus vivendi* and experience that the arrangement delivers positive-sum power, this changes their perceptions. The 1648 treaty of Westphalia was a *modus vivendi* when it was signed. Essentially, it ended a feud between the Catholic South and the Protestant North of Europe, which neither side could win. However, over the *longue durée*, the treaty transitioned into a paradigmatic normative foundation for international-law-cum-justice between sovereign states, as well as a foundation for religious toleration. Out of pragmatic accommodation emerged a whole series of normatively desirable normative principles that underpin the modern international order and liberal political theory. The treaty did not start as a profound normative insight, yet it became normatively thicker over time, as the positive-sum effects became manifest.

This type of process is paradigmatic of the type of pragmatism that underlies practical normative theory, as opposed to abstract theorizing that invariably leads to social systems that subvert the normative intentions of theorists. It is my conviction that liberal democracy did not emerge out of idealism. Rather, it arose out of a slow process of *modus vivendi* buying off of 2-D power conflicts. This pragmatic foundation is not a historical accident; rather, it is fundamental to making the system work.

The slow evolution of power relations towards liberal democratic norms presupposes a succession of *modus vivendi* arrangements. Over time, the process of constant downward buy-out of the revolutionary intent of one group by another confers greater power to the less privileged. Greater commitment to the system by the less powerful reinforces system stability and effectiveness. Once the system increases the power-to of the less privileged, the possibility of a 2-D conflict breakdown of social structures recedes. As the system moves to structured conflict, violence recedes and is replaced by reason-giving that respects citizens' authority.

Rights

A constant danger to democracy is the temptation of the victors to use their power-over to permanently undermine the defeated parties. It is always tempting to convert episodic power-over into permanent dispositional power-over. In order to prevent this, there have to be strict limits upon the powers of the victors. In essence, rights are a form of 2-D structural constraint upon the more powerful that protects the dispositional power of those episodically defeated in democratic contests. Democracy presupposes equality in decision-making, and human rights that limit the powers of government with respect to the individual. While the majority may wish to despoil the minority, rights prevent this. Rights are a condition of possibility for democratic decision-making, while also limiting it.

If the winners in the electoral contest deprive those episodically defeated of a political right, such as free speech and assembly, the less powerful lose dispositional power. Rights are a limit upon power-over, and are normatively justified relative to a shared interest in structuring a positive-sum system in which the least powerful are guaranteed citizen's authority. Losing episodically must deliver dispositional empowerment. If the victors can use their victory to undermine the opponents' ability to fight another day, this fundamentally undercuts citizen's authority. Again, there is feedback from fairness to stability. If the minority are certain of their rights, they will have no fear of conceding defeat. If, in contrast, they have good reason to believe that those empowered will use their power-over to disable minority dispositional power, they will not willingly consent to defeat.

In this theorization rights are not a reified entity. There are no rights-out-there derived from natural law. I agree with Bentham that 'natural rights' are 'nonsense upon stilts' (Bentham 1987: 53). The concept of *natural* rights constitutes an attempt to reify rights. The motivation for character-izing rights in a foundational manner is to reify them; once reified, they appear beyond contestation. The belief that reification is necessary comes from the mistaken belief that convention equals arbitrariness. In contrast, in this theory, we justify rights relative to pragmatist considerations of the conditions of possibility for the social construction of an iterative game of conflict management (democracy). Rights ensure that all members of the polity, including the least powerful, have protection against excessive power-over. Rights enable the least powerful to pass the eyeball test, which guarantees that they will play another round of that iterative positive-sum democratic political game. In short, the only foundation for rights is their usefulness.

If rights are thought of in this pragmatist way, they lose their uncom-promising reified quality. To take an instance, the right to free speech is useful for the preservation of minority viewpoints. However, if free speech is used for the purposes of undermining the democratic process, by demon-izing minorities, free speech is being used to render others subservient, or unable to pass the eyeball test and, in so doing, undermines their citizen's authority. From a pragmatist viewpoint there is no normative problem in limiting free speech in this case. Rights are on a scale. Often they conflict, and so an equilibrium point has to be found between conflicting rights.

This action-oriented approach is consistent with what Amartya Sen would term a capabilities approach to justice (2001 and 2010). Similar to Sen, the capacities for citizen's power-to are not singular. Rather, they are plural. For instance, freedom of speech is not a fully realized right unless it is resourced by universal education, which also qualifies as a right. Because these rights are plural, they are on a scale, rather than absolute.

The *longue durée* process of creating positive-sum-stability-cum-normative-legitimacy

In a binary friend/enemy system, as described by Schmitt (2006), the enemy is a means to an end. If we have a small group of powerful friends dominating a much larger group of subordinate enemies, this is zero-sum power (Schmitt assumes power is zero-sum). In this situation 2-D structural conflict is prevented by coercion. In contrast, imagine a small but powerful group who are continually confronted by rebellious subjects. In order to buy off revolt the powerful individuals single out a particular minority, say, male property owners, and give them a stake in the system, backed by rights. Once these male property owners gain power-to, and confidence that their rights are respected, they become part of the so-called 'friends' within the system, which makes them reliable confirm-structurers. The willingness of the male property owners to buy into the system adds efficiency, stability and positive-sum power to the system. The more powerful learn that giving away power, which is constrained by rights, does not actually mean a net loss in power, as the new group added positive-sum power to the system, giving increased stability and effectiveness. Moving forward, the male workers without property create trade unions and threaten a general strike. In response, unions are recognized as a right, the vote is given, wages are raised and so on, so these workers now also have a stake in the system. As these workers move away from simply being coerced into labour, and start to think of career paths, which are forms of citizen's authority to author their own lives, they become committed to the system, less coerced and more effective. Next, women start to demand and receive power-to and rights, then ethnic and racial minorities and so on.

Let us assume that none of these powers and rights is granted for altruistic reasons, which is a worst-case scenario. The less the members of the system are a means to an end, the more they commit to it. The more powerful buy off an increasing number of people in order to prevent revolt, with the unintended result that they break the friend-versus-enemy dichotomy, as more people feel confident of their citizen's authority backed by rights. They confront each other increasingly as 1-D structured conflict, rather than 2-D conflict over structures, where compliance is based upon 1-D coercion. Being friends does not mean they agree on most things, simply that they are willing to cage conflict systemically as 1-D structural power-over.

As argued by Wilkinson and Pickett (2010), a relatively egalitarian social democratic model benefits both the less powerful *and* the more powerful in society. If the majority population feel they have a stake in the system, the powers of the more powerful do not have to be coercively defended, which creates significant positive effects for the more powerful. However, these positive effects are the unintended effect of intentional action. Historically, the powerful act initially in response to threats of defection and revolution. However, the unintended effect is in their long-term interests. I would argue that the democratic process should be thought of as a structured way of institutionalizing such a virtuous positive-sum power cycle and, in so doing, slowly mitigating domination.

In competition between political systems, there will be a tendency for social systems that generate more positive-sum power to do better than ones that are more zero-sum. The fact that a system is positive-sum means that there is more collective capacity to harness. This, in turn, gives those systems that are more positive-sum an organizational advantage. In other words, I am suggesting a Darwinian evolutionary advantage to democratic systems, which tracks normative desirability. The evolution of democracy associated with modernity is analogous to the evolution of technology in that normative legitimacy confers a competitive advantage in an analogous manner to how advanced technology confers advantage. The implication of this is that the kind of Enlightenment story told by Kant with 'Perpetual Peace' (1985 [1795]) and Pinker in *The Better Angels of Our Nature* (2013), where increasing democracy, and declining violence, came directly out of the Enlightenment project has to be adjusted somewhat. Of course, the Enlightenment ideas are a condition of possibility for democratic societies. However, the reason that democratic society emerged, survived and multiplied (gained evolutionary advantage) was that their positive-sum characteristics gave democratic rights-based systems an advantage over societies that were still largely zero-sum. Democracy won out because it had a power advantage.

Similarly, the decline of violence associated with modernity is not simply the consequence of Enlightenment altruism. It is a consequence of the advantage that positive-sum power has over coercion. If the worst-off comply with power-over because they realize that structural reproduction delivers dispositional power, then they do not need to be coerced. Internal pacification, in turn, confers advantage to the system, as it allows for complexity and flexibility. So, again, the gradual shift from highly coercive political systems to less coercive ones is not simply the victory of the better angels of our nature (as in Pinker 2013), or the story of moral progress.

Power deflation

Contrary to the optimistic story above, power deflation can also occur, even in advanced democracies. Indeed, this is a process that we are currently witnessing. Imagine a system that is highly stable, with a lot of surplus power. Those at the top of this system learn that abuse of trust does not seem to have any immediate effect. So, they award themselves more authority and/or pay themselves bigger salaries. However, unnoticed by the more powerful, support for the system slips from genuine legitimacy to simulacrum legitimacy. For a period, compliance stems from routine compliance to dominant ideology. Those who are most powerful have slipped into the zero-sum category of *elites*, yet compliance is still forthcoming. Unnoticed by these elites, support constitutes a resigned acquiescence, coupled with deep cynicism. Then a specific event triggers resistance. As this resisting group no longer believe in the system, their reaction will be anti-systemic. The result will be the quasi-revolutionary 2-D, as against democratic structurally constrained 1-D.

In a situation of power deflation there will always be a lag between the decline in the legitimacy of power and overt coercion. This is because the routine reproduction of dominant ideology kicks in at first. In the early phase there will be many who are disgruntled but resigned to the system as the natural-order-of-things. They are as yet un-political. However, when a large mass of un-political citizens are offered another vision, they become political, and overt conflict ensues. Arendt argued that the totalitarian movements of the 1930s were the result of previously un-political groups becoming political (Arendt 2004: 421). Today we are witnessing a similar phenomenon in many Western democracies. People who feel marginalized but were previously compliant due to dominant ideology have decided to become political. As they have lost faith in the democratic system, they are willing to listen to those who contest democracy as a sham.

Third and fourth dimensions of power

In our account of the third dimension of power we began with the idea that the interpretative horizons of social actors are divided into practical and discursive consciousness. We argued that relations of domination that are contrary to an actor's interests are often reproduced as practical consciousness knowledge. Once knowledge of social structures is transferred into discursive consciousness it becomes open to contestation. When this occurs, structures are kept stable either by 1-D coercion, or 3-D reification or 4-D ontological disposition, or remain relatively stable through dominant ideology inertia. We saw that social actors are tied into structuration practices through their powers of reasoning, which serve as justification. This was understood minimally as the capacity to be constrained by non-contradiction. For instance, if an actor agrees to stand for election, trying to garner as many votes as possible, they will feel themselves structurally constrained to admit defeat if their party has fewer votes. It would be a performative contradiction, relative to their previous behaviour and discursive principles, not to do so. In short, the soft tissues of the mind bind the political system.

3-D power works through reason, which makes justification central to the democratic process. Imagine that a responding social actor questions a structuration practice; how should the more powerful actor respond? Going back to Levi, if the more powerful actor refuses to respond, or if the request is ignored, this is normatively unjust because it disrespects citizen's authority. As one guard told Levi, 'there is no [reason] why here' (Levi 1991: 35). To be normatively legitimate there must be genuine justification that engages with the justifications of other, thus passes the eyeball test.

In a legitimate system the less powerful should confirm-structure willingly because they *understand* that to do so is in their interests. Understanding means that the act of structuration or confirm-structuration comes from internal volition. To take the other seriously as an end in themselves means that, if required, reasons will be given to explain why that agent should confirm-structure certain forms of status authority. All acts of structural reproduction should be justifiable relative to the power-to goals of a specific field. Episodic power-over should be justifiable relative to the dispositional power-to gain by the responding (confirm-structuring) subject of power.

In our discussion of felicity and infelicity it may have appeared that infelicity was directed solely at exclusion of the less powerful (as exclusion). With respect to the more powerful, the exercise of power outside the intended scope of authority is similarly infelicitous and unreasonable. The scope of authority should be justifiable relative to the objectives of the field and the power-to interests of the least powerful. Accountability requires that those who demand confirm-structuration of their authority can justify that authority in terms of the objectives of that authority as defined by the field.

Justification through reason-giving is crucial to normative justification. As argued by Forst, recognizing others as *human beings* means *recognizing them as moral persons* with a right to *reciprocal and general justification* (Forst 2007: 77). If someone has the Y-status authority of *citizen*, this entails the right to demand justificatory reasons why they should confirm-structure. The exercise of power-over without justification is arbitrary power. Justification suggests that power should always be a*countable*, in the literal sense of a justifiable *account* that respects the confirm-structurer's right to citizen's authority, and is reasonable relative to the objectives of the field. Normatively desirable 3-D entails that when the citizen is bound into the political system through the soft tissues of the mind, this should take place through a process of justification.

Reification

As we have seen, reification is the attempt to make the social construction of structures appear other than conventional. It is a way of asserting that *that which is should be thus because it is inherently so*. This is a way truncating the need to justify, which makes reification inherently normatively objectionable. However, before I make the normative case *against* reification, I wish to acknowledge that reification can have desirable consequences – again, this is not a binary black-and-white theorizing.

Normatively desirable aspects of reification

We have seen that the distinction between sacred and profane constitutes one of the most ancient modes of reification. The classic justification for reification hinges around the idea that once social actors learn that certain social structures are purely conventional, they will conclude that they are therefore arbitrary. Consequently, Socrates, for instance, suggests that the hierarchies and division of labour of the Republic should be made sacred by a myth of metals (Plato 2007: 3.3 414). In consequential terms, Socrates may well be right; perhaps myths of this kind work. Similarly, with regard to the monotheistic faiths, it may well be the case that they performed a pacifying role. Reification through the sacred prevented the constant use of coercion because it made it appear reasonable for social actors to buy into a socio-political system that appeared to them as unchangeable.

The secular equivalent of making sacred is the foundational Truth claim. Social actors are presented with truncated justification. Expert committees use this procedure. Again, this can have beneficial consequences in much the same way as appeals to the sacred. Deep 2-D conflict is averted and stability follows. However, this stability is of lesser normative worth than stability that comes from fuller justification, as we shall see.

Critique of reification

Despite the above acknowledgement, there are serious normative issues raised by reification, both in its sacred and more secular variants.

The first concerns the truncation of the right to justification. In order to qualify as a citizen of equal moral worth, the confirm-structurer is entitled to justification. In contrast, the reification of social structure is a way of subverting that claim to justification. To be told that structural reproduction is *a must* because failure to do so is a profanation of the sacred, or violates the essence of things, or some Truth, is a way of sidestepping justification. A confirm-structurer with citizen's authority over their life has a right to know in what way the social structures that she is expected to confirm-structure contribute to her power-to. The response that a metaphysical socially constructed entity (such as a God, transcendental essence, natural law, Truth or cultural tradition) demands that this is the 'right-order-of-things' is a way of failing to engage with the legitimate question: *how does this social structure empower me?* In substance this is not significantly different from demanding obedience without any justification.

If normative authority can be justified, why is reification required? The suspicion has to be that reification constitutes an attempt to stall justification, by using a trump card. When social actors reify, they make that-which-is beyond critique. Typically, reification constitutes a mask for arbitrary power.

Reification has a second worrying characteristic. If you understand that social structures are social constructions made by people, you are never going to make the mistake of thinking that the structures are more important than the persons who made them. In Marx's theory of alienation, the person is alienated when they think that the thing they create – capital – is more important than they are. Similarly, in Weber's iron cage, bureaucracy becomes an end in itself. Within such a system, which Clegg et al. (2016) characterize as Kafkaesque, the objective of bureaucracy is to reproduce itself, and to use social subjects as a means to do so. A pragmatic approach tells us that social structures should serve the purposes of the people who create them. However, with reification reversal takes place all too easily. If social actors believe that social structures are not social constructions (thus have an independent existence), it is possible to convince them that these structures are more important than they are.

If we look to ancient societies, the perception of self-worth of those societies was generally measured by their conquests. Empires were considered a glorious achievement, irrespective of the cost to individuals. Similarly, great buildings were venerated, while the everyday wellbeing of the persons who built them was deemed of a lesser order of importance. This is symptomatic of societies governed by reification, where the individual was fodder for their own creation. This leads to a state of alienation, whereby the social creation appears as an alien object that dominates its creator.

This process also exists in contemporary society. Nationalism is a way of making a collective identity essentialist (Haugaard 2011), thus a thing-in-itself. As observed by Gellner (1983), most nationalists consider national identity intrinsic and defining of person. Most nationalists try to deny that nations are a relatively recent social construction. Socially constructivist accounts of nations formulated by theorists like Gellner (1983; see Haugaard 2007) are usually rejected by nationalists in favour of primordial accounts, stretching back into the mists of time, to a (supposed) Golden Age of the nation. In contrast to nationalist discourse, if nations are recently made, they can also be unmade. Typically, nationalists believe that individuals should be willing to sacrifice themselves for the nation. It is assumed that if nations are 'mere' social constructions, they are 'arbitrary', thus not worthy of dying for. The nationalist narratives typically emphasize the sacrifice of altruistic nationalists. These call for further sacrifice, making extreme nationalism a kind of tyranny by the dead. Often, nationalists will make the nation sacred, linking it either directly to religion, or some sacred foundational myth. Within this frame of reference, it is altruistic to sacrifice their real living selves for the imagined life of the sacred community. For instance, in the Easter Rising of 1916, the Irish revolutionary leader Patrick Pearse directly linked the insurrection to the Christian ideas of blood sacrifice (Kearney 1978).

As a qualification upon the above, the priority of persons over social structures does not preclude limited community-oriented altruism. Members of a community may, in times of need, legitimately demand sacrifice from its members. However, this sacrifice should not be directed away from the individual towards some alien thing-in-itself. Reification is not normatively required. Justification should explain how individuals benefit from their membership of the community and are therefore expected to give something back. The structures of the community should be recognized as socially constructed, as conventions that could be otherwise. The moral worth of these socially constructed conventions should be measured against the power-to that they deliver. A pragmatic normative approach is commensurable with patriotism of a moderate kind. A pragmatic patriot does not sacrifice himself for some symbol of the nation but may, on balance, place the common good above his individual good. Altruists may even feel pride at the conventions of their community, justified relative to the power-with and power-to of the community. This constitutes a kind of constitutional patriotism envisaged by Habermas (see Muller 2006), which has little in common with the reifications of nationalism.

A third normative problem with reification occurs with regard to the reciprocal fairness of justificatory contestation. If one viewpoint is based upon reification, while others are not, this creates an imbalance of justification. Those holding views based upon reification will be more resistant to compromise because the reified belief cannot be deconstructed. Their reifications are a kind of trump card, which only they hold. Critique by the other that deconstructs the reified social structure is arbitrarily placed outside the frame – a normatively unreasonable 2-D bias. This creates an unbalanced justificatory situation in which the persons, or groups, holding the reified belief will insist that it is impossible for them to compromise because their belief transcends them. Appeals to the sacred, some essentialist views of identity or culture would be typical of this strategy to subvert reciprocity of critique. The use of religion, culture or identity as trump cards that are immune to critique, because of a reified claim that they *just are and therefore must be*, is not normatively justifiable.

A fourth aspect of reification is that it leads to either/or binary thinking. In monotheism the world is divided into some variation of Augustine's two cities: the saved and the damned. In essentialist discourses the world is comprised of similarly either/or sortal concepts. Binary thinking leads to a politics of the extremes where power is perceived as zero-sum.

Currently, populism is socially constructed in a binary manner and entails dangerous reifications. As argued by Muller (2016), populism entails a resistance to pluralism. The populist leader reifies their viewpoint-cum-interests as *the will of the people* and socially constructs those with whom she disagrees as *the elite*. The latter constitutes a negative Y-status that renders them unworthy of justification. This represents a Schmittian turn, where politics is theologized – Schmitt's book is aptly named *Political Theology* (Schmitt 2006). Democratic politics becomes a reified zero-sum field of sacred friends and profane enemies. In contrast, democracy presupposes that those who disagree with you are fundamentally morally equal to you, so therefore must be considered worthy of dialogue.

It is ironic that the social construction of adversaries as 'an elite' is in itself a quintessentially elitist move. Elites can be specified as an ethnic group or a mysterious entity such as the *deep state* or (so-called) *globalists*. While the word *elite* suggests a small minority, they can in fact be numerous, as the (so-called) pro-EU globalists are. Similarly *the people* may fall short of an actual numerical majority. Rather, they are socially constructed as the *silent majority*. In short, populist logic is essentially a form of reverse-elitism. This is a point that is implicitly acknowledged by Mouffe (2018), in her quest to create a Left populism that replicates the logic of Right populism, but without any recognition of the normative problems raised by this form of binary reification.

Deconstructing reification through multiple interpretative horizons

An important aspect of social critique of relations of domination entails showing how it is that we have come to believe the natural-order-of-things. This kind of genealogical deconstruction makes manifest the contingency of social constructions – *that which was made can be unmade*. While this is highly Foucauldian and Bourdieusian, in this framework it is important to add that because social structures are social constructions, this does not mean that they are arbitrary. Structures can be socially constructed for normatively desirable reasons. In that case, deconstruction will show how certain social structures reflect citizen's authority. For instance, a deconstruction of rights will reveal why these social constructions are normatively desirable, relative to their usefulness. This is where grounded critique gives way to pragmatic positive normative theory-building.

One significant mode of deconstructive critique and theory-building is the use of multiple interpretative horizons. In our analysis of practical consciousness we saw that human interpretative consciousness is not composed of a singular interpretative horizon. Rather, our practical consciousness is comprised of a multiplicity of interpretative horizons each appropriate to a specific field. This multiplicity increased with the advance of modernity.

The problem of social critique is always one of perspective. The persons attempting to understand and critique how they came to socially construct the natural-order-of-things have to do so from some perspective or other. There is no outside singular interpretative horizon that constitutes a view from nowhere. In fact, that very idea is a source of reification. In contrast, the social critic has to stand somewhere. The social subject may appear physically singular, but interpretatively they are plural. In a complex modern society there are many cognitive disciplines. So, social subjects can become strangers to themselves by checking to see how things appear from a different interpretative horizon.

The use of a multiplicity of interpretative horizons is a way of extending pluralism to the person. Liberalism is not simply about a plurality of singular persons (as in Rawls 1993: xxv); it is simultaneously about persons who are themselves plural.

Hilberg argued that in order to make the Holocaust happen there were perpetrators, victims and bystanders (Hilberg 1992). The atrocity was not made possible by the perpetrators alone. It required ordinary civil servants do their job conscientiously (see also Bauman 1989: 21). These (so-called) bystanders did their job without questioning the moral basis of what was being perpetrated. The paradigmatic instance is the bureaucrat who is a moral person in the home but ensures that the railways run efficiently, without asking where the trains are going or if they should be going there. This is the phenomenon that Arendt described as the banality of evil (Arendt 2006). In contrast, if those social subjects had allowed their everyday affective familial interpretative horizon to interfere with their work, they would have experienced cognitive dissonance, which could have stimulated critique. Instead of simply doing their job, they could have used other interpretative horizons, supposedly inappropriate to bureaucracy, as a moral reality check.

The Milgram (2010b) experiments were an attempt to recreate the psychic life of the obedient bystanders who facilitate atrocity. As emphasized by Bauman, the Milgram experiments showed that *conflicting information* made the students administering electric shocks more likely to evaluate the morality of the situation, thus to disobey authority (Bauman 1989: 165). This accords with Arendt's observation concerning the change in Nazis living in occupied Denmark (2006: 171–5). Nazi officers facilitated the escape of the Jews from Denmark to Sweden by deliberately leaking information to the Danish underground, including the proposed date for the arrest of the Danish Jews. This information allowed the underground to organize their escape to Sweden. Why did high-ranking Nazis suddenly subvert their cause? Arendt argued that living in Denmark, where Nazi ideology was contested, created interference of interpretative horizon. Thus the racial Nazi interpretative horizon was no longer the natural-order-of-things. It was subject to scrutiny and justification. Consequently, immoral orders did not follow through nearly as effectively.

Modern education entails socialization into a multiplicity of interpretative horizons, appropriate to specific fields and disciplines. This multiplicity makes the person plural and aware that singular descriptions of reality, as the natural-order-of-things, are suspect. In order to gain critical edge, these disciplines should not be reified as separate realms where different Truths reside. Rather, students should learn to think of disciplines as *different ways of describing reality, for different purposes*. From this perspective a description does not represent an objective world-out-there, or natural-order-of-things, but constitutes a social construction conducted for a purpose.

Ironic social subjects

Moving to 4-D, the plural liberal democratic actor I am proposing is akin to the *liberal ironist* described by Rorty (1989) but with a significant difference. For Rorty interpretative horizons are *arbitrary* local ways of life. It is just the way *we happen to do things*. In contrast, because conventions are arbitrary, these are not simply contingent language games. Gestalts all have a purpose that can be subject to justification. To combine Wittgenstein with Kuhn, the gestalts of different disciplines are conceptual tools, which can do their job better or worse. While this perspective is socially constructivist (as in Rorty), it is not relativist (unlike Rorty).

The liberal ironic social subject who I am proposing as suitable for democracy has a sense of irony arising from the realization that there are many descriptions of the world-out-there. Such a sense of irony will make her critical of all attempts to hold on to one single version of reality, including well-intentioned political correctness. Like Rorty's ironist, she is suspicious of any final vocabularies or totalizing worldviews. Yet, her understanding that social construction does not equate to arbitrariness gives her the capacity to fight for what she believes is right, rather than slipping into nihilistic relativism.

Core to the plural self is the realization of the importance of freedom of speech. Like John Stuart Mill (1972: 79), the liberal ironist holds that even mistaken ideas have value in themselves because they accentuate plurality. Consequently, she will, for instance, fight for freedom of speech with a level of conviction she would not if she simply viewed it as an arbitrary Western custom.

The liberal ironist has a number of characteristics, which makes her very different from an ideologue. The liberal ironist loves satire. As a consequence, books of orthodoxy, which cannot be subject to humour, are an anathema. The liberal ironist has a high tolerance for humour that plays with alternate descriptions of reality. Consequently, unlike many liberals of the Enlightenment variety, she does not fear her emotions. Neither does the liberal ironist take offense when confronted with alternate descriptions of reality. To the liberal ironist, so-called 'safe spaces' are dangerous spaces in which plurality and contingency are repressed.

The ironic social subject may have a certain empathy with the *intentions* of those who wish to fix meaning through enforced (so-called) 'political correctness'. However, she will find the exercise futile and wrong-headed. It is futile because there can be no final vocabulary. It is wrong because it is anti-pluralist. There are many descriptions of the world, some may appear offensive, but the ironic response should either be willingness to debate, or laughter, rather than suppression.

The pluralism of the public sphere demands a pluralism of the person. Moving to 4-D state-sponsored formation of persons, education should be plural, not singular. A democratic pluralist society demands a state-funded educational process in which totalizing final vocabularies are constantly subject to scrutiny. Students should be continually made aware of the social construction of all interpretative horizons and encouraged to view them each against other.

In contrast, private single-faith schools encourage singular interpretative horizons with reifications that are never deconstructed. Institutionalized single-faith education is damaging to the process of creating ironic citizens. The intention – to be tolerant of plurality – may be good but the result is to foster groups of people who lack the capacity to see the socially constructed nature of their interpretative horizons. Singular interpretative horizons become reified as the natural-order-of-things. Religious education can take place in schools but it must be plural, introducing a multiplicity of faiths and cultures. Similarly, schools should also be diverse along the lines of class – expensive private education is normatively undesirable.

Multiculturalism encourages a pluralism of *singular* individuals but not plural ironic social subjects. Social actors who are socialized to believe in a single correct interpretative horizon have a weak sense of the ironic. Consequently, they tend to personalize disagreement, taking offence, which has resonance of a feudal honour culture, which is incompatible with democracy. Critique of the order-of-things should never be perceived as insult.

While students need a strong sense of collective solidarity, because it facilitates empathy with the worst-off, schooling should not be nationalistic. Pledges to the flag and so on are a form of reification that is damaging to an ironic sense. Citizens should be aware that nationality is truly just an accident of birth, which could be otherwise.

The idea that a common public pluralist education violates the rights of minorities stems from an over-singular and static view of the person. It comes from the idea of the singular self, who just is the way they are, which is a reification of the person. Rather, social subjects are justifying beings, who act for plural reasons (see Korsgaard 2009: 19) and can revise their practical knowledge. In complex modern societies, where so many situations demand different modes of justification, there is no singular self. Essentialist definitions in terms of religion, gender or sexual orientation render the social subject overly singular. In fact, highly religious groups often have a remarkable ability to switch interpretative horizon, as context demands, when it comes to technology. If the switch is possible between faith and medicine, it is similarly possible to be plural for the sake of democracy.

As a qualification on the above, we also have to recognize that there are very real limits to how much persons already socialized with singular interpretative horizons, especially with a sense of the sacred, can simply turn around and become plural socially constructivist ironists. As suggested by the 4-D discussion of solitary confinement, excessively demanding social change results in ontological insecurity. There are very real limits to how much any social actor can critique their deep socialization. This applies particularly to recent immigrants, or those already fully socialized in a singular-faith community, for whom a socially constructionist worldview may appear arbitrary and profane. Consequently, the social construction of ironic social subjects has to be balanced against the realities of 4-D conditions of possibility. Again, we are dealing with a scale, rather than absolutes, and the objective should always be compromise. Ironic social subjects are formed over time, which may span generations.

Discipline and self-restraint

As was emphasized by Foucault (1979) and Dean (2010), a significant aspect of modern education entails the internalization of discipline and self-restraint, which they view as normatively undesirable. Elias argued that these forms of discipline and self-restraint were the consequence of various groups competing for social capital but implied that the process had normatively desirable elements. Whatever their origins, what are we to

make of these 4-D formations of disciplined social subjects from a normative perspective? Again, there is no single answer. Everything lies on a scale,
and we must evaluate relative to purpose.

Discipline in itself is intrinsically neither good nor bad; what is crucial is
the purpose for which it is used. Is the overall goal to create social subjects
who are willing to accept zero-sum power that renders them comparatively
powerless, or is the objective to form social subjects with dispositions that
enable them to empower themselves? The former is normatively reprehensible, the latter desirable.

An aspect of discipline is the internalization of structuration and confirm-
structuration practices as routine. Through constant repetition the social
subject has an automatic response to certain stimuli, which is socialization
as the internalization of Pavlovian responses. The idea is to maximize practical consciousness over discursive consciousness, and therefore to prevent
critical reflection. Such a socialization distances the person from critical
justification of structural reproduction. The objective is to create a docile
social subject who is automatically compliant. Such docile social subjects
are not predisposed to resist their own domination. Rather, they have
predispositions to be complicit in self-subjectification. Therefore, this specific use of discipline is normatively reprehensible and was what Foucault
had in mind when he wrote *Discipline and Punish* (1979).

In contrast, there are uses of discipline that are normatively desirable.
Discipline can be used to create a social subject capable of long-term forward
planning. Such a social subject becomes capable of deferring momentary
gratification for the purposes of long-term goals. In essence, they develop a
capacity to accept momentarily undesirable episodic power in the interests
of longer-term dispositional power. Elias' description of disciplined social
subjects emerging out of modern complex interdependence constitutes an
account that renders this aspect of discipline visible.

Modernity entails meritocracy (often imperfectly realized) in which education performs a central role. Acquiring such educational qualifications
involves a continual process of deferral of gratification. Within the context of a modern social order, this form of discipline is empowering to social
subjects, as it allows them to author their own lives. In its ideal form, meritocracy is normatively desirable as effort is linked to power-to reward. Thus
discipline leading to meritocracy constitutes a positive-sum system of power.

Obviously, many Western capitalist societies are imperfect in their realization of meritocratic norms. In the UK, the presence of a two-tier educational system is a clear impediment to meritocracy. The solution to this is
not to abandon meritocracy; rather, it is to change the social structures of
society that militate against meritocracy.

Self-subjectification and justice

In our analysis of Elias' account of court society we noted a parallel with Foucault's account of the Panopticon. The creation of a capacity for self-surveillance can be normatively reprehensible when used for the purposes of instilling a sense of paranoia that undermines the person's sense of self. It can be used to create a 4-D climate of fear in which individuals constantly evaluate themselves as falling short. However, these negatives should not blind us to the fact that the capacity to perceive self from the perspective of the other is core to justice. Self-surveillance builds the capacity to distinguish the *I* from the *me* (Mead 2015: 173). The separation of the *I* and the *me* gives the self two different gestalts: one from inside the self, and the other from outside the self. These are two horizons of interpretation upon the self. This capacity is a prerequisite for understanding that the self should abide by rules that can be universalized, which is the foundation of legal justice. In short, the pluralization of the self is the 3-D condition of possibility for the creation of social subjects capable of the 4-D disciplinary methodological bracketing required by a system of justice.

This sense of justice should be embedded in a strong 4-D predisposition towards self-restraint. There is no point in knowing what is fair, cognitively, and not having the self-restraint to act upon that knowledge. This applies both to justice and the democratic process. The 3-D knowledge of universal principles has to translate into a 4-D ontological predisposition not to make an exception of the self. In democracy, turn-taking in elections requires both the 3-D understanding of the meaning of voting *and* the 4-D self-restraint to accept defeat. Once the election has taken place, democracy requires of the victors the 4-D self-restraint not to despoil the losers of their dispositional powers. In already-established democracies, politicians require the self-restraint and sense of fairness not to use their period in office to change electoral boundaries to their advantage, or to target the judiciary, or to undermine the freedom of the press.

Freedom

I wish to conclude our normative theory chapter with a few reflections on the subject of freedom, as this is central to liberal democratic political theory.

In an earlier essay on freedom and power (Haugaard 2017) I distinguished between 'natural' and 'social' freedom. In this chapter I will concentrate solely on Berlin's famous distinction between *positive* and *negative freedom*. Berlin defined negative freedom as follows.

I am normally said to be free to the degree to which no man or body of men interferes with my activity. Political liberty in this sense is simply the area within which a man can act unobstructed by others.

(Berlin 2010: 169)

For Berlin, negative liberty entails 'that a frontier must be drawn between the area of private life and that of public authority' (Berlin 2010: 171). He defines positive liberty as follows: 'The "positive" sense of the word "liberty" derives from the wish on the part of the individual to be his own master. I wish my life and decisions to depend upon myself, not on external forces of whatever kind' (Berlin 2010: 178). In this theorization positive freedom suggests a kind of self-mastery. The classic instance of self-mastery is insistence that we should not be slaves to our passions or unbridled nature, which is an underlying theme for Plato (2007) and to many utopian variants of Christianity and Marxism. Two selves emerge, which can be in conflict with one another. There is the higher self, or the true self (depending upon the utopian vision), and the lower self, which has to be controlled. The higher self constitutes a hypothetical self constructed out of the social whole, represented by 'a tribe, a race, a Church, a State, the great society of the living and the dead and the yet unborn' (Berlin 2010: 179). Berlin sees this as the road to the kind of un-freedom characteristic of utopia-inspired false-consciousness arguments.

With regard to negative freedom, we saw that all forms of resistance require a metaphorical private space – in the case of a slave it was a shack for the family. The whole point of 4-D extreme domination (slavery and solitary confinement) was to deprive the social subject of private space. In Scott's account of subaltern resistance we again see that the dominated social subject realizes autonomy in private spaces. We also saw that the democratic process requires rights that limit the powers of the political victors. For all these reasons, I would agree with Berlin that negative private liberty is normatively desirable. However, I would still reserve significant conceptual space for positive freedom. I would see both forms of freedom as in mutual tension, with balance as normatively desirable.

Berlin views positive freedom as the road to totalitarianism of both the communist and right-wing variety. I would accept that the idea of a higher self (with a true essence) has the possibility of being dangerous when thought of in a reified manner. Those in power can socially construct this human essence, reify it through essentialist claims, and then anyone who does not conform to this social construction has to be forced to be free – to echo Rousseau's infamous phrase. For instance, under Chairman Mao and Pol Pot, *capitalist roaders* had to be re-educated in order to conform to their (supposed) true proletarian nature (see Pina e Cunha et al. 2012 and

2014). It becomes legitimate to oppress and torture in the name of this reified true nature, which serves as a super-ego for the lesser, yet wilful, ego-in-need-of-correction (see Berlin 2010: 180–1).

While we should not downplay the dangers of positive freedom, Berlin's characterization of positive freedom includes reification, and it is the latter that is the normative problem. Reification is equally misguided with respect to negative freedom. Berlin even states that negative freedom should be characterized as a 'sacred ground' (Berlin 2010: 176), which is reification. In the USA, the National Rifle Association's perception of the Second Amendment (the right to bear arms) constitutes a *reification* of negative liberty. It is a sacred ground that has horrendous results. I would argue that both positive and negative liberties are dangerous when reified. Yet, this does not mean that these liberties are not significant when not reified, and theorized as more or less useful social constructions. Rather than asserting the primacy of one over the other, I will argue for a balance between them.

The concept of negative liberty makes sense as an ideal type, which is never realized, but works as a regulative principle. However, if taken literally, the concept presupposes a monadic self, which is inconsistent with the actual socially interactive construction of the self. The social actor gains a capacity for action, or power-to, in collaboration with others. Not only does the solitary individual not have significant capacity for action, their constitution as social agent takes place interactively. These factors bring us to positive liberty as a prerequisite for agency.

Positive liberty has various normative aspects depending upon which dimension of power is in focus. Relative to 1-D power, positive liberty constitutes agency in collaboration with others. As we have argued, the democratic process, and any system of justice, entails social subjects who accept constraints upon their will. The creation of dispositional powers entails accepting short-term episodic constraints upon that will. The reproduction of democratic dispositional power and justice through the rule of law presupposes a social subject who is willing to accept episodic defeat. As we have seen, this entails a 3-D plural ironic worldview and a 4-D self capable of significant internalized restraint. The feudal knight, as described by Elias (1995), did not have (to use Berlin's phrase) the 'higher self' of a democratic social subject. In other words, we should acknowledge that the hypothesis that democracy presupposes an ironic social subject constitutes a claim for a normatively desirable 'higher self'.

Collaboration with others in a positive-sum manner requires 4-D super-ego self-restraint. This does not entail the reifying essentialism of claiming that this represents *true human nature*. In fact, such a 4-D social subject is socially constructed (although based upon biological neural brain capacity). Similarly, the formation of a self-restrained social subject capable of

forward planning is normatively desirable because it is functional to democracy. While re-education according to reified images of human nature in
utopian projects is deeply disturbing, we should acknowledge that everyday
schooling in Western democracies entails subject formation, suggestive
of a higher self. When a student acquires the self-restraint necessary to
master a subject discipline, rather than opting for immediate gratification,
this is a form of positive freedom through social subject formation. What is
at issue is not whether subject formation is right or wrong, as an intrinsic
property. What is at issue is the purpose for which this takes place. As in
Elias' example of the modern highway, the positive freedom of the modern
self-restrained forward-looking social subject (with a sense of *I* and *me*) is
a condition of possibility for the purposes of interdependence in a complex
modern society.

In Bentham's account of the Panopticon (2017), he proposes that the
school Panopticon may be used to perform experiments upon students. In
one school, the students can be taught that two and two make four and
the correct physical description of the moon, while in the second school
the students can be taught that two and two make five and that the moon
is made of green cheese. Then the students can be put together and
observations made (Foucault 1979: 204). This characterization of the use
of the Panopticon school is as an experiment in creating social subjects with
positive freedom dispositions. In the second school, the students are clearly
being used as a means to the ends of the persons conducting the experiment, which is normatively reprehensible. However, in the first school,
taken on its own (without the objective of comparison), the students who
learn mathematics and astronomy are clearly being empowered. Pedagogic
empowerment is not simply with respect to the knowledge acquired.
Pedagogic conditions should be more than simply learning by rote. Hence,
education should emphasize 3-D reflexivity-cum-plurality and 4-D capacity for self-restraint.

Positive and negative freedom should be in balance, and should limit
each other. A Danish study of school children (sample size 20,000,
between ages 5 and 19) examined some of the external influences upon
their ability to concentrate and study at school (Goodyear 2013). Variables
included breakfast, lunch and physical exercise. To the surprise of the lead
researcher (Niels Egelund of Aarhus University), the biggest single factor
that influenced these students' cognitive abilities was exercise, through
cycling or walking to school, not breakfast or lunch. Such simple exercise
before school increased the children's concentration and cognitive power
for four hours after the exercise was completed. In the longer term, the
study found that children in third grade who walked or cycled to school
were the equivalent of six months ahead of their peers who did not cycle.

In contrast to Denmark, in the urban USA most parents would not dare let their children walk or cycle to school, even if the school is only two blocks away (Hoffman 2009). Extending the Elias highway analogy, the metaphor of the modern highway is the conceptual equivalent of the Danish children walking or cycling to school. In contrast, in terms of danger, US streets are analogous to eleventh-century roads. In Denmark there is *less* negative liberty than in the USA, as strong state regulations govern the ownership of firearms. However, the negative liberties afforded by the Second Amendment are a contributory factor in making US streets unsafe, analogous to eleventh-century European roads. Normatively, in Denmark the positive freedom to walk to school has 4-D consequences that positively empower children as social subjects. Being capable of concentrating for longer periods constitutes a form of 4-D social subject formation that is a form of positive liberty. In contrast, with respect to the USA, obesity and stress induced by feelings of lack of safety have negative effects upon children's educational ability, making them less able (see Wilkinson and Pickett 2010: 85–6, 90–1). The latter constitutes an absence of positive liberty, which is an unintended consequence of reifying the negative liberty to bear arms. When we compare the two, it is normatively desirable to limit the negative liberty to bear lethal weapons for the sake of the positive liberties of children to maximize their cognitive capacities.

In this example it is true that there is a positive view of how the social subject should be socialized, which can be described as a 'higher self'. However, this is not really comparable to re-education of *capitalist roaders* (which is the kind of phenomenon that Berlin had in mind).

The problem with positive liberty that Berlin identifies derives from normatively utopian theories. In contrast, positive liberty that is justified relative to pragmatic goals of empowerment constitutes a different matter. Of course, it should be acknowledged that the encouragement of positive liberty has the potential to shade into utopian projects. Therefore, it is paramount that positive liberty is also curtailed by negative liberty.

In conclusion, positive and negative liberties are in tension, and it is normatively desirable to balance them against each other. The balance will never be achieved to perfection. With empowerment there always lurks the shadow of domination. The way to deal with this is not to embrace the chimera of utopian reified models that promise resolution. Neither should we fall for any binary vision, where the (so-called) 'enemy of freedom' can be eradicated. Rather, the name of the game is pragmatic, contextual, purpose-related, plural, ironic reflexivity, which is based upon a sophisticated and nuanced understanding of the four dimensions of power.

References

Abbott, Jack Henry (1991) *In the Belly of the Beast: Letters from Prison*. New York: Vintage Books.

Abercrombie, Nicholas, Stephen Hill and Bryan S. Turner (1980) *The Dominant Ideology Thesis*. London: Harper Collins.

Adams, Douglas (1995) *The Hitchhiker's Guide to the Galaxy*. London: Heinemann.

Agamben, Giorgio (1998) *Homo Sacer: Sovereign Power and Bare Life*. Stanford, CA: Stanford University Press.

Alasuutari, Pertti (2018) 'Authority as epistemic capital'. *Journal of Political Power*, 11(2): 165–90.

Alasuutari, Pertti and Ari Rasimus (2009) 'The use of the OECD in justifying policy reforms: the case of Finland'. *Journal of Power* [now *Journal of Political Power*], 2(1): 89–109.

Alexander, Jeffrey C. (2006) *The Civil Sphere*. Oxford: Oxford University Press.

Alexander, Jeffrey C. (2009) 'The democratic struggle for power: the 2008 presidential campaign in the USA'. *Journal of Power* [now *Journal of Political Power*], 2(1): 65–88.

Alexander, Jeffrey C. (2010) *The Performance of Politics: Obama's Victory and the Democratic Struggle for Power*. Oxford: Oxford University Press.

Alexander, Jeffrey C. (2011) *Performance and Power*. Cambridge: Polity.

Alexander, Jeffrey C. and Bernadette Jaworski (2014) *Obama Power*. Cambridge: Polity.

Allen, Amy (1999) *The Power of Feminist Theory: Domination, Resistance, Solidarity*. Boulder, CO: Westview Press.

Anderson, Benedict (1983) *Imagined Communities: Reflections On the Origin and Spread of Nationalism*. London: Verso.

Arendt, Hannah (1970) *On Violence*. London: Penguin.

Arendt, Hannah (1998) *The Human Condition*. Chicago, IL: University of Chicago Press.

Arendt, Hannah (2004) *The Origins of Totalitarianism*. New York: Schocken Books.

Arendt, Hannah (2006) *Eichmann in Jerusalem: A Report on the Banality of Evil*. London: Penguin.

Aristotle (1941) *The Basic Works of Aristotle*, R. McKeon (ed.). New York: Random House.

Austin, John L. (1975) *How To Do Things with Words*. Oxford: Clarendon Press.

Bachrach, Peter and Morton S. Baratz (1962) 'The two faces of power'. *American Political Science Review*, 56(4): 947–52. Reprinted in Haugaard (2002: 28–37).

Bachrach, Peter and Morton S. Baratz (1963) 'Decisions and nondecisions'. *American Political Science Review*, 57(3): 632–42.

Baldwin, David A. (2015) 'Misinterpreting Dahl on power'. *Journal of Political Power*, 8(2): 209–27.

Bar'el, Zvi (2018) 'With Sissi on the ballot, young Egyptians return to voting with their feet'. *Haaretz*. 2 April (accessed 15 April 2018).

Barnes, Barry (1988) *The Nature of Power*. Cambridge: Polity Press.

Barry, Norman (1982) 'The tradition of spontaneous order: a bibliographical essay'. *Literature of Liberty: A Review of Contemporary Liberal Thought*, 5(2): 7–58.

Bettelheim, Bruno (1986) *The Informed Heart: A Study of the Psychological Consequences of Living under Extreme Fear and Terror*. London: Penguin.

Bashir, Martin (2018) 'Leo Varadkar glad church is "less dominant" in Ireland'. BBC News (online). Available at: www.bbc.com/news/world-europe-45291018 (accessed 10 March 2020).

Bauman, Zygmunt (1989) *Modernity and the Holocaust*. Cambridge: Polity.

BBC News (2017) 'Spain Catalonia: PM Rajoy vows to fight independence vote'. BBC News (online). 7 September (accessed 10 September 2017).

BDS Movement (2018) 'BDS Movement'. Available from: www.bdsmovement.net/. (accessed 25 July 2018).

Beard, Mary and Hilary Clinton (2017) 'Let's talk: a conversation special'. *The Guardian* (online). 2 December (accessed 5 December 2017).

de Beauvoir, Simone (2010) *The Second Sex*. London: Vintage.

Bellah, Robert N. (1967) 'Civil religion in America'. *Daedalus*, 96(1): 1–21.

Bentham, Jeremy (1987) 'Anarchical fallacies'. In J. Waldron (ed.), *Nonsense upon Stilts: Bentham, Burke and Marx on the Rights of Man*. London: Routledge, pp. 46–77.

Bentham, Jeremy (2017) *Panopticon: The Inspection House*. London: Createspace Independent Publishing.

Berlin, Isaiah (2010) 'Two concepts of liberty'. In I. Berlin and H. Hardy (eds), *Liberty*. Oxford: Oxford University Press, pp. 166–217.

Bettelheim, Bruno (1986) *The Informed Heart: A Study of the Psychological Consequences of Living under Extreme Fear and Terror*. London: Penguin.

Billig, Michael (2005) *Laughter and Ridicule: Towards a Critique of Humour*. London: Sage.

Boffey, Daniel and Sam Jones (2017) 'Spain "ready to discuss" greater fiscal autonomy for Catalonia.' *The Guardian* (online). 21 November (accessed 4 December 2017).

Boffey, Daniel and Jennifer Rankin (2018) 'EU publishes plan to keep Northern Ireland in customs union.' *The Guardian* (online). February 28 (accessed February 28, 2019).

Bohr, Nils (1949) 'Discussions with Einstein on epistemological problems in atomic physics'. In P. Schilpp (ed.), *Albert Einstein: Philosopher-Scientist*. Peru, IL: Open Court Publishing, pp. 199–242.

Bourdieu, Pierre (1977) *Outline of a Theory of Practice*. Cambridge: Cambridge University Press.

Bourdieu, Pierre (1989) *Distinction*. Oxford: Routledge.

Bourdieu, Pierre (1990) *The Logic of Practice*. Cambridge: Cambridge University Press.

Bourdieu, Pierre (2000) *Pascalian Meditations*. Cambridge: Polity Press.

Breen, Keith (2007) 'Violence and power: a critique of Hannah Arendt on the "political"'. *Philosophy and Social Criticism*, 33(3): 343–72.

Butler, Judith (1997) *The Psychic Life of Power*. Stanford, CA: Stanford University Press.

Campion, Nicholas (2017) 'How many people actually believe in astrology?'. *Phys Org News* (online). 28 April (accessed 15 May 2018).

Chomsky, Noam (2002) *On Nature and Language*. Cambridge: Cambridge University Press.

Chomsky, Noam (2006) *Language and Mind* (3rd edn). Cambridge: Cambridge University Press.

Christianson, John R. (2000) *On Tycho's Island*. Cambridge: Cambridge University Press.

Clegg, Stewart (1989) *Frameworks of Power*. London: Sage.

Clegg, Stewart, David Courpasson and Nelson Philips (2006) *Power and Organization*. London: Sage.

Clegg, Stewart, Miguel Pina e Cunha, Iain Munro, Arménio Rego and Martha Oom Sousa (2016) 'Kafkaesque power and bureaucracy'. *Journal of Political Power*, 9(2): 157–81.

Clinton, Hillary (2017) *What Happened*. London: Simon & Schuster.

Cooke, Maeve (1994) *Language and Reason: A Study of Habermas' Pragmatics*. Cambridge, MA: The MIT Press.

Cooke, Maeve (2006) *Re-Presenting the Good Society*. Cambridge, MA: The MIT Press.

Connolly, William (1983) *The Terms of Political Discourse* (2nd edn). Princeton, NJ: Princeton University Press.

Cseresnyesi, Laszlo (1996) 'Sum: Borgesian joke'. Linguist List 7.1446. Available at: https://linguistlist.org/issues/7/7-1446.html (accessed 10 March 2020).

Dahl, Robert A. (1957) 'The concept of power'. *Behavioural Science*, 2(3): 201–15.

Dahl, Robert A. (1961) *Who Governs?* New Haven, CT: Yale University Press.

Dahl, Robert A. (1968) 'Power'. In David L. Shills (ed.), *International Encyclopedia of the Social Sciences*, Vol. 12. New York: Macmillan, pp. 405–15.

Dahl, Robert A. (1989) *Democracy and its Critics*. New Haven, CT: Yale University Press.

Dalberg-Acton, John E.E. (1887) Acton-Creighton Correspondence. Online Library of Liberty. Available at: www.oll.libertyfund.org/titles/acton-acton-creighton-correspondence (accessed 12 March 2018).

Darwin, Charles (1998) *The Origin of Species*. London: Wordsworth Classics of World Literature.

Davenas, E., F. Beauvais, J. Amara, M. Oberbaum, B. Robinzon, A. Miadonnai, A. Tedechi, B. Pomeranz, P. Fortner, P. Belon, J. Sainte-Laudy, B Poitevin and J. Benveniste (1988) 'Human basophil degranulation triggered by very dilute antiserum against IgE'. *Nature*, 333 (6176): 816–18.

Dawkins, Richard (2006) *The Selfish Gene*. Oxford: Oxford University Press.

Dean, Mitchell (2010) *Governmentality: Power and Rule in Modern Society* (2nd edn). London: Sage.

Descartes, René (1912) *A Discourse on Method*. London: Dent, Everyman's Library.

Dewey, John (1998) *The Essential Dewey: Pragmatism, Education Democracy, Vol. 1.* Bloomington, IN: Indiana University Press.

Digeser, Peter (1992) 'The fourth face of power'. *Journal of Politics*, 54(4): 977–1007.

Durkheim, Émile (1989 [1897]) *Suicide*. Oxford: Routledge.

Durkheim, Émile (2008 [1915]) *The Elementary Forms of Religious Life*. Oxford: Oxford University Press.

Durkheim, Émile (1982) *The Rules of Sociological Method*. London: Macmillan.

The Economist (2013) 'Slamming on the brakes: drivers push back against a government directive'. *The Economist*. 12 January.

Elias, Norbert (1995) *The Civilizing Process: The History of Manners and State Formation and Civilization*. Oxford: Blackwell.

Elster, Jon (2015) *Explaining Social Behavior: More Nuts and Bolts for the Social Sciences*. Cambridge: Cambridge University Press.

Erdbrink, Thomas (2017) 'Iran bans two soccer stars for playing against Israelis'. *The New York Times*. 10 August.

Erikson, Erik (1995) *Childhood and Society*. London: Vintage Books.

Faculty of Homeopathy (2018) Faculty of Homeopathy. Available at: www.facultyofhomeopathy.org (accessed 12 May 2018).

Faculty of Homeopathy (2018) 'Evidence'. Faculty of Homeopathy. Available at: www.facultyofhomeopathy.org/homeopathy-the-evidence (accessed 12 May 2018).

Fives, Allyn (2018) 'Paternalism and moral conflict: a pluralist analysis of paternal power'. *Journal of Political Power*, 11(2): 151–64.

Flat Earth (2018) *Flat Earth – UK Convention*. Available at: www.flatearth conventionuk.co.uk (accessed 15 March 2018).

Flyvbjerg, Bent (1998) *Rationality and Power: Democracy in Practice*. Chicago, IL: University of Chicago Press.

Ford, Richard T. (2005) *Racial Culture: A Critique*. Princeton, NJ: Princeton University Press.

Forst, Rainer (2007) *The Right to Justification*. New York: Columbia University Press.

Forst, Rainer (2015) 'Noumenal power'. *The Journal of Political Philosophy*, 23(2): 111–27.

Forst, Rainer (2017) *Normativity and Power: Analysing Social Orders of Justification*. Oxford: Oxford University Press.

Foucault, Michel (1970) *The Order of Things*. London: Routledge.

Foucault, Michel (ed.) (1975) *I, Pierre Riviére, Having Slaughtered My Mother, my Sister, and My Brother: A Case of Parricide in the Nineteenth Century*. New York: Pantheon Books.

Foucault, Michel (1979) *Discipline and Punish: The Birth of the Prison*. Harmondsworth: Penguin.

Foucault, Michel (1980) *Power Knowledge: Selected Interviews and Other Writings 1972–1977*, ed. Colin Gordon. Brighton: Harvester Press.

Foucault, Michel (1981) *The History of Sexuality Volume 1: An Introduction*. Harmondsworth: Penguin.

Foucault, Michel (1982) 'The subject and power'. Afterword in H.L. Dreyfus and P. Rabinow (eds), *Beyond Structuralism and Hermeneutics*. London: Harvester Wheatsheaf.

Foucault, Michel (1988) *Politics, Philosophy, Culture: Interviews and Other Writings 1977–1984*, ed. Lawrence D. Kritzman. London: Routledge.

Foucault, Michel (1989) *The Archaeology of Knowledge*. London: Routledge.

Foucault, Michel (1994) *Power: Essential Works of Michel Foucault 1954–1984, Vol. 3*, ed. James D. Faubion. New York: The New Press.

Foucault, Michel (2010) *The Government of Self and Others: Lectures at the Collége de France, 1982–1982*. London: Palgrave Macmillan.

Foucault, Michel and Donald F. Bouchard (ed.) (1977) *Language, Counter-Memory, Practices: Selected Essays and Interviews*. New York: Cornell University Press.

Frankfurt, Harry (2005) *On Bullshit*. Princeton, NJ: Princeton University Press.

Gallie, Walter B. (1956) 'Essentially contested concepts'. *Proceedings of the Aristotelian Society*, 56: 167–98.

Gambetta, Diego and Steffen Hertog (2009) 'Why are there so many engineers among Islamic radicals?' *European Journal of Sociology*, 50(2): 201–30.

Gardner, Howard (1991) *The Unschooled Mind: How Children Think and how Schools should Teach*. New York: Basic Books.

Garfinkel, Harold (1984) *Studies in Ethnomethodology*. Cambridge: Polity.

Gellner, Ernest (1983) *Nations and Nationalism*. Oxford: Blackwell.

Gellner, Ernest (1989) *Plough, Sword and Book*. Chicago, IL: Chicago University Press.

Giddens, Anthony (1984) *The Constitution of Society*. Cambridge: Polity.

Gilabert, Pablo (2018) 'A broad definition of agential power'. *Journal of Political Power*, 11(1): 79–92.

Gilbert, Martin (2008) *Israel: A History*. London: Black Swan.

Giuffrida, Angela (2018) 'Vatican scrambles after Pope appears to deny existence of Hell'. *The Guardian* (online). 30 March (accessed 30 March 2018).

Glynos, Jason and David Howarth (2007) *Logics of Critical Explanation in Social and Political Theory*. London: Routledge.

Goffman, Erving (1971) *The Presentation of Self in Everyday Life*. Harmondsworth: Pelican.

Goodyear, Sarah (2013) 'The link between kids who walk or bike to school and concentration'. *Citylab* (online). 5 February (accessed 16 January 2018).

Gramsci, Antonio (1973) *Selections from Prison Notebooks*. London: Lawrence and Wishart.

Grimes, David Robert (2012) 'Proposed mechanisms for homeopathy are physically impossible'. *Focus on Alternative and Complementary Therapies*, 17(3): 149–56.

Grimwood, Tom (2011) 'Nietzsche's death of God'. In S. Bruce and M. Barbone (eds), *Just the Arguments*. Oxford: Blackwell.

The Guardian (2018) 'Afghan president offers to recognize Taliban to end war'. *The Guardian* (online). 28 February (accessed 1 March 2018).

The Guardian (2018) 'French waiter says firing for rudeness is "discrimination against my culture"'. *The Guardian* (online). 26 March (accessed 28 March 2018).

Guenther, Lisa (2013) *Solitary Confinement: Social Death and its Afterlives*. Minneapolis, MN: University of Minnesota Press.

Haaretz (2017) 'Iranian wrestler says manager forced him to lose to avoid facing an Israeli'. *Haaretz* (online). 28 November (accessed 22 February 2018).

Haaretz (2018) 'Iranian wrestler temporarily banned after intentional loss to avoid Israeli opponent'. *Haaretz* (online). 19 February (accessed 22 February 2018).

Habermas, Jurgen (1984) *The Theory of Communicative Action, Vol. 1*. Cambridge: Polity.

Habermas, Jurgen (1990) *The Philosophical Discourse of Modernity*. Cambridge: Polity Press.

Hahnemann, Samuel (1833) [1796] *The Homoeopathic Medical Doctrine*. Dublin: W.F. Wakeman.

Haugaard, Erik (1966) Anonymous eyewitness account of the Shoah, as related to Erik Haugaard at Kibbutz Shomrat, Israel, in 1966.

Haugaard, Mark (1992) *Structures, Restructuration and Social Power*. Aldershot: Avebury.

Haugaard, Mark (1997) *The Constitution of Power*. Manchester: Manchester University Press.

Haugaard, Mark (ed.) (2002) *Power: A Reader*. Manchester: Manchester University Press.

Haugaard, Mark (2007) 'Power, modernity and liberal democracy'. In S. Malesevic and M. Haugaard (eds), *Ernest Gellner and Contemporary Social Thought*. Cambridge: Cambridge University Press.

Haugaard, Mark (2008a) 'Sociological Lukes versus moral Lukes: reflections on the second edition of Power: A Radical View by Steven Lukes'. *Journal of Power* [now *Journal of Political Power*], 1(1): 99–106.

Haugaard, Mark (2008b) 'Power and habitus'. *Journal of Power* [now *Journal of Political Power*], 1(2): 189–206.

Haugaard, Mark (2010) 'Power: a "family resemblance concept"'. *European Journal of Cultural Studies*, 13(4): 419–38.

Haugaard, Mark (2011) 'Identity and nationalism in a global world: some theoretical reflections'. In M. Boss (ed.), *Narrating Peoplehood Amidst Diversity*. Aarhus: Aarhus University Press.

Haugaard, Mark (2014) 'Power'. *The Encyclopaedia of Political Thought*, pp. 2965–78. Oxford: Blackwell.

Haugaard, Mark (2015) 'Concerted power over'. *Constellations: An International Journal of Critical and Democratic Theory*, 22(1): 147–58.

Haugaard, Mark (2016) 'Two types of freedom and four dimensions of power'. *Revue International Philosophie*, 70(275): 37–66.

Haugaard, Mark (2018) 'What Is authority?' *Journal of Classical Sociology*, 18(2): 104–32.

Haugaard, Mark and Philip Pettit (2017) 'A conversation on power and republicanism: an exchange between Mark Haugaard and Philip Pettit'. *Journal of Political Power*, 10(1): 25–39.

Haugaard, Mark and Kevin Ryan (2012) *Political Power: The Development of the Field*. Berlin: Barbara Budrich.

Hayward, Clarissa Rile and Steven Lukes (2008) 'Nobody to shoot? Power, structure, and agency'. *Journal of Power* [now *Journal of Political Power*], 1(1): 5–20.

Hayward, Clarissa Rile (2000) *De-Facing Power*. Cambridge: Cambridge University Press.

Hayward, Clarissa Rile (2013) *How Americans Make Race*. Cambridge: Cambridge University Press.

Heaney, Jonathan (2011) 'Emotion and power: reconciling conceptual twins'. *Journal of Political Power*, 4(2): 259–77.

Heaney, Jonathan and Helena Flam (2015) *Power and Emotion*. Oxford: Routledge.

Hegel, Georg W.F. (1961) *The Phenomenology of Mind*. London: Allen and Unwin.

Heidegger, Martin (1962) *Being and Time*. Oxford: Basil Blackwell.

Heritage, John (1984) *Garfinkel and Ethnomethodology*. Cambridge: Polity Press.

Hilberg, Raul (1992) *Perpetrators, Victims, Bystanders: The Jewish Catastrophe 1933–1945*. London: Harper.

Hindess, Barry (1995) *Discourses of Power*. Oxford: Wiley Blackwell.

Hobbes, Thomas (1914 [1651]) *Leviathan*. London: Dent, Everyman's Library.

Hoffman, Jan (2009) 'Why can't she walk to school?' *New York Times* (online). 12 September (accessed 17 February 2018).

Hughes, Gillian (2015) 'Fiction in the magazines'. In P. Garside and K. O'Brien (eds), *The Oxford History of the Novel in English*. Oxford: Oxford University Press, pp. 461–528.

Humphries, Conor (2017) 'Three months that shook Ryanair: how cancellations sparked a pilot revolt'. *Reuters Business News* (online). 20 December (accessed 25 May 2018).

Husserl, Edmund (1991) *General Introduction to Pure Phenomenology*. London: Routledge.

Hyland, James (1995) *Democratic Theory: The Philosophical Foundations*. Manchester: Manchester University Press.

Irish Independent (2017) 'How Martin McGuinness and Ian Paisley forged an unlikely friendship'. *Irish Independent*. 21 March.

Irish School of Homeopathy (2018) 'Irish School of Homeopathy – Courses'. Irish School of Homeopathy. Available at: www.ish.ie/courses (accessed 1 April 2018).

Inglis, Tom (1998) *Moral Monopoly: The Rise and Fall of the Catholic Church in Modern Ireland*. Dublin: University College Dublin.

James, William (1981) *Pragmatism*. Indianapolis, IN: Hackett Publishing.

Jenkins, David and Steven Lukes (2017) 'The power of occlusion'. *Journal of Political Power*, 10(1): 6–24.

Johansson, Anna and Stellan Vinthagen (2015) 'Dimensions of everyday resistance: the Palestinian *Sumud*'. *Journal of Political Power*, 8(1): 109–40.

Kant, Immanuel (1985) 'Perpetual peace: a philosophical sketch'. In *Perpetual Peace and Other Essays*. Indianapolis, IN: Hackett.

Kant, Immanuel (2003) *Critique of Pure Reason*. Translated by Norman K. Smith. London: Palgrave Macmillan.

Kant, Immanuel (2012) *Groundwork of the Metaphysics of Morals*. Translated by Christine Korsgaard. Cambridge: Cambridge University Press.

Kearney, Richard (1978) 'Myth and terror'. *The Crane Bag Journal*, 2(1&2): 260–8.

Kettner, Matthias (2018) 'The Forstian Bargain: Overrationalizing the Power of Reasons'. *Journal of Political Power*, 11(2): 139–50.

Korsgaard, Christine M. (1996) *Creating the Kingdom of Ends*. Cambridge: Cambridge University Press.

Korsgaard, Christine M. (2009) *Self-Constitution: Agency Identity and Integrity*. Oxford: Oxford University Press.

Kuhn, Thomas S. (1970) *The Structure of Scientific Revolutions*. Chicago, IL: The University of Chicago Press.

Kuhn, Thomas S. (1977) *The Essential Tension: Selected Studies in Scientific Thought and Change*. Chicago, IL: The University of Chicago Press.

Kuhn, Thomas S. (1985) *The Copernican Revolution*. Cambridge, MA: Harvard University Press.

Kumwenda-Mtambo, Olivia (2018) South Africa's ANC to amend constitution to allow land expropriation'. Reuters (online). 31 July (accessed 1 August 2018).

Landes, Joan B. (1988) *Women and the Public Sphere in the Age of the French Revolution*. Ithaca, NY: Cornell University Press.

Langone, John (1988) 'Science: the water that lost its memory'. *Time Magazine*. 8 August.

Lanzmann, Claude (1985) *Shoah: An Oral History of the Holocaust* (movie). British Broadcasting Corporation (BBC).

Lappin, Chloe (2017) *The Presentation of Everyday Self as a Form of Identity Capital in Disadvantaged Social Contexts* (M.Litt). Galway: National University of Ireland.

Laver, Michael (1997) *Private Desires, Political Action: Invitation to the Politics of Rational Choice*. London: Sage.

Levi, Primo (1991) *If This is a Man*. London: Abacus.

Levi, Primo (2013) *The Drowned and the Saved*. London: Abacus.

Lijphart, Arend (1977) *Democracy in Plural Societies: A Comparative Approach*. New Haven, CT: Yale University Press.

Lijphart, Arend (2008) *Thinking about Democracy: Power Sharing and Majority Rule in Theory and Practice*. Oxford: Routledge.

Los Angeles Times (2016) 'Nancy Regan turned to astrology in White House to protect her husband'. *Los Angeles Times*. 6 March (accessed 15 July 2018).

Lukacs, Gyorgy (2000) *History and Class Consciousness: Studies in Marxist Dialectics*. Cambridge, MA: The MIT Press.

Lukes, Steven (1974) *Power: Radical View*. London: Macmillan.

Lukes, Steven (2005) *Power: A Radical View* (2nd edn). Basingstoke: Palgrave Macmillan.

Lukes, Steven (2018) 'Noumenal power: concept and explanation'. *Journal of Political Power*, 11(1): 46–55.

McCarthy, Tom (2018) 'Hilary Clinton unleashed foul-mouthed tirade in Trump prep session.' *The Guardian* (online). 24 April (accessed 25 April 2018).

McCullough, Michael E., Kurzban, Robert and Tabak, Benjamin A. (2013) 'Cognitive systems for revenge and forgiveness'. *Behavioural and Brain Sciences*, 36(1): 1–15.

McLoughlin, Gavin and Breda Heffernan (2017) 'Ryan Air pilots call off-Christmas strike as airline recognises union'. *Irish Independent*. 18 December.

Maddox, J., J. Randi and W.W. Stewart (1988) ' "High-Dilution" Experiments a Delusion'. *Nature*, 334 (6180): 287–90.

Maddox, John (1988) 'When to believe the unbelievable'. *Nature*, 333 (6176): 787.

Malesevic, Sinisa, and Kevin Ryan (2012) 'The disfigured ontology or figurational sociology: Norbert Elias and the question of violence'. *Critical Sociology*, 29(2): 165–81.

Maltz, Judy (2019) 'Significant majority of Israeli Arabs want representation in next government, survey shows'. *Haaretz* (online). 28 January (accessed 28 January 2019).

Marsh, Henry (2014) *Do No Harm: Stories of Life Death and Brain Surgery*. London: Weidenfeld & Nicolson.

Marshall, Michael (2018) 'The universe is an egg and the moon isn't real: note from a Flat Earth Conference'. *The Guardian*. 2 May.

Marx, Karl (1974) *The German Ideology*, C.J. Arthur (ed.) (student edition). London: Lawrence & Wishart Limited.

Marx, Karl (1976) *Capital*, Vol. 1. Harmondsworth: Penguin.

Maskey, Paul (2018) 'I'm a Sinn Fein MP. This is why I won't go to Westminster, even over Brexit.' *The Guardian* (online). 6 March (accessed 9 March 2018).

Mead, George H. (2015) *Mind, Self & Society*. Chicago, IL: University of Chicago Press.

M.E.M.R.I. TV videos (2018) 'Egyptian TV host kicks atheist out of studio, recommending psychiatric treatment'. *YouTube*. 2 March. Available at: www. youtube.com/watch?v=J5aseBw4BmM (accessed 8 March 2018).

Mennell, Stephen (1989) *Norbert Elias: An Introduction*. Oxford: Blackwell.

Mik-Meyer, Nanna (2007) 'Interpersonal relations or jokes of social structure? Laughter in social work'. *Qualitative Social Work*, 6(1): 9–26.

Mik-Meyer, Nanna and Mark Haugaard (2019) 'The performance of citizen's and organisational authority'. *Journal of Classical Sociology* 1–26, published online. DOI: i1.o0r.g1/107.171/1747/61847689759X5X1919886600111.

Milgram, Stanley (2010a) 'On maintaining social norms: a field experiment in the subway'. In T. Blass (ed.), *The Individual in a Social World: Essays and Experiments*. London: Pinter & Martin, pp. 34–41.

Milgram, Stanley (2010b) 'Some conditions of obedience and disobedience to authority'. In T. Blass (ed.), *The Individual in a Social World: Essays and Experiments*. London: Pinter & Martin, pp. 128–50.

Mill, John Stuart (1972) *Utilitarianism, Liberty, and Representative Government*. London: Everyman's Library, John Dent & Son.

Moi, Toril (2010) ' "The Adulteress Wife". A review of The Second Sex by Simone de Beauvoir'. *London Review of Books*, 32(3): 3–6.

Moriarty, Gerry (2014) 'DUP's Campbell denied speaking rights for "mocking Irish"'. *Irish Times*. 4 November.

Morris, Benny (2001) *Righteous Victims: A History of the Zionist-Arab Conflict 1881–2001*. London: Vintage.

Morris, Benny (2004) *The Birth of the Palestinian Refugee Problem Revisited*. Cambridge: Cambridge University Press.

Morriss, Peter (2002) *Power: A Philosophical Analysis* (2nd edn). Manchester: Manchester University Press.

Morriss, Peter (2009) 'Power and liberalism'. In S. Clegg and M. Haugaard (eds), *The Sage Handbook of Power*. London: Sage, pp. 54–69.

Mouffe, Chantal (2000) *The Democratic Paradox*. London: Verso.

Mouffe, Chantal (2018) *For A Left Populism*. London: Verso.

Muller, Filip (1999) *Eyewitness Auschwitz: Three Years in the Gas Chamber*. Chicago, IL: Ivan R Dee Publisher.

Muller, Jan-Werner (2003) *A Dangerous Mind: Carl Schmitt in Post-War European Thought*. New Haven, CT: Yale University Press.

Muller, Jan-Werner (2006) 'On the origins of constitutional patriotism'. *Contemporary Political Theory*, 5: 278–96.

Muller, Jan-Werner (2016) *What is Populism?*. Philadelphia, PA: University of Pennsylvania Press.

Nietzsche, Friedrich (2006) *The Nietzsche Reader*, K.A. Pearson and D. Large (eds). Oxford: Blackwell.

Northup, Solomon (2012) *Twelve Years a Slave*. London: Penguin Classics.

Palacios, Carlos (2018) 'Freedom can also be productive: the historical inversions of "the conduct of conduct'. *Journal of Political Power*, 11(2): 252–72.

Pansardi, Pamela (2012) 'Power to and Power over: two distinct concepts?' *Journal of Political Power*, 5(1): 73–89.

Pareto, Vilfredo (1935) *The Mind and Society*. London: Harcourt Brace.

Parsons, Talcott (1963) 'On the concept of political power'. *Proceedings of the American Philosophical Society*, 107(3): 232–62. Also Reprinted in Haugaard (2002: 70–112).

Patterson, Orlando (1982) *Slavery and Social Death*. Cambridge, MA: Harvard University Press.

Pettit, Philip (1996) 'Freedom as antipower'. *Ethics*, 106(3): 576–604.

Pettit, Philip (1997) *Republicanism: A Theory of Freedom and Government*. Oxford: Oxford University Press.

Pettit, Philip (2012) *On the People's Terms: A Republican Theory of Democracy*. Cambridge: Cambridge University Press.

Pettit, Philip (2014) *Just Freedom: A Moral Compass for a Complex World*. New York: Norton and Company.

Philips, Amali (2004) 'Gendering Colour: Identity, Femininity, and Marriage in Kerela'. *Anthropologia*, 46: 253–72.

Pinker, Steven (1995) *The Language Instinct*. London: Penguin.

Pinker, Steven (2012) *The Better Angels of Our Nature*. London: Penguin.

Pina e Cunha, Miguel, Stewart Clegg, Arménio Rego and Michele Lancione (2012) 'The organization (*Ângkar*) as a state of exception: the case of the S-21 extermination camp, Phnom Penh'. *Journal of Political Power*, 5(2): 279–99.

Pina e Cunha, Miguel, Stewart Clegg and Armenio Rego (2014) 'The ethical speaking of objects: ethics and the 'object-ive' world of Khmer Rouge Young Comrades'. *Journal of Political Power*, 7(1): 35–61.

Plato (2007) *The Republic*. Translated by Desmond Lee. London: Penguin Classics.

Popper, Karl (2002) *The Logic of Scientific Discovery*. London: Routledge.

Popper, Karl (1976) *Unended Quest: An Intellectual Autobiography*. Glasgow: Flamingo, Fontana.

Prolife campaign (2018) 'Latest research'. Prolife Campaign Ireland. Available at: www.prolifecampaign.ie (accessed 28 May 2018).

Rawls, John (1971) *A Theory of Justice*. Oxford: Oxford University Press.

Rawls, John (1993) *Political Liberalism*. New York: Columbia University Press.

Raz, Joseph (1990) 'Authority and justification'. In J. Raz (ed.), *Authority*. New York: New York University Press.

Read, James (2010) 'Leadership and power in Nelson Mandela's *Long Walk to Freedom*'. *Journal of Political Power*, 3(3): 317–40.

Rein, Lisa (2017) 'Here are the photos that show Obama's inauguration crowd was bigger than Trump's'. *The Washington Post* (online). 7 March (accessed 8 February 2018).

Rorty, Richard (1989) *Contingency, Irony and Solidarity*. Cambridge: Cambridge University Press.

Rosa, Hartmut (2017) 'The philosophy of resonance and the sociology of democratic stabilisation'. Conference paper, Philosophy of Social Science, Prague, Villa Lana.

Ruohomäki, Jyrki (2010) 'Parity of esteem: a conceptual approach to the Northern Ireland conflict'. *Alternative*, 35(2): 163–85.

Rush, Benjamin (1806) *Essays, Literary, Moral and Philosophical*. Philadelphia, PA: Thomas and William Bradford.

Russell, Bertrand (1938) *Power: A New Social Analysis*. London: George Allen & Unwin.

Ryan, Kevin (2007) *Social Exclusion and the Politics of Order*. Manchester: Manchester University Press.

Ryle, Gilbert (2009) *The Concept of Mind*. London: Routledge.

Saar, Martin (2010) 'Power and critique'. *Journal of Power*, 3(1): 7–20.

Said, Edward (2003) *Orientalism*. London: Penguin.

Sartre, Jean-Paul (2000) *Nausea*. London: Penguin.

de Saussure, Ferdinand (1960) *Course in General Linguistics*. London: Fontana.

Savery, Daniel (2015) 'Power to the people: freedom as non-domination, disabling constraints and the eyeball test.' *Journal of Political Power*, 8(3): 363–84.

Schutz, Alfred (1967) *The Phenomenology of the Social World.* Evanston, IL: Northwestern University Press.

Scott, James C. (1987) *Weapons of the Weak: Everyday Forms of Peasant Resistance.* New Haven, CT: Yale University Press.

Scott, James C. (1990) *Domination and the Arts of Resistance: Hidden Transcripts.* New Haven, CT: Yale University Press.

Searle, John (1996) *The Construction of Social Reality.* London: Penguin Books.

Searle, John (2007) 'Social ontology and political power'. In *Freedom and Neurobiology: Reflections on Free will, Language and Political Power.* New York: Columbia University Press.

Sen, Amartya (2001) *Development as Freedom.* Oxford: Oxford University Press.

Sen, Amartya (2010) *The Idea of Justice.* Cambridge, MA: Belknap.

Schmitt, Carl (2006) *Political Theology: Four Chapters on the Concept of Sovereignty.* Chicago, IL: University of Chicago Press.

Sharp, Gene (2010) *From Dictatorship to Democracy: A Conceptual Framework for Liberation* (4th edn). Boston, MA: The Albert Einstein Institution.

Sinha, Pawan, Margaret M. Kjelgaard, Taban K. Ganhi, Kleovoulos Tsourides, Annie L. Cardinaux, Dimitrios Pantazis, Sidney P. Diamond and Richard M. Held (2014) 'Autism as a disorder of prediction'. *Proceedings of the National Academy of Sciences of the United States of America,* 111(42): 15220–5.

Smith, Philip (2008) 'Meaning and military power: moving on from Foucault'. *Journal of Power* [now *Journal of Political Power*], 1(3): 275–94.

Spruyt, Hendrik (1994) *The Sovereign State and its Competitors: An Analysis of Systems Change.* Princeton, NJ: Princeton University Press.

Taylor, Charles (1989) *Sources of the Self: The Making of Modern Identity.* Cambridge: Cambridge University Press.

Terreblanche, Sampie (2002) *A History of Inequality in South Africa, 1652–2002.* Pietermaritzburg: University of Natal Press.

Tharoor, Ishaan (2015) 'Nethanyahu's awkward relationship with the two-state solution.' *The Washington Post* (online). 19 March (accessed 12 February 2018).

Thoren, Victor E. and John R. Christianson (1990) *The Lord of Uraniborg: A Biography of Tycho Brahe.* Cambridge: Cambridge University Press.

Thrall, Nathan (2018) 'BDS: how a controversial non-violent movement has transformed the Israel-Palestine debate.' *The Guardian* (online). 14 August.

Tilly, Charles (1990) *Coercion, Capital, and European States.* Cambridge: Cambridge University Press.

Vazquez, Maegan (2018) 'Trump says that military parade would be great for country's spirit'. *CNN Politics* (online). 25 February (accessed 27 April 2018).

Walters, Joanna (2018) 'Gene Sharp, US scholar whose writings helped inspire Arab Spring, dies at 90'. *The Guardian* (online). 31January (accessed 2 February 2018).

Washington Post (2015) 'Homeopathic Drugs: No Better than Placebos?'. *The Washington Post.* 21 December.

Washington Post (2017) 'Washington Post-ABC News Poll Oct. 11–15'. *The Washington Post.* 16 October.

Watt, Nicholas (1999) 'Thatcher gave approval to talks with IRA'. *The Guardian* (online). 16 October (accessed 6 January 2018).

Weber, Max (1970) 'The psychology of the world religions'. In H.H. Gerth and C. Wright Mills (eds), *Max Weber: Essays in Sociology*. London: Routledge, pp. 267–301.

Weber, Max (1976) *The Protestant Ethic and The Spirit of Capitalism* (2nd edn). London: George Allen & Unwin.

Weber, Max (1978) *Economy and Society (Vol. 1), An Outline of Interpretive Sociology*, eds G. Roth and C. Wittich. Berkeley, CA: University of California Press.

Weber, Max (2011 [1904]) '*Objectivity of Social Science and Policy*'. Anthropos-Lab. Available at: www.anthropos-lab.net/wp/wp-content/uploads/2011/12/Weber-objectivity-in-the-social-sciences.pdf (accessed 11 November 2018).

Wilkinson, Richard and Kate Pickett (2010) *The Spirit Level: Why Equality is Better for Everyone*. London: Penguin.

Willis, Paul E. (2016) *Learning to Labour: How Working Class Kids Get Working Class Jobs*. Oxford: Routledge.

Wittgenstein, Ludwig (1967) *Philosophical Investigations*. Oxford: Oxford University Press.

Wollstonecraft, Mary (2014) [1792] *A Vindication of the Rights of Women*. New Haven, CT: Yale University Press.

Wrong, Denis H. (2009) *Power: Its Forms, Bases and Uses*. New Brunswick, NJ: Transaction Publishers.

Wylie, Christopher (2018) 'Cambridge Analytica whistleblower: Vote Leave "cheating" may have swayed Brexit referendum'. *The Guardian* (online). 27 March (accessed 28 March 2018).

Yeats, William Butler (1933) *Collected Poems of W.B. Yeats*. London: Macmillan.

YouGov Survey Results (2015) Internal Results, Zodiac, 20150701, 30 June–1 July.

Zexer, Elite (2016) *Sand Storm* (film in Arabic). Israel: 2-Team Productions.

Zimbardo, Philip (2009) *The Lucifer Effect: How Good People Turn Evil*. London: Ebury, Random House.

Index

EU authorised representative for GPSR:
Easy Access System Europe, Mustamäe tee 50,
10621 Tallinn, Estonia
gpsr.requests@easproject.com

www.ingramcontent.com/pod-product-compliance
Lightning Source LLC
Chambersburg PA
CBHW072000260326
41914CB00004B/877